Naval Power

Also by Jeremy Black
Eighteenth-Century Britain, 1688–1783, 2nd revised edition

Naval Power

Jeremy Black

palgrave
macmillan

First published 2009 by
PALGRAVE MACMILLAN

Palgrave Macmillan in the UK is an imprint of Macmillan Publishers Limited, registered in England, company number 785998, of 4 Crinan Street, London N1 9XW.

Palgrave® and Macmillan® are registered trademarks in the United States, the United Kingdom, Europe and other countries.

ISBN-13: 978–0–230–20279–5   hardback
ISBN-13: 978–0–230–20280–1   paperback

This book is printed on paper suitable for recycling and made from fully managed and sustained forest sources. Logging, pulping and manufacturing processes are expected to conform to the environmental regulations of the country of origin.

A catalogue record for this book is available from the British Library.

A catalog record for this book is available from the Library of Congress.

For Colin Gray

Contents

List of tables

List of abbreviations

Add   Additional Manuscripts
BL   London, British Library
NA   London, National Archives
RA   Windsor, Royal Archives
SP   State Papers

All dates given are new style aside from those indicated as old style (os).

Foreword

Jeremy Black's *Naval Power* emphasises the important role that control of the sea has played globally in shaping the history of nations, individually and collectively, over the last five centuries. Notably, securing access to the sea in facilitating world trade is a central theme, and one that remains very relevant today. Support to, and protection of, maritime trade and commercial interests has always underpinned the exercise of British naval power and is a theme that echoes down the years, linking the Royal Navy warships of the 1850s, countering piracy in the Malacca Straits, to their successors in the Gulf of Aden today.

More generally, naval power, and the regular deployment of such power, has been critical during the last half-millennium to the development of far-flung economic and political systems. This was not only about building empires; naval power was employed to protect trading links, undertake scientific exploration and research, prevent and contain potential crises, and promote and influence international co-operation. This ability, which finds its expression in the naval and mercantile capacity of maritime nations, remains crucial to global development, albeit naval forces will likely find increased roles in protecting the marine environment, its resources and the burgeoning coastal populations reliant upon those resources.

Naval power was, and is, the sharp edge of maritime capability and effectiveness in combat; at sea, from the sea and in support of operations ashore. Thus, the history of campaigns and battles, and ensuring the free flow of goods and materials, is intimately linked with the story of investment in naval infrastructure. Professor Black's account indicates the importance and interaction of this multiple effectiveness. His is a history that is central not only to that of Britain, but also of other major powers. His study is particularly valuable not only because his account is so very up-to-date, but also because of his consideration of the future trajectory of naval developments. As such it deserves attention from all those interested in naval power and its strategic and historic ramifications.

Admiral Sir Jonathon Band GCB
Formerly First Sea Lord and Chief of Naval Staff, Royal Navy
2006–2009

Preface

This book aims to provide a short, accessible account of naval power and its linkage with international relations, not least in the shape of power-projection. The emphasis is not on the techniques of ship construction nor on the social history of naval power, important though they are, but rather on navies as instruments of power and what they indicate about the nature of state systems, strategic cultures, and the necessary domestic contexts for such power. The space available imposes severe constraints, not least because there is an effort to give due weight to non-Western naval power. This approach, however, has to take note, as I do, of Western preponderance throughout the period.

There is no perfect way to organise this book and, rather than implying that the coverage that follows is the obvious one, I want to highlight the different courses that could have been followed. In particular, other chronological divides could have been adopted, notably the move to steam and iron in the mid-nineteenth century. Another divide might have been that of the beginning of the nuclear age at sea in the late-1950s. My preference for the use of conflicts as signposts, notably the start of the War of American Independence (1775), the end of the Napoleonic Wars (1815), the beginning of the First World War (1914) and the end of the Second World War (1945), reflects a deliberate attempt not to put the focus on technology, and, instead, to look at the formative role of conflict. This role relates not solely to periods of high-intensity conflict between major fleets, as in 1778–82, 1793–1815, 1914–18 and 1939–45, covered in Chapters 4 and 6, but also to the type of conflict that pertained during periods when one navy was clearly dominant – the British in the period of Chapter 5 and the American in that of Chapter 7. The importance of goals and tasks is a key theme, as is their relationship with political structures, interests and ideas.

I have benefited from the opportunity to discuss ideas considered in this book presented by lectures to the Australian

Defence Force Academy and on the *USS Missouri* and from giving the 2009 Midway lecture at the Naval War College in Newport, Connecticut. One of my pleasantest memories is of a day spent with Jan Glete on which we visited the *Vasa*. I would like to thank Guy Chet, Michael Duffy, Maria Fusaro, Jan Glete, Richard Harding, Patrick Kelly, Nicholas Rodger, Doug Smith, Larry Sondhaus, Sam Willis and two anonymous readers for their comments on an earlier draft and Howard Fuller, Colin Gray, Heinz Dieter Jopp, Duncan Redford and Matthew Seligmann for their comments on particular chapters. The encouragement of these fine naval historians has been of great value to me. They are not responsible for any errors that remain. I am also grateful for advice from Julian Lewis and John Lynn.

It is a great pleasure to dedicate this book to Colin Gray, a good friend who is also one of the world's leading experts on strategic studies, a scholar who expertly bridges the fields of history and international relations.

Jeremy Black

1 Introduction

The Water Planet. That was the image created by Athelstan Spilhaus in his *Atlas of the World with Geophysical Boundaries Showing Oceans, Continents and Tectonic Plates in their Entirety* (1991), the first version of which was devised in 1942. Spilhaus emphasised the sea more than other map-makers and also challenged the control of the map provided by edges and edging, concepts that mean little as far as the oceans are concerned. Indeed, he mapped what he termed 'a water planet': the world ocean uninterrupted by the limits of the map. To do so, Spilhaus produced a three-lobed map, centring respectively on the Atlantic, Pacific and Indian Oceans, with the map joined around Antarctica.[1] A related, but different, reconceptualisation of the relationship between land and sea has been offered by challenges to the organisation of the world in terms of continents,[2] and the stress, instead, on oceanic-based systems, such as the South Atlantic and the Indian Ocean. These approaches lead to a strong emphasis on oceanic links, maritime interests and naval power.

Man lives on land but the seas of the world are crucial to his lot. As a result, power, the power of man over his environment and of man over man, has frequently had a maritime component, which has ranged from fishing and whaling to the naval capability intended to give effect to ambitions to control trade and project power. Invasions are the most overt, but not the sole, form of the latter. The history of such capability is a long one, and some of it overlaps with such questions as the migrations of people in ancient and indeed more recent times. This book is devoted to the last half-millennium but it is useful to offer some preliminary comments about earlier naval conflict, not least because it differed from that of the dominance of sailing vessels for much of the period 1500–1850, let alone from what came later.

Instead, prior to the period 1500–1850, and overlapping with much of it, came an emphasis on oared shipping, shipping that might employ sails but that also had an important oared capacity. This shipping varied greatly in scale and sophistication, a variety that made it particularly amenable to operating not only in deep waters but also in the shallower waters of coastlines, deltas, estuaries, lakes and rivers, which together comprise a maritime world that tends to be greatly underplayed in naval history.[3]

Variations in scale and sophistication were linked to crucial contrasts in roles and tasks. Indeed, a central problem with the idea of organising any treatment of naval history in terms of types of vessel, for example Age of Sail followed by Age of Steam, is that it can lead to an underplaying of the importance of distinctive roles. Crucial differences arose from the contrast between essentially predatory naval forces that attacked trade and coastlines and the navies of empires. The former ranged in scale from the Sea Peoples, who allegedly caused a crisis for the Bronze Age Mediterranean, to pirates, such as the Japanese *wako* of the sixteenth century, or the Europeans who sought, in the sixteenth to eighteenth centuries, to exploit the new wealth of the American colonies.[4] The imperial navies included those of Classical Rome, Song China (960–1279), nineteenth-century Britain, and the modern USA. Some great naval powers, such as ancient Athens or nineteenth-century Britain, have been described in terms of thalassocracy or maritime empire, but naval strength is not necessarily centrally linked to the existence of such an empire, as both Song China and the modern USA demonstrate. The protection of maritime interests, however, can still be a key function, as is certainly the case with the USA.

The development of specialised warships reflected the profit to be made from attacking or defending trade in areas, such as the Mediterranean, where it was large-scale by the first millennium BC. At the 'high-spectrum' end, oared vessels could be formidable warships, although a lack of adequate sources makes it difficult to write with authority, and there is a danger of glossing over all sorts of complexities in ancient naval warfare. Nevertheless, modern full-scale reconstructions of triremes, a type of galley used for Classical warfare in the Mediterranean, have helped greatly in understanding the options faced by the commanders of that period. The oarsmen were seated on up to three levels, and between two and sixteen men pulled on the oars in each vertical group. The Athenians used the tactic of steering for an opposing trireme, then veering to one side just before colliding bow-on to break off the oars of their opponent, maiming or killing many of the latter's rowers in the process. This attack was followed by grappling and boarding. The success of this tactic led to it being copied by the other Greek and Persian navies. Galleys had rams on their prows which could be used to devastating effect, but the preferred tactics were to bombard and then board: using catapults, archers and javelin throwers to weaken resistance, before trying to board.[5] Yet, as a reminder of variety, whereas the Greeks and Phoenicians did not pack their galleys with troops and artillery, the Romans did.

The necessity for considerable manpower to propel these vessels by rowing them, however, greatly limited the cruising range of such ships, as they had to stop to take on more water and food. As a result, combined with the absence of living and sleeping quarters, galleys rarely abandoned the coastline and generally beached every night. As a consequence of their inability to remain at sea for weeks at a stretch, the projection of naval power required safe ports as bases, without which it was impossible to blockade or besiege opposing ports. The nature of naval possibilities in this period ensured that nineteenth- and twentieth-century concepts of control of the sea cannot be applied. That, however, does not mean that fleets were without value. Instead, in combination with troops, fleets played a key role in amphibious operations aimed at seizing positions. Doing so brought both profit and also the opportunity to restrict the possibilities for naval action by rivals.

Although the nature of logistical restrictions changed across history, notably with the move to smaller crews (for size of ship), with sail and then steam, such restrictions were (and are) of continuing importance in naval history.[6] As far as galley warfare was concerned, these restrictions remained pertinent until its demise in the eighteenth century.[7] Indeed, the logistical problems of galley warfare hindered the efforts of the Ottoman Turks to operate into the western Mediterranean in the sixteenth century, and helped explain their effort to capture Malta from the Knights of St John in 1565 so as to use it as a major naval base in the central Mediterranean and in support of moves further west.

Naval warfare played a key role in the fate of the Classical Mediterranean world, with the two crucial battles being Salamis

(480 BCE) and Actium (31 BCE). The former indicated the dependence of the Persian invaders of Greece on naval power. Having provided a bridge across the Hellespont, a massive fleet of about 1,200 warships supported the large Persian invading army, escorting the supply ships, but, after the Persians occupied Athens, the Greek fleet assembled by the nearby island of Salamis. The subsequent battle indicated that, as so often in naval history, numbers of warships alone were not the key issue. In the face of the larger Persian fleet (about 800 ships from Persia's subjects and allies to the Greek 300), the Greeks decided to fight the Persians in the narrows of Salamis rather than in the open water, as they correctly anticipated that this position would lessen the Persians' numerical advantage. The Persians indeed found their ships too tightly packed, and their formation and momentum were further disrupted by a strong swell. The Greeks attacked when the Persians were clearly in difficulties, and their formation was thrown into confusion. Some Persian ships turned back while others persisted, and this led to further chaos, which the Greeks exploited.

The Persians finally retreated, having lost over 200 ships to the Greeks' 40, and with the Greeks still in command of their position. As a result of this battle, Xerxes, the Persian ruler, returned to Anatolia (now Asian Turkey) with the remnants of his navy and part of his army. Yet, again as is generally the case with the use of naval power, Salamis had not settled the war,[8] as Xerxes left a force in Greece that had to be defeated, on land, at Plataea in 479 BCE. Conversely, as the historian Herodotus noted of 480 BCE, it was unclear what advantage the Greeks could derive 'from the walls built across the Isthmus [of Corinth] while the king [Xerxes] was master of the sea'.

Subsequently, naval power provided Athens with the opportunity to dominate the Aegean while, during the Peloponnesian War with Sparta (431–404 BCE), the fleet protected Athens' trade routes, notably its grain supplies from the Black Sea. However, this naval power could not be used to defeat Sparta, very much a land power, and, instead, led to the strategic overreach of the unsuccessful attempt to capture Syracuse in Sicily (415–413 BCE).

Subsequently, the Macedonians also demonstrated the strength of land powers against those reliant on navies, although, in capturing Tyre (332 BCE) and defeating the Athenian fleet off Amorgos (322 BCE), the Macedonians fundamentally benefited from their ability to deploy allied and captured naval forces.

The Roman state for long did not place an emphasis on sea power, but eventually had to do so in order to contest the Carthaginian position in the central and western Mediterranean, initially, more particularly, the waters off the island of Sicily, where Carthaginian control was well established. At the start of the three Punic Wars, in 264 BCE, Rome had no significant naval tradition, but was faced with war against Carthage, a maritime state based near modern Tunis. In battle, the Romans rammed their opponents and then used the plank-like corvus, which had a spike that attached it to the enemy ship so that the latter could not escape, to form a bridge between ships and thus enable rapid boarding of the enemy vessel. War at sea was thereby transformed into land battle afloat, and the Romans used their skills in land fighting.

By 200 BCE, Rome had considerable experience in naval conflict and had exploited her naval strength to project troops into Sicily, Spain and North Africa, and, at the same time, denied Carthage the ability to unite her disparate territories and campaigns. The Romans had also triumphed in major naval battles such as Encomus (256 BCE). The Punic Wars, which closed with the destruction of Carthage in 146 BCE, were won convincingly by Rome, a result that is a testament to the ability of a traditionally land-based power to wield sea power with sufficient investment and dedication to its development and use.[9]

The defeat of Carthage left Rome the leading Mediterranean maritime power, enhancing its central position, and also ensured a naval experience that was to be useful in subsequent operations, including Julius Caesar's expeditions against Britain in 55 BCE and 54 BCE. Indeed, in AD 83 or 84, the first circumnavigation of Britain was allegedly undertaken by the Roman fleet, and Roman naval activity was certainly important in the acquisition of geographical information about the British Isles, as well as in military operations.[10]

Rome developed a considerable capability for force projection by sea, but this capability was closely linked to her ability to deploy effective armies, as with the successful conquests of Greece in the second century BCE and of Britain from AD 43. This relationship between sea and land power was also the case with civil war in the Roman empire, for example Julius Caesar's conflict with Pompey (50–48 BCE) and that between the triumvirate that succeeded Caesar and the conspirators who had killed him (43–42 BCE). Most prominent was the struggle between two members of the triumvirate, Mark Antony and Octavian, later Augustus Caesar, a conflict best remembered for the battle of Actium (31 BCE), which was fatal for Antony because his naval breakout from a blockade on the coast of Greece entailed the abandonment of his army there. Augustus' naval capability enabled him to exploit this victory by the conquest of Egypt, which left Rome as *the* Mediterranean naval power, which was a key attribute of its geopolitical position and imperial strength.

The preference, both in Europe and elsewhere, was for operations across narrow waters, as was shown in the invasions of Britain by Angles, Saxons and Vikings from the fifth to the eleventh centuries AD, the Norman invasion of England in AD 1066,[11] and, far less successfully, the Chinese invasions of Japan mounted in AD 1274 and AD 1281. The last were launched by the Mongols, who had taken over China, from the subsidiary kingdom of Korea against Kyushu, the closest of the main Japanese islands. The expedition in 1274 was wrecked by a storm, while that in 1281 landed troops before another storm proved fatal. In 1281, there was some conflict with Japanese vessels, but this fighting was small-scale compared to operations on land and the impact of the storm. Although unsuccessful, the Mongol attacks were indicative of the willingness, seen also with Alexander the Great of Macedon, the Romans and the Byzantines, of land-based powers to take to the sea to realise their imperial ambitions. The Mongols also created an effective river navy in the thirteenth century in order to help overcome the use of defensive river lines in southern China by the Southern Song empire.

The Chinese, first under the Mongols and then under the Ming dynasty, made no subsequent attempt to conquer Japan, but, in the early fifteenth century, they deployed the most powerful fleets then seen. Cannon had possibly been carried on the Ming Chinese fleet from the 1350s, and were available for the series of seven expeditions sent into the Indian Ocean between 1405 and 1433. The largest ships carried seven or eight masts, although claims that they were nearly 120 metres (400 feet) in length are questionable, not least as the dimensions do not correspond to the figures for carrying capacity, tonnage and displacement. Nevertheless, they were possibly the largest wooden ships built up to then, and, thanks to watertight bulkheads and several layers of external planking, these ships may well have been very seaworthy. The Ming warships more than matched Henry V of England's contemporary fleet of great ships, impressive though that was.[12]

Although claims that they circumnavigated the world are farfetched, the Ming Chinese certainly travelled longer distances than European vessels of the period, and reached Aden and Mogadishu, as well as successfully invading Sri Lanka in 1411 on the third expedition. However, in response to a shift in strategic culture towards an emphasis on the landward challenge of the Mongols, and to related political changes within China, as well as to demographic and fiscal problems, the Chinese gave up this long-range naval power projection in the 1430s.[13]

Chinese naval activity takes the limelight, but there were other naval powers in medieval Asia, for example Srivijaya, centring on eastern Sumatra from the seventh to the eleventh century, and the Chola empire of southern India in the eleventh century. The key theme in much naval activity, for example that of the Cholas, was the use of amphibious operations in order to mount raids.[14]

Comparisons between Chinese achievements in the Indian Ocean and those of the Europeans there from the 1490s need to note that the Europeans achieved much more with much less, in part because their activities were located in a different socio-economic framework and were guided in part by a search for profit. In contrast, there was domestic criticism in China that vast resources were spent to no useful purpose. It is not surprising that the Chinese voyages stopped, as the incentive for spending enormous sums with very small returns must have been limited. These expeditions in some respects were like modern space programmes, with prestige, curiosity and technological achievements pursued as ends in themselves alongside military and political benefits. In their place, the capability for long-range naval power projection was taken by the Western Europeans, a key development in naval affairs, power projection, and the history of the world.

2 1500–1660

An account of change driven by military technology and operational considerations would argue that the prime means of, and reason for, change was the rise in Europe in the sixteenth century of the large, specialised, sailing, cannon-armed warship, built and maintained just for war, rather than also acting as a peacetime trader. These ships, able to take part in sustained artillery duels at close range, were expensive to build, administer and maintain. As a consequence of this cost and the related need for political support and organisational sophistication, the number of potential maritime powers was restricted, and, by the late seventeenth century, the powerful naval state was no longer coterminous, as it had earlier been, with the commercial territory or port; although, nevertheless, particular ports and related entrepreneurial groups were crucial to the operation of these states.[1]

In medieval Europe, maritime warfare was not a state monopoly. With the exception of some piracy, such as that of Sextus Pompey (43 BCE–36 BCE) – which, in turn, was an aspect of the civil war for control of the Roman empire – this warfare had been such a monopoly in the ancient Mediterranean because of the size of the galleys involved, but, thereafter, there was a dominance of European waters by large sailing ships, ships which could also be merchantmen. As a result, it became possible for pretty much anyone with enough cash to raise an armed maritime force. As a separate point, medieval maritime warfare was largely not about conflict at sea but about troop projection, which was the prime concern of rulers. This situation was changed by the rise of specialised armed warships, and the high cost of guns was a key factor in the chance, for whereas, for example, Henry VIII of England (r. 1509–47) could afford to arm his ships with hundreds of guns, no one else in England could match him.

This approach helpfully links technological changes with those in the wider political context, but it possibly suggests a more automatic process of development than was in fact the case. The lesson from shifts on land was that there was no such process, and that it was far from clear what at any particular stage was the most effective weapons system, form of combat, and, indeed, military organisation. As with land warfare, this issue was further complicated by the range of factors involved in effectiveness and, in particular, the need for trade-offs between mobility, armament and firepower. However, the range of factors in naval effectiveness was more extensive than those appertaining to land warfare, and was more complex than the combination of mobility, armour and firepower that applied to cavalry. This range of factors entailed the need to balance cargo capacity, which was a factor even for warships, with sea-keeping quality, speed, armament types and numbers, optimum size of crew and draught; and these relationships, moreover, depended on the likely role of the ship.

As a result, the specifications of warships varied greatly. European purpose-built warships were typically 500–600 tonnes in the second half of the sixteenth century, while armed merchant vessels were in the 200–300 tonnes range. Assumptions about likely needs interacted with the possible range of specifications. For example, Portuguese East Indiamen relied on their vast size for defence, while Spanish *fregates* trusted to speed for their safety. Spanish treasure galleons needed room for treasure, while English warships of the late sixteenth century were built for speed and for attack, including attack on such galleons.

As another instance of the role of choice or agency, it is also necessary to consider why particular states chose to develop their naval power. Issues of identification and image played a major role, alongside the dynamics of imperial ambition. Thus, assessing increases in naval power, it is appropriate not only to discuss states and political cultures that placed an emphasis on commercial interests, but also to underline the importance of particular conjunctures, notably geopolitical strategies and the choices of individual rulers and ministers. The role of choice was especially apparent in the case of powers that had to prioritise between Mediterranean and Atlantic commitments, especially Spain under Philip II (r. 1556–98)[2] and France under Louis XIV (r. 1643–1715).

Ships

Naval strength entailed a commitment of resources which was often greater than that required for warfare on land. Sailing warships were costly, but the great costs of naval operations were food and wages. Fleets could not live on local resources like armies, for example wayside grass for the draught animals; instead, they had to be provisioned. The wooden warship equipped with cannon, whether driven by sails, muscle-power (for galleys) or both (for galleys were equipped with masts and sails), was the single most costly, powerful and technologically advanced weapons system of the period; although galley construction itself was relatively cheap: the great cost was personnel, as galleys required enormous crews.

Naval capability posed challenges as well as providing opportunities. The introduction of large numbers of cannon on individual ships was a challenge for ship design, made maritime technology more complex, and greatly increased the operational and fighting demands on crews. The need for cannon accentuated the extent to which the construction, equipment, manning, supply and maintenance of a fleet required considerable financial and logistical efforts.[3] These problems were enhanced by the nature of the available technology. The construction of large warships using largely unmechanised processes was an immense task and needed large quantities of wood. The capital investment was formidable, but ships generally had a life of only 20–30 years. Maintenance was also expensive, as wood and canvas rotted while iron corroded.

Warships therefore demanded not only, by the standards of the day, technologically advanced yards for their construction, but also permanent institutions to manage them. The construction and logistical infrastructure of a fleet constituted the major 'industrial' activity of the sixteenth century, with a requirement for a commensurate administrative effort to support it. This requirement applied to all countries involved in the creation and support of fleets. The resulting scale of activity is apparent in the surviving arsenals in Copenhagen and Venice,[4] and was also well recorded in contemporary drawings. The effort was judged worthwhile because warships provided effective mobile artillery platforms that lacked an equivalent on land, and an individual vessel might carry heavy firepower capacity comparable to that of an entire army.

The demands upon naval power also changed. Whereas the Mediterranean had dominated the trade of medieval Europe, with its maritime outliers reaching to the North Sea, and, more distantly the Baltic, the trading wealth unlocked by the 'Age of Discoveries', as the Europeans created trade routes to South and East Asia and the Americas, encouraged the development of naval strength to both protect and attack long-distance trade routes.[5] Warships were also the most effective means of attacking distant hostile bases. In European waters, the strategic commitments of many powers involved maritime links, for example, in the sixteenth and seventeenth centuries, between Spain and both Italy and the Low Countries, or between Sweden and the eastern and southern Baltic.

From *c*.900, the Europeans had been able to apply force across the Mediterranean against the Muslim powers, most dramatically with the Crusades,[6] but, from the later fifteenth century, it was a case of force applied across the oceans. There had been no earlier examples by Europeans, as the Viking presence in North America was very limited. Modernity indeed has been seen as arriving in the late fifteenth and sixteenth centuries in the shape of heavily armed warships capable of sailing long distances. There was also an important organisational dimension, as the sixteenth century saw the establishment and growth of state navies, as well as the greatly increased use of heavy guns in galleys and sailing warships.

The cannon carried on some European warships from the middle of the fifteenth century were made with a particular concern for their use at sea in a fashion distinct from that of land-based weaponry. This was an important aspect of specialisation; although it is important not to exaggerate the differences between guns for siege warfare, fortifications and naval warfare as, to a large extent, they were interchangeable, although the cannon mountings had to be altered. Field artillery, in contrast, was different as it had to be as light as possible. The increase in cannon size mounted in European sailing ships in the first two decades of the sixteenth century was impressive, although the cannon did not compare in size to the fortress artillery that, for example, the Knights of St John employed in their unsuccessful defence of the island of Rhodes against a large-scale Ottoman amphibious attack in 1522.

Sailing warships had important advantages over galleys, the most important ships in the Mediterranean, although even English Atlantic sailors held the sea-fighting capability of galleys in some respect well into the sixteenth century. Indeed, English warships of the 1560s–70s were built with forward and rear firing cannon to meet the threat posed by cannon-armed galleys. Large sailing ships with three masts required fewer bases than galleys, which relied on human power: thanks to a reliance on the wind, the crews of sailing ships were smaller than galleys, and their larger hull capacity allowed them to carry more food and water. With their shallow draught, galleys were also particularly vulnerable to storms,[7] while ships with three-mast rigs could sail closer to the wind. Able, as a result of their relatively small crews, to transport a large cargo over a long distance at an acceptable cost, sailing ships, thanks to their cannon, could also defend themselves against attack, without requiring a large crew or the support of soldiers to do so.

In the medieval period, it had been common to board rival warships; and boarding was not suddenly replaced by firepower in the sixteenth century. Instead, the capture of prizes, by boarding, both from galleys and from rigged warships, remained a fundamental of maritime war. Moreover, very few naval battles were concerned to sink the enemy, as there was little gain to be had in it. Prizes could be taken by artillery: warships often struck their colours when the rig was severely damaged and the ship could not escape, nor turn its guns on the enemy. Large warships were difficult to sink with the gunfire of the period, but they could be reduced to defenceless hulls. Moreover, there was no incentive to sink an enemy; it was always better to capture the ship. Even during the Spanish Armada of 1588, there was a determination to capture vessels by the English, and the rich booty from the *Rosario* demonstrated why. Equally, the Spaniards tried hard to capture the English *Revenge* off the Azores in 1591 by boarding her. The naval clashes off Terceria in the Azores, as Philip II of Spain in 1581–3 drove off French warships supporting a Portuguese claimant, and some of the clashes in the Baltic war between Denmark and Sweden in 1563–70, were the exceptions to the rule.

There was therefore a very long transition to bombardment-only exchanges between ships, and, instead, boarding followed a missile exchange, now conducted by gunpowder weaponry instead of archers, remained the norm. However, there were now different fighting requirements for boarding and bombardment. Moreover, an emphasis on cannon had obvious implications in terms of ship-killing capabilities and requirements: for armament, supply and tactics.

Heavy guns were carried in the Baltic and by English and French warships from the early 1510s. Carvel building (the edge-joining of hull planks over frames), which spread from the Mediterranean to the Atlantic and Baltic from the late fifteenth century, replaced the clinker system of shipbuilding using overlapping planks. This change contributed significantly to the development of hulls which were stronger and better able to carry the heavy guns that challenged stability and seaworthiness by needing to be carried high in the hull.[8] The potential size of European warships also grew. The English *Henry Grâce à Dieu* (also known as *Great Harry*), a very large wooden ship, had a 1514 specification of 186 guns, although the majority of these guns were hand-weapons. Indeed, sixteenth-century gun inventories are often misleading, if compared to those from later centuries, as many of the guns were weapons of a size comparable to muskets. The Danish, French, Lübeck, Maltese, Portuguese, Scottish, Spanish and Swedish navies all included ships of comparable size during the course of the seventeenth century.

Portuguese naval power

Initially, the most impressive sixteenth-century naval power was Portugal, the first state in the world to have colonies in Asia, Africa and the Americas, and the first transoceanic state to rely on warships to articulate such an empire. Portugal's naval strength was based on sailing ships which were strong enough to carry heavy wrought-iron cannon capable of sinking the lightly-built vessels of the Indian Ocean: this heavier armament was crucial in the face of the numerical advantage of their opponents. There was no comparable opposition to the Portuguese in African or Brazilian waters.

Drawing on late fourteenth- and fifteenth-century developments in ship construction and navigation, specifically the fusion of Atlantic and Mediterranean techniques of hull construction and lateen and square-rigging,[9] as well as on advances in location-finding at sea, the Portuguese enjoyed advantages over other vessels, whether the latter carried cannon or not. These advantages were a reminder of the extent to which technology was not a simple process involving changes only in one element. Moreover, developments in rigging permitted the Portuguese greater speed, improved manoeuvrability, and a better ability to sail close to the wind.

Information also played a major role in Portuguese effectiveness. This was a role that is consistently significant in naval power, requiring, as it does, the ability to project strength over considerable distances, and to understand the locational issues involved. Thanks to the use of the compass and other developments in navigation, such as the solution in 1484 to the problem of measuring latitude south of the Equator, it was possible to chart the sea and to assemble knowledge about it, and therefore to have greater control over the relationship between the enormity of the ocean and the transience of man than ever before. The Portuguese made a major effort to accumulate information that would aid navigation, and also to keep it secret from rivals.

This information policy was an aspect of a more general process of state direction. The Portuguese fleet was a state-owned and controlled body, with the ships built in the royal dockyards at Lisbon and Oporto. As with the Spaniards at Havana, the Portuguese also discovered the value of a far-flung production and organisational system, developing colonial dockyard facilities, which were useful both for constructing vessels from durable tropical hardwoods, such as western Indian teak, and for repairing warships locally. The Portuguese built a large 800-tonne ship at Cochin in India in 1511–12, established a major dockyard at recently conquered Goa in India in 1515, and developed shipbuilding facilities at Damao in India and Macao in China.

A key element in the Portuguese expansion along the coast of Africa and into the Indian Ocean was its string of fortified naval bases. They replicated the role of the ports that were so indispensable to Mediterranean galley operations, but over a vastly greater distance. Portuguese sailors knew that they could replenish in safety at a series of 'way stations' on their long voyages to and from Asia. Their 'sea lines of communication' rested on their bases, a policy that the Dutch and English copied in the seventeenth and eighteenth centuries. For example, Cape Town, established as a base in 1652, was developed by the Dutch in part as an area to grow green vegetables to replenish their ships sailing between the South Atlantic and the Indian Ocean.

The Portuguese initially relied on the caravel, a swift and seaworthy, but relatively small ship, ideal for coastal exploration and navigation, as well as the *nau* or 'great ship', a very large carrack-type vessel, but they then developed the galleon as a vessel able to sail great distances. It was longer and narrower than earlier carracks, with a reduced hull width-to-length ratio, and was faster, more manoeuvrable, and capable of carrying a heavier armament. The cannon were fired from the side of the vessel, a change that owed much to the development of the gunports just above the waterline and of waterproof covers for them. These covers ensured that guns could be carried near the waterline as well as higher up, thus reducing top-heaviness and increasing firepower. Such cannon, moreover, could inflict serious damage near the waterline and thus hole opposing warships.

The Portuguese navigator Vasco da Gama arrived in Indian waters in 1498, dropping anchor near Calicut on 20 May, with vessels carrying cannon that Asian warships could not resist successfully in battle. This technological gap helped give the Portuguese victory over the Calicut fleet in 1503, although the latter was supported by Arab vessels. Portuguese gunfire saw off boarding attempts. The Portuguese were also successful over other Indian fleets, those of Japara and Gujarat, in 1513 and 1528, respectively. An Egyptian (Mameluk) fleet, partly of galleys, sent from Suez in 1507, and supported by Gujarati vessels, initially defeated a greatly outnumbered Portuguese squadron at Chaul in 1508, but was largely destroyed off Diu in 1509 by Francisco de Almeida, the first Viceroy of Portuguese India.[10]

The Egyptian, and later Ottoman (Turkish), vessels that sailed to the west coast of India or between the Red Sea and the Persian Gulf were different to the Portuguese ships in their long-distance capability, and were also less heavily gunned. Indeed, whereas there was considerable diffusion of new weapons and techniques to non-Western powers in land warfare in the sixteenth century, there was no comparable diffusion of naval weaponry and techniques. The Western European combination of ships with hull-mounted cannon, and fortresses with garrisons, remained particularly effective.[11]

This effectiveness did not mean that European warships were invulnerable. In African, Indian and Indonesian waters, heavily-gunned Portuguese vessels, with their deep draught and reliance on sails, were vulnerable to shallower-draught oared boats, for example in the Straits of Malacca, where the Sultan continued to resist after the loss of the city of Malacca to a Portuguese amphibious attack in 1511. More generally, deep-draught Portuguese warships, like those of other European powers, frequently had only limited value in the important inshore, estuarine, deltaic and riverine waters of the world, a situation that was not to change until the introduction of shallow-draught steamships carrying steel artillery in the nineteenth century. However, earlier, there was some effective European usage of shallow-draught ships. In Europe, the Dutch used shallow craft effectively in their successful riverine war with the Spanish Army of Flanders, especially in its early phases in the 1570s. The Russians also had a capability for river operations: flotilla expeditions were sent down the Don against Azov and the Khanate of the Crimea from 1646.

Moreover, the problems faced by deep-draught European warships outside European waters could be matched in the latter, and this point serves as a reminder of the continuing diversity of naval warfare within Europe. Thus, the long-established Viking tradition of (shallow-draught) longship-building continued in the islands off west Scotland until the late sixteenth century: in an analogue of the cavalry forces of the Cossacks on land, the Hebrideans had a military system that relied on mobility and was able to support itself by raiding. In 1533, the English attempt to impose their power by using the new technology failed when the *Mary Willoughby* was captured by longships off the Shetlands.[12] The use of Viking-style longships by the Western Islemen, notably the MacDonalds, enabled them to transport mercenary *redshanks* from the Western Isles into Ulster, using Lough Foyle as their landing area, throughout the sixteenth century. Attempts to intercept the fleets with English sailing ships were unsuccessful, as were efforts to penetrate into the lochs of the Mull of Kintyre to attack the vessels at source. Only the occupation of Lough Foyle by English troops finally solved the problem. Galleys were not solely used by the Western Islemen: in 1594, they played a role in the English siege of Enniskillen Castle, while, in the Baltic and the Mediterranean, the continued need for galleys also reflected the importance of inshore waters.

Moreover, South-East Asian rulers responded to the threat posed by European warships not only by attempting to copy them but also by building bigger armed galleys whose oars gave them inshore manoeuvrability. A fleet of about fifty Cochin-Chinese galleys destroyed three Dutch warships in 1643. In response to the local rulers, the Portuguese, in turn, developed coastal fleets composed of local oared vessels or small sailing ships at Goa, Diu and in the Persian Gulf. These fleets, in turn, were of great value when the Portuguese resisted Dutch and English attack in the seventeenth century, as they could be used to harass English and Dutch big ships and could circumvent blockades by them.[13]

In turn, Francis Drake and other English privateers took small, oared, prefabricated raiding vessels with them to assist with operations in the inshore waters of the Caribbean against Spain in the late sixteenth century. Such small ships do not appear in lists of naval strength as the latter focus on what became ships of the line, but this limitation is a reminder of the need to be cautious in assuming any one measure of naval power, and, in particular, in treating such power simply in terms of battle-winning or of the ability successfully to transport amphibious and expeditionary forces over long distances. This point remains relevant today.

Nevertheless, despite their limitations inshore, European vessels in deep waters were difficult to attack successfully, and, on the oceans of the world, there was little challenge to European military technology. In part, this lack of serious challenge reflected the absence of interest shown by China, Japan and Korea in developing a long-distance naval capability to match their powerful short-range effectiveness; while in Mameluk Egypt (which was conquered by the Ottomans in 1517) the commitment to a social order based on mounted warfare led to a rejection of the idea of seafaring and to a failure to become a naval power of much significance.[14] A Chinese fleet employing cannon defeated a Portuguese squadron off Tunmen (Tou-men) in 1522, but Tunmen is in Chinese waters near Macao. The Portuguese were fortunate they did not reach the Indian Ocean when the Chinese deployed fleets there in the early fifteenth century, as Chinese ships were sturdier than Indian ones, but, by the sixteenth century, although the Chinese had an important inshore naval capability, they no longer deployed distant fleets. The Portuguese were to have a fleet defeated off Johor (in modern Malaysia) in 1603, but by the Dutch, and not by an Asian power.

The short-range effectiveness of Asian naval power was amply demonstrated in 1592 when the Japanese fleet covering the invasion of Korea was defeated in the Battle of the Yellow Sea by a Korean fleet, commanded by Yi Sun-Shin, that included some of the more impressive warships of the age: Korean 'turtleships', oar-driven boats, possibly covered by hexagonal metal plates in order to prevent grappling and boarding, that may also have been equipped with rams. In turn, the Japanese rapidly deployed cannon on their warships, and used them with effect in 1593 and 1597, but in 1598 the Koreans were supported by a Chinese fleet under an artillery expert and the Japanese were defeated in the Battle of the Noryang Straits: the Koreans appear to have had a lead in cannon. This battle helped bring the Japanese invasions of Korea to an end and demonstrated the role of gunned warships off East Asia.[15] In this context, the deliberate move by Japan away from foreign links in the following century was a powerful cultural and political rejection of maritime identity and interests, and one that was important to the distribution of naval power on the global scale. So also was the Manchu conquest of Korea.

The Korean war may seem less important than the European ability to project power over a long distance. For example, a Portuguese presence was an issue for both China and Japan, but not vice versa, although this argument, however, has to be handled with care: Viking power extended to Newfoundland but to scant effect. More generally, the definition and basis of naval power are again at issue, as they are throughout this book. This power was a function of ships, manpower, bases, logistical support, funding and political support, each of which was intimately related to the others, and it is important not to adopt a single definition of naval power. The understanding of the use of naval power can also be overly simple. There is a temptation to think only of the gains to be made through the use of this power, namely acquiring resources through violence and of trade as a power relationship.

This tendency, however, has to be related to the mutually beneficial nature of trade, as well as to the need for maritime powers to accommodate themselves to the demands and opportunities of land-based economic systems, if they were to be much more than transient plunderers. After technology had given them an initial advantage, the Portuguese sought this accommodation, and it also proved important for the Dutch and the British in Asian and African waters. In the very different context of today, this point may still be pertinent when discussing the limitations of naval power.

Naval warfare

The rising importance of firepower led to a shift towards stand-off tactics in which ships less frequently came into direct contact, and boarding therefore became more difficult. The Portuguese were the first systematically to exploit heavy cannon to fight stand-off actions against superior enemies, a development often incorrectly claimed for the English at the time of the Spanish Armada (1588). In northern Europe, the shift towards stand-off tactics can be seen by contrasting the Anglo-French war of 1512–14, in which the fleets fought in the English Channel in the traditional fashion, with the gunnery duel in which they engaged off the English naval base of Portsmouth in 1545. This shift had important implications for naval battle tactics (although truly effective ways of deploying naval firepower were not found until the next century), and it further encouraged the development of warships primarily as artillery platforms.

Fleets, nevertheless, continued to contain ships that were not specialised warships. The Dutch, for example, used their fleet to great effect in the second half of the sixteenth century, but some of the ships were still armed merchantmen, although there were also warships well suited for river and shallow-water warfare. The considerable force of French and Spanish ships that engaged in what was essentially an artillery duel off Terceria in the Azores in 1581 were a mixture of types, but with armed merchantmen and privateer vessels from a variety of sources predominating. More generally, the term 'ship of the line' is applicable to the seventeenth rather than the sixteenth century. Certainly the French, English and Scottish kings built large specialised warships in the first decades of the sixteenth century, but these were as much statements of royal power, even fashion, as functional warships.

Yet, there were also signs of change. The English constructed purpose-built warships along new technological lines in the 1570s, which were essentially for the defensive task of dominating the English Channel, although they were hired out by Queen Elizabeth for commerce raiding on an *ad hoc* basis. The Portuguese, who constructed vessels of similar size and capability, built them for Atlantic convoy escorts, while the Spaniards only began to build royal warships in the same class, such as the 'twelve apostles', during the last decade of the century. The Danes, the Swedes and the Hanse merchants of Lübeck built large specialised warships that fought artillery duels during the naval war in the Baltic in the 1560s, but they also sought to board each other's vessels.

At the same time, it is important to avoid any teleological assumption that it is only if ships were able to use gunfire to sink others that they were effective, and that therefore there was a revolution in naval warfare with the development of the more powerful 'ship-killing' warships.[16] Instead, it has been argued that, as with land warfare, fifteenth-century developments were also important, and that it is necessary to focus on a 'process of technological and tactical evolution which began with the advent of gunpowder weapons on land, and then progressed through the placement of these guns on board ships, their use in naval engagements as anti-personnel weapons, their increase in size and numbers, and, finally, their changes in technology, separate from similar weapons used on land, in order to produce weaponry that was effective by contemporary criteria'.[17] Early cannon fire was not broadside fire, but, instead, firing from fore and aft,[18] and the English flagship the *Mary Rose* may have sunk in 1545 as a result of taking on water through a hole made by a cannon on a French galley. It is also unclear, if naval revolution(s) are being sought, whether the focus should be on shipping or weaponry. If the former, changes in ship construction and design in the fourteenth and fifteenth century, particularly the increase in the number of masts, the number of sails per mast, the variety of sail shapes and the spread of the sternpost rudder,[19] may be seen as more important than those in the sixteenth century.

The introduction of cannon was certainly a difficult process. Wrought-iron cannon were dangerously unreliable. They were not much in use after the third quarter of the sixteenth century and, judging by evidence from the Danish, English and Swedish navies, they were probably scrapped by the end of that century, as navies converted to 'copper' guns. The manufacture of large cast-iron weapons was initially beyond the technological scope of the period, but, from the mid-fifteenth century, firepower was increased by the development of large cannon cast, instead, from lighter, more durable, and workable 'brass'; actually bronze, an alloy of copper and tin. These cannon were thick enough to withstand the high pressure from large powder charges and were able to fire iron shot with a high muzzle velocity and great penetrative force. The stone shot used in early cannon was phased out. In most European languages, the word for cannon made from bronze was normally copper, possibly because the tin was a much smaller part of the alloy than in other types of bronze and the gun metal probably looked very similar to copper.

From the 1540s, cast-iron cannon were produced in England. They were relatively cheap. Cast-iron guns imported from England were in use in Denmark from the 1560s. The Dutch were able to produce cast-iron cannon by the 1600s, but such cannon were preferred for merchantmen and not for warships, as they could burst when overheated through rapid firing. In Sweden, cast-iron technology was developed by foreign, predominantly Walloon (Belgian) technicians, with the royal family (Duke Charles, later Charles IX) acting as entrepreneur. In the 1610s, the Walloon-born Louis de Geep became interested in this as a promising commercial enterprise, while the Swedish state was ready to lease out or sell its industrial enterprises. A major expansion in production followed, but the important effects of that were not seen until the 1640s. Even in England and Sweden, which had domestic cast-iron gun production, 'copper' guns dominated in the navies until the third quarter of the seventeenth century. After that, more determined efforts were made to replace even the heavier types of copper guns (18–36-pounders) with cast-iron guns.

Cast-iron cannon did not become the leading naval cannon until after 1650: a list of the cannon on English warships at sea in 1595 revealed that 80 per cent were brass and only 20 per cent cast iron. The early cast-iron guns were usually of small or medium calibres, and the rapid development of successful Dutch and English armed merchantmen for trade in dangerous areas, especially the Mediterranean and the East Indies, was closely connected with the spread of cheap, small and medium cast-iron guns; while the growth of the big battle fleets after 1650 would have been more expensive if cheap large-calibre cast-iron guns had not been available. Demand from buyers interacted with the development of cast-iron technology, a classic instance of the relationship between goals and capability. In addition, the process of modification and improvement in naval ordnance, especially the major drop in cost, helped to give the Europeans an important comparative advantage in naval capability on the world scale. Simultaneously, significant improvements in gunpowder increased the range of cannon.[20] Nevertheless, the main driving forces behind the great expansion of the European navies were political: intense power struggles dominated by warfare involving battle fleets, as well as the stronger aggregation within states of interests supporting maritime power.

It is important not to assume that the development of rigging, muzzle-loaded cast-metal cannon, and heavy cannon on the broadside, all occurred at once, and were mutually dependent. Indeed, by the mid-fifteenth century, galleys were being built to carry cannon, and in 1513 these showed their ship-killing capability at the expense of the English fleet off Brest.

Mediterranean warfare

For long, the imaginative character of naval conflict prior to the Spanish Armada (1588) was dominated by galley warfare in the Mediterranean, not only because of the issues at stake but also because it involved Europe's two leading naval powers, Spain and the Ottomans, the latter better known as the Turks. The Ottomans had created a fleet to help prevent Constantinople (the capital of the Byzantine or eastern Roman empire; now Istanbul) from being relieved when they attacked it in 1453; an earlier

Ottoman fleet had been destroyed by the Venetians in the nearby Dardanelles in 1416. Once the city fell to land attack in 1453, the Ottomans used it as their capital, and this move to a port-capital whose support depended on maritime links led to an increased role for naval concerns. Indeed, the Ottoman fleet was swiftly a major force in the Aegean Sea, and was crucially employed to support amphibious attacks on Mitylene (1462) and Negroponte (1470).[21]

The Ottomans subsequently developed their fleet for more distant operations beyond the Aegean and to carry cannon, which they used with effect to defeat the Venetians at the Battle of Zonchio in 1499. Yet, as a reminder of the need for caution before focusing on cannon, contemporary images of Zonchio also show the hurling of spears and the firing of arrows, while rocks and barrels of, probably, quicklime, are thrown from the fighting tops. The battle ended when the ships were burned, which was not caused by the cannon, which fired stone shot.

In their war with Venice of 1499–1502, the Ottomans successfully combined a strong fleet, which was more powerful than that of Venice, and was intended to support amphibious operations rather than to seek battle, with heavy siege cannon moved by sea. As a result, they were able to drive the Venetians from their bases in the Peloponnese (southern Greece): Lepanto fell in 1499 and Modon and Coron, 'the eyes of Venice', in 1500, and in 1503 Venice sought peace.[22]

In the sixteenth century, the emphasis on firepower in galley warfare increased.[23] These cannon were carried forward and supplemented the focus on forward axial attack already expressed by the presence of a metal spur in their bow. This spur might damage enemy oars and could be pressed into the hull of an enemy galley if a boarding was attempted. The strengthened and lengthened prow provided the access/boarding ramp onto an enemy ship. These spurs could not sink ships as (underwater) rams were intended to do, but the latter was a weapon of the Classical period that had disappeared. Like spurs, cannon were intended to disable the opposing ship as a preparation for boarding.

Galley conflict was not unchanging. Aside from the introduction of cannon, galleys became easier to row in the mid-sixteenth century, as one-man oars (with the typical galley having three men on a bench with one oar each) gave way to rowing *a scaloccio*, in which there was one large oar for each bench, and this oar was handled by three to five men. This change, which reflected the shift from skilled volunteer oarsmen to convicts and slaves, led to an increase in the number of rowers, and also made it possible to mix inexperienced with trained rowers without compromising effectiveness. Experts were long divided about the respective success of the two systems, which is a reminder of the need for caution when assessing the likely value of competing military methods.

The effects of prevailing wind patterns, currents and climate in the Mediterranean ensured that voyages were easiest if they began near the northern shore. As a result of these wind patterns, shipping was generally restricted to a certain number of routes, affecting strategic and operational options and leading to pressure to control nodal points on these routes.[24] Carrying soldiers greatly increased galleys' consumption of food and water, and therefore affected their range. Few harbours and anchorages were able to support and shelter large fleets transporting substantial numbers of troops, a situation that affected operational methods and strategic goals. The seizure of these harbours was crucial.

The rapid Ottoman conquest of Egypt, and particularly of the vital port of Alexandria in 1517, as a result of an invasion by land from Palestine, facilitated and encouraged a major growth in Ottoman naval power and in the merchant marine. Links between Constantinople and Alexandria, like those between Classical Rome and Alexandria, were only really viable by sea, and this encouraged the Ottoman determination to dominate the Mediterranean.[25] Cyprus became a tributary in 1517, and Rhodes was captured in 1522, after a lengthy siege. The Ottomans also extended their control along the North African coast, allying with Khair-ed-Din (known to Westerners as Barbarossa), who dominated Algiers and was appointed admiral by the Ottoman ruler, Suleiman the Magnificent (r. 1520–66).

The Ottomans benefited from the decline of Genoese and Venetian naval power, neither of which were able any more on their own to mount a powerful resistance. As a result, Christendom's naval capability was reconfigured away from the city-state maritime empires of the later Middle Ages. The weakness of Genoa and Venice enabled the Ottomans to dominate the Aegean and seize its islands. Karpathos and the northern Sporades (1538) and Naxos (1566) were captured from Venice, and Samos (1550) and Chios (1566) from the Genoese. Neither Venice nor Genoa had the capability to protect such exposed positions, which was a far cry from the naval reach enjoyed by both powers during the Middle Ages, a reach that had extended into the Black Sea.

In response to the Ottoman advance, Venice, Charles V (the Habsburg ruler of Austria and Spain) and the Papacy deployed a combined fleet, in 1538, against the Ottomans in the Adriatic, but the Ottomans were able to check them at the Battle of Prevesa on 27 September. The battle demonstrated the importance of tactical problems in naval warfare: the Ottomans had withdrawn their galleys onto the beach under cover of their fortress guns, with their forward galley guns facing out to sea, which immediately robbed the Genoese admiral, Andrea Doria, of the initiative, as his crews were consuming their food and water as they tried to hold their station outside the port on the open sea. He had the choice of attacking the Ottomans in their fixed position, with the Ottomans able to fire from stable gun platforms with a secure retreat, or landing troops and attempting to storm the fort and its outer defence works with inadequate siege equipment. As neither option offered much prospect of success, his only realistic option was retreat. The moment he began to withdraw, however, Doria exposed his sailing vessels to the Ottoman galleys, whose fresh crews were able to overhaul and board them. Instructively, accounts of the battle vary, which is more generally true of naval (and land) battles in this period and thus make it difficult to judge the particular factors that led to successful capability. Recriminations among the allies were linked to these different accounts.[26]

In 1541, Charles V led a crusade against Algiers, a major amphibious expedition that was a considerable logistical achievement. However, attacking late in the year, his fleet was badly damaged by an autumnal storm and the expedition failed. In 1542–4, Khair-ed-Din, with 110 galleys, co-operated with the French against Charles V, raiding Catalonia (1542), capturing Nice (1543) and harrying the Italian coast (1544). Tripoli (in modern Libya) fell to the Ottomans in 1551, and in 1552, when Henry II of France attacked Charles V, the Ottomans sent about a hundred galleys to the western Mediterranean. Each year until 1556 and again in 1558, the Ottomans sent large fleets, although for logistical reasons they returned each winter to Constantinople. This return gave their opponents opportunities to 'share' the sea, so that in 1553 the Ottomans invaded Corsica, only for Genoese control to be re-established when the fleet left.

Unlike their attacks on Rhodes (1522) and Malta (1565), the Ottomans did not use these expeditions to seek to accumulate conquests that might establish a permanent position, but the expeditions created grave problems for the articulation of the Spanish empire and for the coastal communities in the region. During the period 1540–74, the number and scale of amphibious operations mounted in the Mediterranean by all of the major combatants was impressive. The size of armies that were transported, the distances they were moved and the speed of transit were all striking, and highlighted a degree of competence and capability that was largely due to the experience of the commanders and sailors involved.

In 1560, Charles V's son, Philip II of Spain (r. 1556–98), launched an expedition to regain Tripoli, but it was surprised at Djerba by the Ottoman fleet with devastating consequences. In turn, in 1565, Suleiman the Magnificent sent a powerful expedition of 140 galleys and about 30,000 troops to capture Malta, the principal Christian privateering base in the Mediterranean, and a threat to Ottoman trade. Naval power provided the power projection, but, hampered by divided leadership, specifically the failure of the Ottoman land and sea commanders to agree and implement a coordinated and effective command structure and plan, as well as the summer heat, and logistical difficulties, including in the supply of drinking water, the Ottomans could not prevail over the determined defence. The latter, especially the extraordinary heroism of the defenders of St Elmo, which delayed the Ottomans for two weeks, was crucial to the logistical problems the attackers encountered, and also gave the Spaniards sufficient time to mount relief attempts. The defenders could only repel the attacks: they were not strong enough to mount a sortie, but a Spanish relief force was sent from Sicily. Forced back twice by bad weather, the Spaniards, 11,000 strong, eventually landed and the besiegers retreated, unwilling to face the new foe. The Ottomans never again attacked Malta.[27]

Effective resistance combined with relief by sea from a nearby base had saved Malta; not a naval battle. The strength of the Spanish response in 1565 reflected the major effort made by Philip II in the Mediterranean in the early 1560s. This effort included operations on the coast of North Africa. Aside from the Djerba expedition, the Spaniards broke the blockade of Spanish-held Oran in 1563 and sent an expedition to gain the Peñón de Vélez in 1564.

Cyprus was an easier target for Ottoman conquest than Malta. It was closer to the centres of Ottoman power and the Venetian rulers appeared less formidable. In 1570, Suleiman's successor, Selim II, sent 116 galleys and 50,000 troops, who rapidly overran the island, but a substantial garrison continued to hold Famagusta. Its defences were on a par with those of Malta, and it contained one of the best ports in the eastern Mediterranean, as Richard I – the Lionheart – of England had been quick to spot in 1191 during the Third Crusade. Although gunpowder stores ran down, Venetian relief vessels did break through with supplies during the siege, and there is good reason to believe that the city would hold out. Ottoman cannon fire had failed to breach the land walls and they had been forced to commence mining operations. Had the garrison realised that the Ottomans would not honour the terms of their surrender, it is unlikely that they would have surrendered, and the relief vessels that were en route could have changed the outcome of the siege.

In response to the Ottoman attack, a Holy League of Spain, Venice and the Papacy was organised by Pope Pius V in May 1571. The Christian fleet, under Philip II's illegitimate half-brother, Don John of Austria, found the Ottoman fleet at Lepanto off the west coast of Greece. The Ottomans, under Müezzinzade Ali Pasha, had probably more ships, about 282 (although recent Turkish work has reduced that figure to about 230) to about 236, but fewer cannon, 750 to 1,815. The Ottoman fleet was disease-ridden, while Don John had made modifications to his ships to widen their field of fire. More than 100,000 men took part in the battle on 7 October, a reminder of the major manpower requirements of naval power when strength was a function of a large number of ships, certainly in comparison to the situation for sail and steam warships. In the latter cases, numbers of ships and of men were both still important but not to the same degree.

At Lepanto, Don John relied on battering his way to victory, although he also benefited from having a reserve squadron, which permitted a response to the success of the Ottoman offshore squadron. Superior Christian gunnery, the fighting qualities and firepower of the Spanish infantry who served on both the Spanish and the Venetian ships, and the exhaustion of Ottoman gunpowder, all helped to bring a crushing victory in four hours' fighting. The cannon of six Venetian galleasses played a particularly important role in disrupting the Ottoman fleet. These galleasses were three-masted, lateen-rigged, converted merchant galleys which were longer and heavier-gunned than ordinary galleys, and they carried firing platforms at poop and prow and sometimes along their sides. Their height also gave them a powerful advantage as they could fire down on opponents. If they were able to crash into the side of, or sweep away the oars of, an enemy galley, the impact of their weight was much larger than that of a normal galley. The deployment of galleasses, to break the force of the Ottoman assault, represented a considerable tactical innovation, especially when it was combined with a reserve squadron.

The willingness of both sides to engage in an open sea battle was important. The Ottomans could have pulled back under the guns of the fortress at Lepanto and forced the Christian forces into a risky amphibious assault. Good morale and determined leadership characterised both sides, and this may have led to a riskier approach being taken by both commanders: the normal caution of the Christian galley commanders was overridden by the charismatic and determined leadership of Don John, who brought a land perspective to the battle. Casualty figures vary greatly, and the limited extent of the Ottoman sources is a serious problem, but all agree that the Ottomans lost far more men, possibly **30,000** dead (including the admiral) to maybe **9000** Christians, while the freeing of maybe **15,000** Christian galley slaves accentuated the disruption to Ottoman naval manpower. The Ottomans lost about 113 galleys sunk and 130 captured, as well as their cannon and naval stores, whereas the victors lost only about 12 galleys.[28]

The battle was applauded as a triumph throughout Christian Europe, a decisive victory over a feared foe. However, it was to serve as an important reminder of the complexities of naval power, particularly the extent to which, as on land, triumph in battle did not necessarily lead to success in war. Lepanto occurred late in the year, and could not be followed by the recapture of Cyprus, let alone, as Don John hoped, by the liberation of Palestine, the Crusader goal. More modestly, an attempt to retake the port of Modon failed in 1572. The Ottomans avoided battle in 1572–3, and rapidly constructed a new navy which included mahones, their version of galleasses. By April 1572, about 200 galleys and 5 mahones were ready for action. In order to improve the firepower of the Ottoman fleet, there was a stress on an ability to use handguns among those called on to serve in the fleet.

The role of alliance dynamics was also crucial, as so often in naval conflict, for example the position taken by the Dutch and Spain during Anglo-French conflicts from 1689 to 1815. The outcome of Lepanto, although disappointing from the Christian viewpoint, was fatally undermined by the Venetian decision to sue for a unilateral peace with the Ottomans: in 1573, Venice recognised the loss of Cyprus. Tunis, which had fallen to the Ottomans in 1570 and been regained by Spain in 1573, fell to the Ottomans the following year: they deployed 280 galleys and 15 mahones.[29] Under serious pressure, especially from the Dutch Revolt in the Low Countries, Philip II was unable to respond, and, instead, Spain followed with a truce in 1578. Lepanto was decisive more for what it prevented – a possible resumption of the Ottoman advance in the Mediterranean and Adriatic – than for pushing the balance of military advantage towards the Christians. The loss of skilled Ottoman manpower was also important. The end result was the de facto establishment of Spanish and Ottoman spheres of influence in their respective halves of the Mediterranean.

Large-scale naval warfare between Ottomans and the Mediterranean Christian powers did not revive until the mid-seventeenth century. Although the Ottomans and the Austrians were at war in 1593–1606, they did not fight at sea at any serious level, and Spain crucially did not use the opportunity to join Austria in attacking the Ottomans (although an unsuccessful assault on Algiers was launched in 1601). This absence of conflict can be seen as a sign of a more widespread stagnation of Mediterranean galley warfare,[30] but, as always when discussing naval power, it is also necessary to give due weight to the other commitments of the combatants and the potential combatants.

These commitments, for example, help explain why the Spanish galley fleet in the Mediterranean declined, while, until 1645, the Ottoman fleet was able to concentrate on action against privateers and other defensive tasks. There was no need for major force projection.[31]

In 1645, in contrast, the Ottomans invaded the Venetian-ruled island of Crete, sending over 100,000 soldiers and a massive fleet of about 400 ships, of which, however, solely 106 were warships, the remainder being *karamursel*, ships used only for transport. Most of the island was rapidly captured, but the siege of the capital, Candia, lasted until 1669. The Venetians sent reinforcements, including 33,000 German mercenaries, while political divisions undermined the Ottoman war effort. The Venetians also responded with forward naval power, blockading the Dardanelles (the approach to Constantinople) in 1648, which helped to precipitate the fall of Sultan Ibrahim, and again from 1650. An Ottoman fleet which evaded the blockade was defeated off Naxos in 1651 and, in 1656, the Venetians largely destroyed the Ottoman navy off the Dardanelles. However, leadership as so often was a key factor in mobilising and using resources: the vigorous Mehmet Köprülü became Grand Vizier and rebuilt the fleet, and the blockade was broken in 1657.

Baltic warfare

Meanwhile, 1563–70 saw the first modern naval war between sailing battle fleets in European waters, as Denmark and Sweden fought for control of invasion routes in the Baltic. The Danes were supported by the semi-independent German city of Lübeck, no longer the great sea power it (like Genoa and Venice) had been, but still able to make an important contribution. Both sides sought to destroy the opposing fleet, and seven battles were fought between 1563 and 1566, a very high tempo of conflict and one that was unusual for subsequent European warfare, although such a tempo was seen in the Pacific between Japan and the USA in the Second World War. In general, the Swedes, under Klas Kristersson Horn, with their modern bronze artillery, systematically used stand-off gunfire to block Danish boarding tactics: sheer weight of metal was decisive. However, at the battle of Oland (30–31 May 1564), the Swedes lost their new flagship, the *Mars*, after repeated Danish–Lübeck attacks. The *Mars* was successfully boarded on the second day of the battle, caught fire, and blew up.

Both navies expanded greatly and, by the late 1560s, the Swedes may have had the largest sailing fleet of the period. At the same time, the conflict indicated the limitations of naval power. It proved difficult to coordinate with land operations, and the vulnerability of warships to weather was shown in 1566 when several ships in the Danish–Lübeck fleet were wrecked during a gale when at anchor off Visby; although intense summer gales were very unusual in the Baltic.[32] Subsequently, the Danish navy was greatly expanded under Christian IV (r. 1588–1648), and it and its Swedish rival competed in the struggle for Baltic primacy.[33]

Atlantic warfare

During the period of the great Mediterranean galley wars, there was a great deal of naval activity in the Atlantic area of operations, including Anglo-French naval conflict in the 1540s and 1550s and English amphibious operations against Scotland during the reign of Edward VI (r. 1547–53). These culminated, under Elizabeth I (r. 1559–1603), in 1560, when an English fleet was decisive in leading to the defeat in Scotland of the French attempt to suppress the Protestant Lords of Congregation who had rebelled against Mary Queen of Scots, the wife of Francis II of France. The English under William Winter cut links across the Firth of Forth (leading the French to abandon operations in Fife), before successfully blockading Leith. The English land assault failed, but the naval blockade led the French to negotiate the withdrawal of their force.

As a reminder of the nature of economic warfare and the related need for naval forces, the Habsburg government of the Low Countries co-operated with Amsterdam and the States (Estates or Parliament) of Holland in the 1550s to ensure that fleets were deployed to protect their shipping from French and Scottish privateers.[34] The potential of naval power in these waters was shown during the Dutch Revolt. Philip II had sold his Dutch navy after peace with France in 1559, and was therefore unable to respond to the privateering attacks of the Protestant Sea Beggars that began in 1568. In some respects, this failure indicated a lack of responsiveness to the potential and threat of maritime power, but Philip had pressing problems in Spain (the Moriscos Revolt) and the Mediterranean (from the Ottomans), and the Duke of Alba, the Governor, appeared to have restored order in the Low Countries.

The crisis that began in 1572, when the Sea Beggars took over the port of Brill and the Dutch Revolt spread, however, revealed the deficiencies of a Spanish system that relied on hiring and requisitioning armed merchantmen. Alba had done so, mostly from Amsterdam, but these warships were defeated, particularly in a battle in 1573, which led to a crucial lack of Spanish control in Dutch waters. In turn, Philip II prepared a fleet in northern Spain in 1574, only for the scheme to be shelved when illness hit the sailors. In the absence of Spanish naval power, it required a huge military effort by the Duke of Parma to recapture the key port of Antwerp in 1585.

The fleet of 1574 was not the end of plans for Spanish naval action, but other problems and options came to the fore and the major effort the Spaniards mounted in the Atlantic in 1582–3 was the conquest of the Azores, a Portuguese island-group in the Atlantic. The outbreak of war with England in 1585 ensured that now Spain had an enemy that could only be decisively attacked by sea. Philip decided to mount an invasion of England, although it had to be postponed because in 1587 the English under Sir Francis Drake successfully attacked Cadiz. The Spaniards were also delayed by the immensity of the necessary preparations.

The Armada

The Armada of 1588 was of a totally new order of magnitude for Spain and for Atlantic expeditions. Spanish preparations translated earlier hopes into an organised ocean-going force, and replaced the small force that had landed in Ireland in 1580 (it was swiftly defeated by the English) with a bold plan for large-scale concerted operations against England. Anglo-Spanish naval hostilities contrasted with the minor role of naval forces in the French Wars of Religion. However, in 1588, Philip failed to coordinate adequately two disparate plans: one for an amphibious invasion of England from Spain by the Duke of Medina-Sidonia's fleet, and the other for a crossing from the Spanish Netherlands (Belgium) by the Duke of Parma's army. The final plan was for the Armada to proceed up the Channel and then cover Parma's landing, but the details of how the two elements were to co-operate had not been adequately worked out.

Philip underestimated the difficulties facing Parma. He could not keep his troops sitting in their invasion barges for extended periods, and he required a significant period of time to load them. Parma worked on the assumption that the time would be available, once the Armada had destroyed the English fleet guarding the Channel, and also the Dutch ships that were blockading his embarkation ports. The vulnerability of his open barges to attack by Dutch *flybotes* in the shallow waters around the ports of Ostend and Sluys were never appreciated by Philip.

On 28 May 1588, the Armada of 130 ships and 19,000 troops left Lisbon. Storm damage necessitated refitting in Corunna, and it was July before the slow-moving fleet appeared off the Cornish coast. The Spanish warships then headed for Calais, maintaining a tight formation to protect their more vulnerable vessels, and harried by long-range English gunnery. This bombardment did little damage, and, during nine days of engagements, the Spaniards retained their formation. With the advantage of superior sailing qualities and compact four-wheeled gun-carriages, which allowed a high rate of fire, the English fleet suffered even slighter damage. It was, however, threatened by a shortage of ammunition and food. In contrast, many of the Spanish guns were on cumbersome carriages designed for use on land.

When Medina-Sidonia anchored off Calais, he found that Parma had been able to assemble the transport vessels necessary to embark his army for England, but that they could not come out of their anchorages until after the English and Dutch blockading squadrons had been defeated. Before it could act, the Spanish fleet, however, was disrupted by an English night attack using fireships, and the English fleet then inflicted considerable damage in a running battle off Gravelines. The brunt of the battle was borne by the galleons of the Portuguese navy, which were in Spanish service: they were experienced in stand-off gunnery. A strong south-westerly wind drove the Armada into the North

Sea. With no clear tactical objective after Parma's failed embarkation, the disappointed Spanish commanders ordered a return to Spain via the hazardous north-about route around the British Isles. However, a succession of violent and unseasonal storms lashed the fleet as it passed north of Scotland and down the west coast of Ireland; 28 ships were smashed or driven ashore, and only part of the fleet reached Spain.

The loss of so many trained and experienced men was a serious blow for the Spaniards, but, as with the Ottomans after Lepanto (p. 29), and, again as a reminder of the importance of organisational capability, especially that of raising and directing funds, the fleet was rapidly rebuilt, not least because Spanish losses in men and material in 1588, though considerable, are sometimes overstated. The renewed Spanish fleet was not as powerful or effective as its Ottoman counterpart which regained Tunis in 1574, but Spain was able to prepare fleets for English and nearby waters in 1596 (in large part directed against Brittany) and 1597, although both expeditions were stopped by autumnal storms.[35]

The English themselves found it difficult to win lasting naval victory. In 1589, Elizabeth I authorised a counter-stroke against Philip II, but the heavy expenditure on the fleet in 1588 had resulted in shortages of money, and the expedition was funded as a joint-stock enterprise. This funding exacerbated the clash of objectives that is inherent to many naval (and land) operations, not least if they reflect a coalition of interests. Elizabeth's aims, to destroy the remnants of the Spanish fleet, were at variance with those of the force commanders, while the presence of the pretender to the throne of Portugal offered the prospect of driving the Spaniards from Portugal, and gaining commercial access to Lisbon. This aspiration was the motivation behind the substantial funding put up by merchants from the City of London. The result was the worst possible compromise, and ultimately nothing of substance was achieved.

The Queen backed a major shipbuilding programme after the Armada, which led to a major increase in the size of the English royal fleet, but she continued to try to make the maritime war pay for itself, an aspiration that can be seen as a 'pre-modern' form of naval policy and procurement. The English naval effort was an uneasy co-operation between government and private maritime interests. This co-operation worked effectively in 1588, but less so in offensive operations when disparate goals became more apparent. However, the ability to draw on privateers was an important aspect of English naval capability. Privateer operations brought an important synergy to English naval capability. They provided an indispensable pool of highly capable leaders and battle-trained seamen. Spain had no equivalent source of manpower to draw on.[36] In the 1590s, however, improved Spanish fortress defences and a fleet of purpose-built warships meant that the English failed to intercept the *flota* (the Spanish treasure fleet), although they came close to it on several occasions.

A resurgence of activity by the Spaniards and the English occurred in 1596–7. The threat of a Spanish Armada led to a pre-emptive strike being mounted against the coast of Spain in 1596 by a large Anglo-Dutch amphibious force. The English were lucky as the Spanish fleet was dispersed by storms, repeatedly a key element in the Age of Sail, and their own force achieved the most significant gains of the maritime war. Having won surprise, the fleet fought its way past a Spanish force of modern galleons and galleys, supported by the guns of the city of Cadiz, and conducted a successful opposed landing, followed by the storming of the city. This was a considerable achievement. However, the concentration on the landing allowed a fleet of merchant vessels, sheltering in the inner harbour, to be burnt by the Spaniards, with the loss of much valuable booty for the expeditionary force. The loot from the city was still immense, but the commanders failed to control their troops, and the Queen did not get her share of the proceeds, a share that would have helped finance the war effort. Again, the differing goals of the coalition of interests that made up naval power were at issue.

An attempt by Drake and Hawkins to achieve a similar success in the West Indies was thwarted at San Juan, Puerto Rico by the improved naval and fortress defences. However, the Earl of Cumberland, using an indirect approach, did manage to capture San Juan a year later when he attacked its landward approaches. Yet as a reminder of the difficulty of moving from success to lasting gains, neither Cumberland at Puerto Rico nor the Earl of Essex at Cadiz could sustain a garrison in the cities they had captured. It was beyond the capability of sixteenth-century logistics, and therefore the overall result was minimal, and degenerated into acrimonious arguments with Elizabeth over the division of the booty. As with 1589, such amphibious attacks led to no permanent gain.

There was no equivalent to the Portuguese bases in Africa or the Indian Ocean, nor to the English position at Calais from 1347 to 1558, nor was any attempt made to provide them. However, the role of the English navy in the successful campaign at Kinsale in 1601 against a Spanish expeditionary force and its Irish allies did have an impact that was strategic in its consequences, by ending effective resistance to English rule in Ireland.

The war with Spain, which continued until 1604, illustrated the limitations of naval power in this period, not least its vulnerability to storms, the problems of combined operations, and the heavy supply demands posed by large fleets. The defeat of the Armada also demonstrated the growing technical skill of English and Dutch seamanship and naval warfare, and underlined the importance of superior naval gunnery and appropriate related tactics and leadership.

Dutch naval power

In the early seventeenth century there was a major development in aggregate European naval strength, especially on the part of the United Provinces (modern Netherlands; Holland was the most important province), which became the leading naval power in Europe.[37] This strength gave the Dutch a powerful advantage in war with Spain, one seen in the victory over a Spanish fleet off Gibraltar in 1607, although the resistance of the Spanish navy should not be underrated and the Spaniards built up their navy in the late 1610s and early 1620s.[38] The extent of Dutch maritime power was such that other states seeking warships tried to hire them from the Dutch. In 1625, the French hired 12 Dutch ships as part of the fleet that drove the Huguenot (French Protestant) navy from French waters, a crucial step in exerting pressure on the Huguenot stronghold of La Rochelle.

Dutch power rested in large part on its maritime strength and dynamism. The United Provinces became an entrepôt for European and global networks of trade, in which comparative advantage brought the Dutch profit. Economic strength became a source of power,[39] but this wealth, in turn, made the Dutch a tempting target for other powers, and also encouraged these powers to try to match the Dutch in the synergy of commercial expansion and maritime strength. They also challenged Dutch naval power.

Alongside the treatment of naval conflict, and thus capability, in terms of battle, it is necessary to give due weight to the role of commerce-raiding, and this was a particularly important tool for the opponents of the Dutch. Without trade and fishing, maritime activity would cease, and both presented a tempting target for Spanish attack. The ability of the Spaniards to respond, particularly from Flanders, to the opportunities provided by Dutch maritime links, indicates the danger of assuming that the Spaniards had somehow become redundant at sea. Dunkirk, Spain's North Sea harbour, which was developed to accommodate more and larger vessels, was able to serve Spain not only as a major privateering base, but also as the linchpin of an offensive war at sea, a harbour for large battle fleets.[40]

In what was the first global war at sea[41] the Dutch, however, were not only able to mount a major series of offensives against Spanish and Portuguese interests and possessions around the globe, but also, in Europe to protect their coastline and their maritime links, and to cut the naval link between Spain and the Spanish Netherlands (Belgium). The Dutch campaign against the sea lines of communication culminated in a major naval victory at the Battle of the Downs on 16 September 1639. This battle was sought by the Spaniards as a decisive fleet engagement designed to transform the strategic situation between Spain and the Dutch. In the battle, the Dutch kept their distance, preventing the Spaniards from closing and employing boarding tactics. In the ensuing artillery exchange, the Dutch inflicted greater damage, in part thanks to superior command skill, but both sides ran out of ammunition. The battle demonstrated that, for all their improvements in ship design, the Spaniards had still not adopted a policy of naval combat with artillery, and clung to the tactics of boarding. This practice may well have reflected the tendency for military commanders to hold authority over their naval counterparts. The Spaniards took refuge in the Downs, where they were attacked with heavy losses on 21 October: in the confined waters, the Spaniards were vulnerable to fireships and to the more manoeuvrable Dutch warships.

The French navy

In the 1620s, the French developed a permanent battle fleet for the first time since the 1560s, but their navy did not match Dutch strength, in large part because, despite royal interest in naval matters,[42] the French focused on their armies. France's Spanish opponent could be better attacked by land. However, due in part to the support of Richelieu, the leading minister, the French did acquire a valuable capability to project their strength in the western Mediterranean and in Atlantic waters. In 1626, he created the post of Grand Maître de la Navigation et Commerce for himself, and he used the navy in the operations against La Rochelle that were crucial to the consolidation of royal power. The first ships of the permanent royal fleet created by Richelieu were four warships bought from the Duke of Nevers in 1624, an indication of the shift towards naval power as being under the control of territorial rulers. The French developed an ability to project their power in the Mediterranean, and this enabled them in the 1640s to support the Catalan Revolt against Spanish rule and to intervene against Spain in Italy, for example in attacks on Finale and the Presidios (Spanish coastal forts), and in the dispatch of fleets to Naples in 1647–8. By 1646, there was a standing French fleet of 36 ships, including 17 above 500 tons and with 30 or more cannon.[43]

English naval power

Further afield, the Dutch and English deployed their heavily-armed sailing ships with increasing regularity. Philip II banned Dutch trade with Lisbon in 1594, encouraging the Dutch to seek spices at their Asian sources. The first English ships in the Indian Ocean arrived in 1591. Thanks to the autonomous structure of their East India Companies, mercantile enterprises with naval and military strength, the Dutch and English were able to use the profits of their East Indies trade to support their forceful stance.

The English remained an important naval power throughout the period, although amphibious expeditions against Spanish (Cadiz 1625) and French (relief of La Rochelle, 1627) targets in Europe in the 1620s were unsuccessful. The withdrawal of royal support for the navy by James I (r. 1603–25), and his antagonism towards piracy and privateering, removed the underpinning of naval capacity, and the expeditions of the 1620s showed that, within a quarter-century of Elizabeth I's reign, the naval capability of England had been severely diminished, with a dramatic decrease in the competence of its commanders.

In the 1630s, disputes over financing the expanding navy accentuated distrust of Charles I,[44] but the republican 'Rump' parliamentary government which replaced him after the Civil War developed a formidable naval power: between 1649 and 1660, some 216 vessels were added to the fleet: many were prizes, but half were the fruits of a shipbuilding programme. The earlier dependence on large merchantmen ended with the establishment of a substantial state navy, which, in 1653, employed almost 20,000 men. The English navy had become the largest in the world by 1650.[45]

Six years earlier, in contrast, as a reminder of the extent to which the fate of great powers did not necessarily involve naval operations, the Ming dynasty had come to an end in China as a result of domestic rebellion and foreign invasion neither of which had a naval dimension: the invasion was by the Manchu from the steppe to the north. This point may seem irrelevant in a naval history, but it underlines the need to put naval capability in context.

In 1652–4, England fought the Dutch in what was to be the First Anglo-Dutch War. Traditionally explained as a mercantilist struggle largely due to commercial and colonial rivals, this conflict has more recently been discussed in terms of the hostility of one Protestant, republican regime towards a less rigorous counterpart.[46] It was a war of fleet actions in European waters, fought with heavy guns, as well as of commerce raiding and colonial strikes. Attempts to preserve or cut trade links, crucial to the financial and military viability of the two powers, played a major role in the war. English victories closed the Channel to Dutch trade and this closure helped lead the Dutch to peace. But, because the English warships were larger than the Dutch, they were unable to mount a close blockade of the Dutch ports. On the other hand, being larger, and having a higher ratio of cannon per ton than the Dutch, made the English warships particularly effective. The sole major Dutch victory in 1653 was the destruction of an English squadron off the Mediterranean port of Leghorn (Livorno), a battle that showed the range of fleet action.[47] Both sides greatly increased their naval strength with the construction of new and larger ships.

Having replaced the Rump Parliament, Oliver Cromwell was happy to negotiate peace, but he subsequently used English naval power elsewhere. Robert Blake, the leading English admiral of the period, destroyed a Barbary pirate squadron with minimal losses at Porto Farina on the Tunisian coast (1655) and seized Tenerife (1657). More lastingly, the English also captured Jamaica from Spain. Naval power enabled the English to play a role in the Baltic rivalry of Denmark and Sweden; although Dutch intervention was more important and broke Swedish blockades of Danzig (1656) and Copenhagen (1658).

The development of line-ahead tactics for warships, which the Dutch employed at the Downs in 1639, was an important change at the close of the period. In 1653, the English fleet was ordered in its fighting instructions to provide mutual support. While this was not an instruction to fight in line-ahead, it encouraged the line formation that maximised broadside power. The stress on cohesion reflected a move away from battle as a series of struggles between individual ships. In part, certainly in the case of the English, the line formation reflected a transfer of military models to sea, as commanders with experience of combat on land sought to apply its lessons and to devise a formation that permitted control and co-operation during the battle. In practice, the nature of conflict at sea made it very difficult to maintain cohesion once ships became closely engaged.[48]

The wars between England and the Dutch were fought at sea and in the colonies. There was no land conflict between the two sides in Europe. As a consequence, the conflicts are somewhat atypical of the use of seapower in the period; although it could also be argued that there was no dominant paradigm and instead a variety of uses. It was more generally the case that, as today, seapower was supposed to act in direct support of land operations. This support took two forms. One was an attack or invasion in which the entire land force was transported by sea, as with the English attack on Cadiz in 1596. The other was the use of shipping to assist a land invasion, as with most French operations against Italy. Thus, in 1494, Charles VIII of France invaded Italy by land, but, after the French fleet had repulsed its Neapolitan opponent off Rapallo, the French siege train was moved by sea from Marseilles to Genoa and then on to La Spezia. As so often, ships provided a lift capacity that could not be matched on land, or, today in the air, although, when France lacked naval predominance, it had to rely on overland invasions of Italy, as in the 1620s, 1630s, 1690s, 1700s, 1740s, 1790s and 1800s.

The presence of English and Dutch squadrons in the Mediterranean in the 1650s was part of a longer-term process in which improvements in armaments and rigging and sail patterns helped to ensure that sailing ships, rather than galleys, became more important in Mediterranean warfare, although the French and Spanish sailing ships that clashed off Orbitello on 14 June 1646 were towed by galleys in very light winds. Like steamships as opposed to sailing ships in the nineteenth century, galleys were also more manoeuvrable in inshore waters, for example in the Aegean, and the difficulties the English encountered in the 1660s in opposing Moroccan corsairs off Tangier led to interest in the use of Mediterranean galleys. In 1663, half of French naval expenditure was on the galleys.[49]

Sailing ships, however, freed warships from dependence on a network of local bases, and carried more cannon than galleys. They were also less susceptible to bad weather, a capability that was to be taken further with steamships. The English and Dutch roundship, or *bertone*, that introduced new methods into the Mediterranean, was copied by the local powers; first by the North African Barbary states, especially Algiers, which adopted Atlantic naval technology from the late sixteenth century through the intermediary of English and Dutch privateers. Venice hired 12 armed Dutch merchantmen in 1618, and both Venice and the Ottomans hired Dutch and English armed merchantmen in their war of 1645–69. Indeed, the Venetian fleet in this war was increasingly a sailing fleet of hired merchantmen. By the mid-seventeenth century, both Venice and, more slowly, the Ottomans were shifting their force structure away from galleys, the Ottomans being influenced by the advantage gained by the

Venetians in the war. However, the Order of St John, the rulers of Malta, did not decide to introduce a squadron of square-rigged men-of-war until 1700: the first two were ordered at Toulon and sailed back to Malta in 1704.[50] As with the Atlantic naval powers, differing strategic cultures affected the use of naval power. For example, the Barbary ships, like those of the Omani Arabs based in Muscat from 1650, were essentially commerce raiders, rather than the more regimented and standardised fleets of the European navies with their heavy, slow ships designed for battering power. These fleets were especially intended for littoral warfare in European waters rather than for trans-oceanic operations.

A naval revolution?

European warships became more heavily gunned in the seventeenth century. Instead of relying on converted merchantmen, the English, French and Dutch increasingly used purpose-built warships, heavily gunned, and built accordingly with strong hulls. This emphasis on purpose-built warships led to a professionalisation of naval officership, senior ratings and infrastructure, but also ensured that less heavily-gunned vessels, such as those of the Dutch in the First Anglo-Dutch War (1652–4), were rendered obsolete, prefiguring the *Dreadnought* revolution of the 1900s (see pp. 143–4).

These fleets were the product of state activity, and underlined an important shift across the period as a whole and one that was to define modern naval power at the upper end of the spectrum, namely the concentration of naval force in the hands of territorial rulers able to deploy considerable resources. These financial resources were most useful if they could be combined with the already strong naval traditions of major maritime centres, not least because fleets required large numbers of sailors. Thus, at Lepanto, about a quarter of the Spanish galleys were rented from Genoese entrepreneurs.

However, by 1650, these centres were less able to deploy large quantities of naval strength alone, although the process was more pronounced on land where cities lost their military independence. Thus, in the Baltic, Lübeck had been overshadowed by the strength and competition of Denmark and Sweden, while, in the

Mediterranean, although Genoa and, particularly, Venice remained a naval presence, they were overshadowed by the fleets of territorial states.[51] In the case of Genoa, the shift was dramatised in 1453 when, in taking Constantinople, the Ottoman ruler, Mehmed II, captured the Genoese Old Arsenal at Pera, which was part of the city. By the following century, Pera had replaced Gallipoli as the leading Ottoman naval dockyard and was expanded in capacity, enabling it to construct or maintain about 250 galleys.[52] In response, Genoa established in 1559 the *Magistrato delle Galere*, a permanent institution charged with maintaining a state-owned navy. However, it proved impossible to create the large galley force that was planned.[53] Successfully bombarded by the French fleet in 1684, Genoa sold its last galleon in 1689.

It would be mistaken to exaggerate the novelty of this shift towards territorial rulers. Fleets furthering the interests of these states had been important prior to 1494, notably with Classical Rome, but fleets became more permanent and more clearly under government control in the early modern period. The relationship between maritime interests and states had shifted. Thus, in Spain, the Crown came to take more control over shipbuilding from 1598. This control permitted more government direction for the system in which the Crown used private ships, which they had rented, and frequently also requisitioned. The scale of naval administration in England was indicated by Chatham Dockyard alone spending £22 in 1604 on paper, ink, wax, sand, quills and counters for the clerks to write and reckon with.[54]

At the same time, it is important not to exaggerate the extent of state direction and control. Although he emphasised the achievement of larger political units in mobilising resources to develop effective navies, Jan Glete argued that navies organised by European states were far from universally successful in comparison with private solutions to the problem of protecting trade, as well as pointing out that navies closely controlled by private interests were efficient, and that there were wide differences in quality between different states. Indeed, private Dutch and English shipping often proved superior to Spanish naval power in the Mediterranean. In addition, Dutch and English armed merchantmen (of advanced types and purpose-built to carry a substantial gun armament) were frequently successful against Portuguese warships in the Indian Ocean.

Moreover, Carla Phillips suggested that a permanent navy was not necessarily better than a private/public system as it could be difficult to maintain financial support for such a navy. Phillips also pointed out that best practice was not clear, as it depended on the ability to ensure such support without weakening the state,[55] a point that remains very pertinent.

Repeatedly, indeed, it is the difficulties of early modern European governments in creating, sustaining and controlling naval resources that emerges; which is not surprising, given the continued reliance on private interests and the lack of consistent or comprehensive state financial support. This point is a variant on the argument that, whatever its impact on the world scale, changes in land warfare in Europe in the sixteenth and early seventeenth centuries did not amount to a military revolution. Thus, in the United Provinces (Netherlands), where there were five separate Admiralties (three in Holland, one each in Friesland and Zeeland) from 1598, the degree of coordination by the States General or by the Admiral General, a member of the Orange family, was frequently less than the impact of local pressures and interests. Furthermore, the deficiencies of the state system, the Admiralties, not least a lack of co-operation between them and also shortfalls in anticipated income, were such that, from 1631, another form of public/private partnership was created that lasted until 1656: groups of merchants began to fit out heavily-armed merchantmen in order to escort shipping which was charged for the service.[56]

Such systems and problems were not, however, the same as naval weakness, as the Dutch clearly demonstrated at the expense of Spain in 1639. More generally, the Dutch navy had an impressive level of effectiveness and there was more coordination of naval activities between the Admiralties by the second half of the century. The Dutch navy was very large, not only in comparison to the population but also compared with much larger states, and the mercantile marine it had to protect dwarfed anything else in Europe. Furthermore, funded by customs revenues, the Dutch navy, prior to the mid-seventeenth century, was the sole European navy that even attempted to protect its merchantmen around all European coasts. Private solutions to trade protection do not undermine this point as they were normal in Europe, and indeed the counterpart of the extent to which violence was an aspect of commercial competition; and the Dutch state was ahead of its time when it tried to protect all Dutch trade in Europe: the English started to do so under William III in the 1690s. Dutch 'private navies' were only a supplement to the Admiralty-run forces and a useful addition to the national war effort.

The Dutch state was certainly deficient compared to an ideal image of state organisation and activity, but, contrasted with other states of the period, Western and non-Western, it was a model of efficiency. Indeed, in the 1620s, 1630s and 1640s, the Dutch navy of purpose-built sailing warships was normally the second largest in the world, and, after the dissolution of the Spanish-Portuguese union in 1640, for some years the largest. The Dutch mercantile marine was gigantic, and perfect protection against asymmetric warfare against Dutch trade was almost impossible to achieve. Even the British mercantile marine was to suffer losses from such attack when the British navy was enormous.

The English navy that fought in the First Anglo-Dutch War (1652–4) was also an impressive force, but, rather than looking for a major state navy prefiguring it and, indeed, also the leading Western European navies of the 1660s, and, even more, 1690s, in some linear account of development, it is more appropriate to note the continuing European ability to devise different workable solutions. Alan James's point about the French navy in the 1650s, that it was an effective instrument of royal policy, and also that it proved possible to construct a consensus in maritime affairs, is more generally relevant.

Yet, what has been seen as a new age of naval warfare defined by the Anglo-Dutch conflict changed the situation,[57] so that a workable early seventeenth-century system proved less so from mid-century. This assessment contributes to the idea that, in so far as there was a process of significant military change in the period 1500–1800, let alone, as sometimes claimed, a Military Revolution, the key developments occurred in the second half of the period.[58] This argument indicates the divide in the mid-seventeenth century that testified to the formative nature of the period 1660–1760, although, in the case of naval power, this period should be seen as beginning in the 1650s.

Another aspect of the growth of government control over naval activity was provided by the struggle with piracy.[59] Thus, Spain, Genoa and Tuscany tried to protect the west coast of

Italy from corsair raids, especially from North Africa. This struggle can be located in a wider international context of resisting privateers and pirates that served Ottoman or French interests, but opposition to piracy was also an aspect of the wider-ranging attempt by rulers to control naval forces, or at least to prevent hostile naval developments from within their own territories. Thus, the organisation of an independent Huguenot admiralty in 1621 was a challenge to the French Crown, not least because it was followed that October by the successful operations of the Huguenot fleet against Breton warships in royal service.

The major challenge to the control of naval conflict by the territorial states was from semi-independent naval forces with an international dimension. The Barbary Pirates or Corsairs of North Africa were linked to the Ottomans, while their opponents could call on the Knights of St John, from Rhodes and, later, Malta, and, to a certain extent in the Adriatic, on the piratical Uskoks of Senj. Such raiders tended to maintain a high level of violence; indeed, conflict was integral to their economy and *raison d'être*, as it had been for earlier maritime predators, such as the Vikings. The economy of Senj was based almost entirely on plunder. To supply the town, the Uskoks needed regular and profitable booty – or regular payments from tributaries in exchange.[60] The Uskoks and the Knights of St John were both perfectly willing to attack Venetian vessels if they thought they were trading with the Ottomans, despite their Christian crews.

Similarly, from the late sixteenth century, the Dnieper and Don Cossacks began to raid the Ottoman positions on the Black Sea. As an example of the more general point about the limited value of deeper-draught vessels, and the problem of measuring naval power by counting them, the Cossacks employed portable rowing boats with flat bottoms and no keel, which were able to use shallower waters than those of the Ottoman galleys. This capability had a major affect on Ottoman attempts to pursue the Cossacks in 1614–15. As a consequence, from the 1630s, the Ottomans copied the Cossack boats; while, as with the Spaniards against English privateers, fortifications also played a role in strengthening their position on the rivers, with the Ottomans recapturing Azov and refortifying Ochakov.[61]

Although attacks by Barbary corsairs, Uskoks and Cossacks lacked the scale of the operations of the Ottoman or Spanish forces, and all three could be seen as more akin to brigands than to competing states, it is important not to adopt overly rigid definitions about early modern naval warfare. At the same time, on the other side of the continuum, piracy, or robbery at sea, was possibly nearly as common between Christians in the Channel as in the Mediterranean and was, perhaps, more an unavoidable hazard of seaborne trade than evidence of a state of war between nations, states or creeds.[62] Moreover, rebellion and civil war across much of Europe ensured that there was a host of authorities able to issue letters of marque to licence as privateering what might otherwise be seen as piracy. For example, the privateering frigates of Randall, Marquess of Antrim in the 1640s have been described as doubling as the Irish navy.[63]

In so far as the concept of an early modern European military revolution is helpful, it is more pertinent to apply it to naval than to land capability, which is a reminder of the problem of treating the two as if they conformed to the same pattern. Yet, at the same time, the extent of privateering during the mid-seventeenth-century global crisis that has been discerned in the 1640s and 1650s serves as a warning against stressing the extent of any such transformation towards state-controlled naval force. Rebellion and civil war, for example in France in the 1570s, also greatly lessened the ability of states to suppress piracy and to protect trade and therefore revenues. As a result, although there are no comprehensive figures, it is possible that the European stock of seagoing vessels fell considerably. Far from there having been a major shift, the situation in the Channel in the 1560s was akin to the position in the 1650s. In the 1560s, the Huguenot Prince of Condé, the English Earl of Warwick and the Prince of Orange all granted 'letters of marque' to privateers, and the sailors of the English West Country, La Rochelle, the Breton ports and Zeeland were only too willing to take them up.

The extent to which governments encouraged privateering was a response to the opportunities for commercial warfare against their opponents, and also a product of their own weakness, and the resultant need to tap any military resources that might be available, even at the cost of very limited control. From a different perspective, the creation of large fleets using partnership arrangements with commercial and investment interests, as well as the retention of capability by state-sponsored piracy, each indicated a degree of originality in European thinking as well as organisational flexibility that had parallels with the military entrepreneurs of the period who raised substantial forces of mercenaries; although there were important historical anticipations.

To turn to tactical issues, comprehensive fighting instructions existed in the 1590s, for example for the English Cadiz expedition of 1596. These instructions were steadily developed as line-ahead tactics evolved, but a high degree of discipline and organisational cohesion were present as early as the Armada battles in the English Channel in 1588. Looking ahead from the 1650s, it is possible to see fighting instructions and line tactics as instilling discipline and encouraging a new stage in organisational cohesion that permitted more effective firepower,[64] one that was further enhanced when merchantmen ceased to appear in the line of battle of European fleets in the late seventeenth century. However, it is necessary not to read back from this situation to the more inchoate position earlier, as governments struggled to create and maintain effective fleets in a difficult political and organisational context and were faced with the particular resource requirements of naval strength.

3   1660–1775

Britain became the leading naval power in Europe, and thus the world, in the period 1690–1715, a position it was to sustain until the Second World War. This achievement reflected British policies and priorities, those of other states, and the course of wars. British naval history therefore is the dominant theme in this chapter, both because more is known about Britain than about other states and because it is possible to use Britain as a case study for the domestic aspects of naval power and their interaction with strategic concerns. The growth of English naval power in both the sixteenth and the early and mid-seventeenth centuries had equipped England with an important navy and a tradition of maritime power that subsequently affected political assumptions and views about the necessary identity and desirable policies of Britain (the correct term after the Parliamentary Union of 1707 with Scotland) as a military power.

1660–90

England showed its naval strength during the republican Interregnum (1649–60) and, more specifically, in the ability to contest naval mastery with the Dutch, the foremost naval power in the world, in the three Anglo-Dutch wars of 1652–4, 1665–7 and 1672–4. Yet there had been a relative decline in English naval power in the 1660s when, thanks to French and Dutch ship-building, the English went from leading to third most important naval power;[1] although discussing warships in terms of numbers is problematic unless the quality of ships and crew is also considered, a point that remains pertinent today. English naval strength greatly revived in the late 1670s, thanks to a major shipbuilding programme, but the French navy remained larger in the 1680s and launched more warships than England in the early 1690s.

The French fleet had declined during the *Frondes*, the civil conflicts of mid-century, but was revived from the 1660s, notably by Jean-Baptiste Colbert who, in 1669, became Secretary of State for the Navy, a new post. Colbert organised a system for the conscription of sailors, purchased warships and recruited skilled shipbuilders from the Dutch, founded training schools, developed dockyards and administrative systems, and oversaw a major expansion in the size of the French navy, so that by 1675 it was the largest in the world. Indeed, there was a series of successful naval engagements with Dutch–Spanish squadrons off Sicily in 1675–6. He encouraged the development of Rochefort, La Rochelle, Quebec, Brest, Lorient and Sète as a system of naval ports.

In contrast, for internal political reasons, Spain did not take part in the development by the leading powers of larger and more effective battle fleets.[2] There had also been a shift in the geographical focus of naval development. Judged by the criteria of administrative sophistication, the mobilisation of men and the implementation of technology, the level and intensity of Mediterranean naval conflict in the 1560s and 1570s was far in advance of the campaigns in the Atlantic and North Sea in the 1580s and 1590s,[3] but this situation certainly did not pertain a century later.

The 1690s

During the late 1690s, English naval power increased, not least relative to that of the other two leading naval states, France and the Dutch. Between 1689 and 1698, the English launched 61 capital ships. The situation was initially less promising in 1689–92, but, as a result of an Act of Parliament of 1691 sponsoring new construction, England, from 1695, had a definite lead in new launchings over both France and the Dutch, and by 1700 the English fleet was larger than that of France.

Furthermore, there was a significant improvement in logistical support, while English naval capability also increased with a rapid and expensive programme of dockyard construction. Portsmouth, which already had two dry docks that acted as a double dock, was expanded with the creation of two new dry docks and two wet docks. At Plymouth, where the naval facilities had hitherto been primitive, a new dockyard, including a dry dock and a wet dock, was constructed. Initially, in 1689, it was decided that the Plymouth dry dock should be capable of receiving up to third-rates, but in 1691 the dock contract was upgraded so as to be able to take the biggest ships of the line.[4] The expansion of facilities at Portsmouth and Plymouth supplemented the Restoration concentration of naval facilities on the Medway and the Thames, at Chatham, Deptford and Woolwich. The latter had faced the Dutch, the enemy in three wars from 1652 to 1674, while the Western Approaches of the English Channel, the Atlantic and beyond, were the key to conflict with France. Improvements at Portsmouth and Plymouth permitted the stronger projection of English naval power into the English Channel and Western Approaches in the 1690s.[5] In contrast, Chatham declined, while France was greatly outnumbered by Britain in the number of dry docks.

British naval expenditure reflected the role of credit and trade in raising resources that could be used for the navy. The general financial position of the British navy also improved with the development, from the 1690s, of stable parliamentary-backed national finances anchored on the Bank of England, which was founded in 1694. These finances enabled a cut in the interest rates on government borrowing, providing a much more stable basis for naval expenditure than that of more autocratic societies such as France, Spain and Russia. Thus, alongside similarities between states in naval armament came significant differences in organisational systems. Dockyards were crucially dependent on funds, as were the recruitment and support of the large number of sailors required.[6] Moreover, England, like the United Provinces, witnessed the development of a naval professionalism that was less apparent in France and Spain, where noble privilege played a greater role.[7]

The impact of improvements in English capability was accentuated by changed priorities affecting the French and Dutch navies. Having covered a Dutch invasion of England in 1688, a strategic step that led to William III of Orange replacing James II in Britain, the Dutch navy was affected by a concentration of expenditure on the army, an expenditure made necessary by war with France for most of the period 1688–1713.

As a result, whereas in the abortive defensive treaty of 1678 the ratio of Dutch to English capital ships had been fixed at 3:4, in 1689 this ratio was lowered to 3:5, and, during the War of the Spanish Succession (1702–13), the Dutch were generally more than halfway below their quota, and, even then, the ships often arrived late. This was a stage in an operational retrenchment that reflected the resources available.[8]

Furthermore, from 1694, the French, then at war with England, the Dutch, Austria and Spain, concentrated on the army, and at sea on privateering. Rather than needing warships to protect France's coasts, it was clear that fortifications as at Brest and troops could fulfil these tasks. Prior to that, there had been a short-lived, but intense naval crisis for William III that exacerbated the dangers posed by Jacobitism, the cause of the exiled Stuarts. In 1689, after the indecisive Battle of Bantry Bay, in which Admiral Herbert and 22 ships of the line were unable to defeat a French fleet of 24 ships of the line covering a landing of French troops in Ireland to support James II, the English fleet had to return to Portsmouth for repairs, because there was no dry docking in the Channel further west. This situation gave the French a major advantage, as, from their Atlantic bases at Brest and Rochefort, they could challenge the English in the Channel and in Irish waters, and also attack shipping routes. Two months later, the French threat was accentuated when the able Anne-Hilarion Count of Tourville evaded the English fleet off Brittany to lead much of the Toulon (Mediterranean) fleet into Brest, creating a threatening concentration of French strength.

In 1690, the French successfully escorted another force of troops to Ireland, and were victorious off Beachy Head over a greatly outnumbered Anglo-Dutch fleet. The French, however, did not have an invasion force ready and Louis XIV was more concerned about the conflict on land with England and its allies in the Spanish Netherlands (Belgium). Indeed, Louis only once went to sea, embarking briefly on the *Entreprenant*, a ship of the line, during his visit to Dunkirk in 1680; the sole occasion after 1660 that he saw a ship. Moreover, Louis's earlier failure to maintain financial support for the navy was linked to its institutional weaknesses in the mid- and late 1680s, and to its consequent operational limitations in 1690.[9]

In addition, the concentration of French troops on the Spanish Netherlands did not lend itself to an invasion of England, because French naval power was based further west, in Brest. It was not until 1692 that French invasion forces were prepared, but secrecy was lost, delays in the invasion preparations hindered Tourville, and he was compromised both by a failure to unite the French naval forces and by rigid instructions enforcing conflict even if outnumbered. A far larger Anglo-Dutch fleet under Admiral Edward Russell attacked the French off Barfleur on the Cotentin peninsula. Russell was able to gain the initiative, but the French fought well before withdrawing. Twenty-two of the French warships reached the harbour of St Malo through the hazardous race of Alderney, but many of the damaged warships took shelter under the forts at St Vaast and Île Tatihou in the bay of La Hougue on the east side of the peninsula. In turn, they were attacked and burned by small boats sent in by Vice-Admiral Sir George Rooke, one of the most successful small-boat operations of the period, but one made possible by the division and demoralisation among the French fleet caused by their earlier pummelling from the larger Anglo-Dutch fleet. Fifteen warships, and the transports, were destroyed.

After Barfleur, English warships were in firmer control of Irish waters, but already they had played a key role there in support of the army, relieving Londonderry, helping John, Earl of Marlborough take Cork and Kinsale, blockading Limerick and co-operating in the capture of Duncannon Castle. This activity reflected the potential of naval power for affecting operations on land and helped ensure that the Jacobites were defeated in Ireland, repeating the situation in Ireland at the start of the century (see p. 36).

Barfleur not only dashed French invasion prospects, but also led to a major shift in European naval history. Although Tourville took large fleets to sea in 1693 and 1694, he achieved little: war in Ireland ended with success for William III, a French invasion of England appeared a less promising prospect, and, in 1694, there was little for Tourville to achieve in the Mediterranean. Under pressure from the economic crisis of 1693–4, which hit government finances, and influenced by the limited benefits from recent naval operations, the French refocused their naval strategy from the *guerre d'escadre*, the war of squadrons in which they had sought battle, to the *guerre de course*, in which privateering attacks on trade took top priority, particularly in the War of the Spanish Succession in 1702–13.[10]

These attacks could be very damaging. English trade was hit hard, which affected the economy and public finances, both helping to cause and exacerbating a major financial crisis in 1696. Three years earlier, over eighty English and Dutch merchantmen were lost when the Smyrna convoy was intercepted by the main French fleet off Lagos in Portugal. However, privateering did not provide a serious challenge to English naval power, certainly not one as grave as that posed by the French fleet in 1690. There was no comparison with the more deadly German submarine assault on British trade routes in the Second World War. Conversely, the German invasion threat in 1940 was weaker than that of France in 1692.

The shift in French priorities interacted with a rise in English naval power and confidence, but also created problems because it ensured that there was not generally a French battle fleet at sea for the English to engage and defeat, and that in a political culture in which such victories were necessarily in order to affirm power and maintain domestic support. As a result, although French weakness enabled the English to prepare for a projection of naval power, it proved difficult to follow up Barfleur. As so often, naval advice clashed with governmental optimism, leading to Russell's loss of command after the 1692 campaign. Amphibious attacks were launched at St Malo and Brest in 1692 and 1694, respectively, but without success. Subsequently, a policy of bombarding French ports such as Calais (1696), St Malo (1693, 1695) and Dunkirk (1695) was found less costly. However, such bombardments had only a limited impact and did not distract the French from their campaigns in the Spanish Netherlands, the key area of activity on land. This point is a reminder of the peripheral (at worse) and indirect (at best) strategic impact of naval power.

Far more strategic benefit was gained from the dispatch of a large English fleet under Russell to the Mediterranean in 1694, which was followed by its wintering at Cadiz: Spain was then allied to Britain.[11] In both 1694 and 1695, the fleet stiffened Spanish resistance to French pressure on Catalonia and helped keep Spain in the war.[12] The interests of Austria, France and

Spain in the western Mediterranean ensured that it was the cockpit of European diplomacy, and, in the half-century from 1694, it was to be a major sphere of British naval power, setting the pattern for public assumptions about this power. English warships had been to the area previously, especially under Blake in the 1650s, and, thereafter, to protect English trade from the Barbary pirates of North Africa, but, from 1694, such naval deployment was more closely linked to strategic confrontations with other European states, principally France but also Austria and Spain.

English naval forces ranged widely in the 1690s. In 1697, a small squadron was sent to the Caribbean, but disease claimed the commander, all the captains and half of the sailors. The effectiveness of English naval operations varied, but there was a common theme of gaining the initiative, mounting attacks, protecting English trade and attacking that of France. The range of English naval activity was maintained after peace was negotiated in 1697. A squadron was sent to Newfoundland to protect

Table 3.1   Size of navies: displacement in 1,000 metric tons

	1690	1695	1700	1710	1720	1730	1740	1745	1750	1755	1760
England	124	172	196	201	174	189	195	235	276	277	375
Netherlands	68	106	113	119	79	62	65	65	62	58	62
France	141	208	195	171	48	73	91	98	115	162	156
Spain	30	25	20	10	22	73	91	55	41	113	137

Source: J. Glete, *Navies and Nations: Warships, Navies and State Building in Europe and America, 1500–1860* (Stockholm, 1993).

Table 3.2   Relative size of navy as a percentage of the total size of European navies

	1690	1695	1700	1705	1710	1715	1720
England, later Britain	25.1	25.6	25.8	25.9	26.4	29.2	28.3
Netherlands	13.7	15.8	14.9	14.2	15.6	14.2	12.9
France	28.5	30.9	25.7	23.9	22.4	15.7	7.8

Source: J. Glete, *Navies and Nations: Warships, Navies and State Building in Europe and America, 1500–1860* (Stockholm, 1993).

English trade. This new-found confidence led in 1700 to the dispatch of a joint Anglo-Dutch fleet to the Sound, where it helped to enforce a settlement of Dano-Swedish differences that prevented Charles XII of Sweden from crushing Denmark.

The War of the Spanish Succession, 1702–13

English naval strength was barely contested by the French during the War of the Spanish Succession, in large part because French expenditure continued to be dominated by the army. This situation enabled the English, who took part in the war from 1702 to 1713, to inhibit French invasion planning, to maintain control of maritime routes to the Low Countries,[13] the crucial axis of the Grand Alliance against France, and to project power, especially into the Mediterranean. But for the English navy, there would have been no war in Iberia (Portugal and Spain), not least because the threat of naval action, underlined by the fleet's success at Vigo in 1702, led Portugal to abandon its French alliance in 1703. Thanks in part to the availability of a harbour at Lisbon, the English fleet under Sir Cloudesley Shovell entered the Mediterranean in 1703, encouraging Victor Amadeus II of Savoy-Piedmont to abandon Louis XIV. Naval force therefore acted as a key force multiplier.

The French made one major attempt to contest English naval predominance when in 1704 they challenged the newly established English position at Gibraltar, but the French were checked at the battle of Malaga. No ships were sunk, casualties were heavy on both sides, and several English ships ran out of ammunition, but this battle, although operationally indecisive, was strategically decisive, because, in its outcome, it greatly limited major French fleet action in the region. It thus had the same effect as Barfleur in 1692.

Combined operations were important. In 1705, the English fleet supported the successful siege of Barcelona, landing cannon and seamen. The following year, the arrival of the fleet led the French to abandon their siege of Barcelona: the French fleet did not stay to fight the English. Thus, the English fleet greatly affected the war on land, leading to pressure for it to winter nearby.[14] In 1706, the fleet went on to assist in the capture of

Alicante, Majorca and Ibiza, while, in the following year, the English fleet under Shovell supported the Austro-Savoyard army in its crossing of the River Var en route for Toulon, and later covered its retreat. Although Toulon was not captured, the French destroyed most of their warships in the harbour and thus further improved the English naval position.[15] In addition, from 1709 the French built no ships of the line during the war. As in the previous war, the English fleet also devoted much time both to protecting trade from the damaging ravages of French privateers[16] and to attacking French commerce.

This period of naval superiority was not without its problems, not least those posed by the expectations raised by allies, Austria and Savoy-Piedmont, problems that were (and are) a frequent aspect of naval power and one underplayed by the tendency in some of the literature to focus on battles rather than policy. In 1701, one of the English Under-Secretaries, John Ellis, wrote to George Stepney, the envoy in Vienna, expressing interest in the possibility of using Austria's Adriatic ports, adding:

> I cannot but join with you in thinking that nothing considerable can be done in that part of the world, without a force at sea in the Mediterranean, to procure respect from the princes and inhabitants of the coast, and to set them at liberty from the apprehension and constraints they lie under from the marine power of France and Spain in conjunction.[17]

Yet, the following year, the English felt obliged to resist Austrian pressure for the dispatch of naval forces to Spanish-ruled Naples, which the Austrians were seeking to conquer. Focusing on the need to reconcile differing commitments, the English cited the need to retain naval superiority in the English Channel, while William Blathwayt, the influential Secretary-at-War, drew attention to the problem of detaching squadrons: 'You say right of our noble fleet and number of seamen but I don't conceive how you think we can venture twelve sail alone in the Mediterranean unless it be for a sacrifice',[18] a reference to the threat posed by the French fleet-in-being at Toulon. Instead, the English sought to intercept the Spanish treasure fleet from the New World. By thus deploying the bulk of their fleet in Channel and Atlantic waters, they were also able to keep an eye on the

French in Brest, whose position threatened the Irish Sea and the Channel approaches.

If the 1700s revealed the difficulties of combining naval strategy and operations with the exigencies of alliance politics, the war also indicated the problems facing naval forces operating outside that context, but within that of a different but often more difficult alliance, that with the English army, a point that was relevant for the twentieth century, for example for the troubled relations between the American navy and army in the Pacific in 1944. In 1703, Blathwayt wrote to Stepney about English attacks on the wealthy French West Indies:

> our attempt upon Guadaloupe under the command of Captain Codrington has been so far unsuccessful that after plundering and spoiling the greatest part of the island we were forced to retire to our own islands by the fresh succours the French had received from Martinique. This they say has been chiefly occasioned by the disagreement of the sea commander with our land general which has been the bane of all expeditions from that against Hispaniola [now Haiti and the Dominican Republic] in Cromwell's time [1655] downwards to this last instance but the influence of the Admiralty will always prevail to make it so.[19]

Twenty-two warships under Vice-Admiral John Benbow had been sent to the Caribbean in 1701. Spain was no longer a British ally as she had been in the Nine Years' War, and the possibility of seizing her treasure ships offered profit to naval commanders, bullion for Britain, and the dislocation of the Bourbon financial system. Further north, in a different form of economic warfare, British warships wrecked the highly profitable French fishery off Newfoundland in 1702. In 1711, an amphibious attempt was mounted on Quebec, the major French base in Canada, but it failed in part due to poor navigation in the St Lawrence River. The experience in amphibious operations that the British were to display in mid-century was missing earlier.[20]

In contrast, the Great Northern War (1700–21) in northern Europe saw successful amphibious operations by Sweden and its opponent Russia, albeit at a shorter range. With its new capital and naval base at St Petersburg, Russia was essentially a new naval power whose development owed much to the vision and determination of Peter the Great (r. 1689–1725), and to his ability to direct resources in his quest to copy Western European naval technology. He succeeded in overturning Swedish naval dominance in the eastern Baltic and in using his naval power both to support his land operations against the Swedish empire and to raid Sweden's coasts.

The Anglo-French Alliance, 1716–31

Despite the problems it faced in translating output into out-come, Britain remained the strongest naval power, helped by French naval weakness and then by the Anglo-French alliance (1716–31). Furthermore, Spain was the seat of war during the War of the Spanish Succession and, although the Spanish navy was revived under Philip V (r. 1700–46), the crushing British victory over it off Cape Passaro in 1718 demonstrated that Britain was the strongest naval power in the Mediterranean. In this victory, 20 British ships of the line and 2 frigates, under Admiral Sir George Byng, destroyed a poorly deployed fleet of 13 more lightly gunned of the line and 8 frigates, and captured 7 ships of the line, leading to euphoria about British naval capabilities.[21]

The *Weekly Journal*, a Whig London newspaper, in its issue of 18 October (os) 1718, claimed: 'This single action renders the King of Great Britain as much master of the Mediterranean as he has always been acknowledged to be sovereign over the British seas.' An account of naval operations in this period, the third edition of which appeared significantly in 1739, the year when war with Spain next broke out, misleadingly exulted over 'the war of Sicily, wherein the fleet of Great Britain bore so illustrious a part, that the fate of the island was wholly governed by its operations, both competitors agreeing, that the one could not have conquered, nor the other subdued without it'.

The extent to which Britain was the leading naval power of the period was demonstrated by her most intractable problem, the difficulty of defeating Peter the Great of Russia when his navy refused to fight, prefiguring the Russian naval strategy during the Crimean War of 1854–6. Such problems in the Baltic were a far cry from 1690–2, when France had challenged Britain effectively for control of the Channel. Even so, in the 1720s, the British were mistakenly confident that their navy would prevent the Russians from dominating the Baltic and attacking Britain's allies, Denmark and Sweden, as it was assumed that through the use of naval power Britain could solve her foreign policy difficulties. Twice during the reign of George I, the British ministry chose to intervene in distant quarrels by means of the navy: the dispatch of Byng to the Mediterranean in 1718 and the decision to use the navy as part of the 1719–21 diplomatic offensive to force Russia to return some of her conquests from Sweden as a part of the peace between the two powers. In both cases, the government miscalculated the impact of naval intervention, demonstrating a common flaw in navalist arguments.

In 1718, the government hoped that the threat of British action would persuade Spain not to attack Sicily, but Philip V, who, like Peter the Great, saw naval power as crucial to power projection and geopolitical interests, called Britain's bluff. Although Philip lost his fleet off Cape Passaro, this did not and could not lead to the reconquest of Sicily, a point made then and again, in similar circumstances, when Spain threatened and then successfully invaded Sicily during the War of the Polish Succession (1733–5). The British were able to do little in 1719 to aid the reconquest of Sicily by the Austrians, and the war with Spain indeed led to financial and political problems in Britain. There are instructive comparisons with the operational strengths and strategic limitations of British naval power in the Mediterranean in 1941 when under attack from Italy and Germany.

The 1718–20 crisis in the Mediterranean also revealed what was to be underlined in 1733–5, and again in 1740–1, that, without a permanent squadron in that sea, British intervention would tend to be too late. In 1741, the British were unable to stop the dispatch of Spanish forces to Italy across the Mediterranean. Foreign policy commitments, especially treaty obligations, in southern Europe could only be effected by naval force, but the capabilities of naval preparation and warfare did not permit as rapid a mobilisation and deployment of naval forces as politicians envisaged, a problem that, despite a very different technological context, was to be echoed over the last century. Contributing to the problem was the degree to which, whereas former army commanders held important political posts – George I, George II and Secretaries of State such as Stanhope and Harrington, this was not true of former naval officers.

Moreover, a successful naval strategy that matched political expectations called for Mediterranean bases where a major squadron could be based permanently, repaired completely and victualled adequately. Neither Gibraltar nor Minorca, captured in 1704 and 1708, respectively, and ceded to Britain by the Peace of Utrecht of 1713, was suitable. Gibraltar was small and some of the Bay was exposed to Spanish artillery fire, Minorca was vulnerable to attacks by the French Toulon squadron, and both were dependent for grain on precarious supplies from the Barbary states (Morocco, Algiers, Tunis, Tripoli). Britain lacked the well-positioned, well-supported naval base in the Mediterranean that its foreign policy required, although this policy also relied upon allied land forces to be effective. In contrast, in the nineteenth and early twentieth centuries, the British had valuable bases in Malta (from 1800) and Alexandria (from 1882).

The attempt to force Russia to restore her Baltic conquests was similarly problematic. Naval action was seen as crucial to the fulfilment of the British diplomatic strategy, but naval opinion was contrary, to the disgust of one politician: 'Sir John Norris has in a manner protested against it. He has now 17 ships of the line ... he comes out like all your blusterers a very very little man.'[22] This criticism was unfair, for the hope that Norris could sink the Russian fleet was defeated by Peter the Great's unwillingness to fight. Furthermore, bombarding coastal towns would have been pointless for, as with the Anglo-Russian Ochakov crisis of 1791, the principal targets would have been the warehouses of British merchants. In truth, the blusterers were the members of the ministry who had negotiated themselves into a false position and failed to devote sufficient attention to what the navy could achieve, a situation with modern parallels.

In diplomatic circles, there was still considerable faith in naval power and, looking toward the nineteenth-century use of such power on the world scale, the politics of bombardment were regarded by several diplomats as perfectly possible. Just as, in 1717–18, the British considered bombarding the Papal port of Civitàvecchia in order to ensure the release of the Earl of Peterborough held by the Papacy at Bologna, so the idea recurred in 1727 when the Stuart Pretender, 'James III', was sheltered in the Papal town of Avignon. John Hedges suggested during a dispute with the government of Genoa: 'if 10 or a dozen men of war made them a short visit it would convince them there were other people in the world, besides a family with a great lip [the Habsburgs]'. James O'Hara, envoy in Lisbon, was also a strong believer in the efficacy of violence. In 1729, he proposed that the Portuguese should be brought to reason 'by the roughest means', meaning naval attack, adding that, as Portugal lacked allies, nobody would intervene if George II 'had a mind to lay this country to ashes'.[23]

Prefiguring British policy from 1815, and American from 1945 and, also, 1991, when situations were similar, actual use of the British fleet was far more cautious, although naval power was not restricted to international confrontations. Instead, the Royal Navy was employed to fight piracy and stop smuggling. Many small, fast ships were built to patrol home waters, while warships were deployed to the Caribbean and other waters in order to capture pirates. Policing the seas was important to the British understanding of naval power. The large-scale pirate attacks in the Caribbean mounted in the 1670s, 1680s and 1690s, when cities had been attacked, had become far more small-scale by the 1710s, but piracy continued, not least because it was profitable.[24]

Moreover, naval capability remained the most important aspect of British military preparedness and projection. In 1726, when Britain was in a state of cold war with Austria, Russia and Spain, the navy was mobilised in a truly impressive display of strength, and deployed in several areas of the world in a marked demonstration of numerical and logistical capability. None of the hostile powers nor any combination of them could match this strength. In the Baltic, a squadron helped to dissuade Russia from an attack upon Sweden, in an attempt to secure the alliance of the latter, while in home waters the fleet threatened both Spain and the potential Austrian invasion port of Ostend with attack. A squadron in the Caribbean blockaded the Spanish treasure fleet in Porto Bello. Charles, Viscount Townshend, the Secretary of State for the Northern Department, wrote with some satisfaction:

> It is indeed a reflection which must afford His Majesty a great deal of comfort and satisfaction as it redounds highly to the glory of the British nation and the honour of our navy, that whilst one of his fleets is preserving the tranquillity of the North against the ambitious and pernicious designs of the Czarina [Catherine I], and

another is keeping the Spanish treasure in the West Indies and thereby preventing the Emperor [Charles VI, ruler of Austria] and Spain from disturbing the peace of the South, the very report of a third squadron going out has caused such alarm and confusion in the Austrian Netherlands [Belgium], and has put Spain, in the low and miserable condition of their finances, to the trouble and expense of marching their troops and fortifying their seaport towns.[25]

A high level of naval activity was maintained over succeeding years. In 1727, fearing a Spanish-supported Jacobite invasion, and angry about Spanish intransigence in peace negotiations, the British kept a strong squadron off Cadiz, and Sir Charles Wager was ordered to destroy the Spanish fleet if it should sail towards Britain.[26] In 1729, a powerful squadron was prepared and based at Spithead, ready to sail against Spain,[27] although the fleet, which was reinforced by a Dutch squadron, did not sail, thus provoking Opposition derision about its cost, lack of action and lack of effectiveness.[28]

Despite these preparations, the government deliberately avoided action, in part by keeping the navy away from stations that might have provoked confrontation. In 1726 and 1730, there were no amphibious attacks upon Austria's Italian possessions, while, in 1727, British ships were withdrawn from the approaches to the Baltic, not to reappear there for many years. In 1729, Townshend blocked the sailing of Wager's fleet. In place of active confrontation, the naval strategy was one of a threat of violence to be suggested by naval armaments, again a policy with modern parallels. The *Weekly Medley* claimed on 19 July (os) 1729 that 'the British squadron without going out of our ports can incomparably hasten matters towards a conclusion much quicker than bare negotiations'. Three years earlier, Thomas, Duke of Newcastle, Townshend's fellow Secretary of State, thought that the dispatch of Admiral Sir John Jennings's squadron towards Cadiz in 1726 would have a great effect even though he was not to commit hostilities, 'for his barely appearing in those seas, which would not fail to alarm them, might in the uncertain conditions they are in at present, produce the best consequences imaginable'.[29]

Nevertheless, there was scepticism in Europe about the effectiveness of naval power, scepticism that prefigured the relative lack of interest in British naval power displayed by the Qialong Emperor when Lord Maccartney visited Beijing in 1793 and presented him with a model of a warship. In 1726, Frederick William I of Prussia, fearful, instead, of attack by the Russian army, told the British envoy: 'as to your fleet, it is of no manner of service to me'.[30] Two years later, the Duke of Parma, who had angered Britain by his Jacobite sympathies, was reported as claiming 'he did not fear the English, for their fleet could not come to him at Parma'.[31] Moreover, Jacobites and Jacobite sympathisers, keen to persuade Austria and/or Spain to support an invasion of Britain in the period 1725–9, claimed that the British navy could not guarantee control of home waters.[32]

As in the modern world, the very decision not to use the fleet for conflict kept its potential strength a mystery, and therefore enhanced its value as a diplomatic counter. This policy also meant, however, that unrealistic public estimations of naval capacity could be maintained, specifically that talk of seizing parts of the Spanish Empire without difficulty could continue. Had such a policy been attempted and failed, as it doubtless would have given the logistical difficulties of the task, the primitive state of amphibious warfare and the strength of the Spanish West Indies, then public attitudes to naval strategy would have had to have been reconsidered. They were not, and this contrast in the domestic situation in Britain, the state with the most developed public politics, between popular attitudes – continued faith in naval power and in the Blue Water strategy of self-sustaining maritime power – and, on the other hand, ministerial scepticism and disinclination to accept the risks and cost of naval warfare, continued into the 1730s. This situation was to be repeated in the late nineteenth century until naval panics about the strength and plans of other states reduced the expectations of the British public. More recently, the focus has been on expectations of air power.

Conflict with the Bourbons, 1739–48

Prefiguring the consequences of the deterioration of American relations with China and Russia in the early 2000s, the international naval situation abruptly changed for Britain with the collapse of the Anglo-French alliance in 1731, because naval capability was dependent on political circumstances. The immediate response was war panic at the prospect of a French invasion on behalf of the Jacobites.[33] The longer-term consequence was a realisation that naval superiority and strategic security would require war with France, if, as seemed likely, there was no reconciliation with her. Lacking a substantial army, the British position was very parlous, as it would be necessary to keep the fleet in home waters to prevent invasion.[34] This situation put a premium on the destruction of the French navy, lending military point to the sense of humiliation and dissatisfaction that followed failures to achieve this end. The nature of naval operations in the Age of Sail was not, however, conducive to forcing an unwilling opponent to fight in a position of inferiority.

The continued existence of the French fleet had considerable, potentially crucial, strategic consequences at the time of the Jacobite invasion under Charles Edward Stuart (Bonnie Prince Charlie) in 1745, first of Scotland and then of England. This existence reflected the build-up of the French fleet in the 1730s under Maurepas, the Minister of Marine, and the British failure to defeat the French in 1744 when there had been opportunities both in the Channel and in the Mediterranean. The Brest fleet under de Roquefeuil had moved down the Channel to cover a projected invasion of England, but the British attempt to defeat the French fleet had been wrecked by a storm that hit both fleets, and also sank many of the invasion transports in the Channel ports.

In 1745, the continued existence of a powerful French navy increased the danger of a French landing on the south coast of England. In August 1745, Newcastle's private secretary, Andrew Stone, observed: 'We hope we shall soon have a pretty strong squadron in the Channel: But I know too well, the great delays and uncertainties that service is liable to, to depend very much on it.' That December, Stephen Weston, an Exeter cleric, added: 'We must pray therefore for a North East or North West wind to shut up the western ports of France, since a South East or South West brings our enemies upon us, and at the same time denies us the assistance of our friends.'[35] These fears were to be justified in part. The Duke of Cumberland's pursuit of the retreating Jacobites was to be constrained by the fear of an invasion across the Channel.[36]

Nevertheless, the British were able to take for granted the use of the sea to move their troops up the east coast of Britain and back across the North Sea, thus avoiding many of the problems posed by an invasion when most of the British army was abroad, and also enabling British forces to operate or maintain a presence in two spheres at once. British naval power also blocked French invasion schemes.[37] No crisis comparable to the '45 was ever to recur. During subsequent French invasion attempts on England in 1759, 1779 and 1805, there was no indigenous pro-French activity and, therefore, the strategic situation was very different.

During the remainder of the War of the Austrian Succession (1743–8 for Britain), there was an obvious divergence between growing British naval superiority and the dismal progress of the Allied campaigns in the Low Countries. In consequence, and in marked contrast to the situation during the War of the Spanish Succession, the hope developed that naval success could compensate for continental defeats. This expectation placed a new politico-strategic burden on the navy, for it was now required to obtain and ensure transoceanic advantages, an obligation that necessitated a mastery of home and European waters that would permit the transoceanic dispatch of major naval and army forces. In part, these ideas were of long standing, reflecting a traditional optimistic public assessment of naval capability, but the political need for them can be traced to 1745. It was then that the hopes of defeating France on the Continent that had been so marked in 1742–3, especially after victory in the battle of Dettingen in 1743, were replaced by the realisation that it would be difficult to stop the French triumphing by land. This situation prefigured British policy against France in 1795–1802 and again in 1803–12, when the awareness of disasters in Europe was counteracted by hopes of the conquest of French colonies.

In 1745, the French lost Cape Breton Island and its major naval base of Louisbourg to a force of New England colonists supported by British warships under Sir Peter Warren. The proposition of an exchange for French gains in the Austrian Netherlands [Belgium] as part of a peace, based on the *status quo ante bellum* [situation prior to the war], emerged speedily, and underlined the strategic and political burden on the navy posed by the defence of Cape Breton. That burden led to problems the following year when the French sought to regain the island.[38] In 1746, Newcastle complained:

> Should they [the French fleet] go to North America, and make conquests there, we shall lose both the means of making peace or war. For when once they have either retaken Cape Breton or taken Newfoundland or Nova Scotia (which will be the equivalent for it) we have no longer in our hands the means of purchasing peace of France; or of inducing this nation to carry on the war.[39]

Anville's squadron, however, was wrecked by bad weather and disease,[40] and, from 1747, the British kept more warships to the west of the Channel approaches, which proved crucial in affecting the course of the war at sea. On 3 May 1747, Vice-Admiral George Anson defeated La Jonquière off Cape Finisterre. Anson, with a fleet of 14 of the line, had been long cruising off the Cape, waiting for the French fleet which was instructed to escort ships sailing for both the New World and the East Indies: the French could not keep their fleet simply in being in Brest if they wished to maintain an imperial commercial and political system. The French were heavily outnumbered off Cape Finisterre. Rather than fight in line, Anson ordered his captains to close with the French as fast as they could, and thereafter fight in a series of individual actions, in order to prevent the French from escaping under cover of darkness. The French warships were captured, and Anson gained great prestige and a peerage.[41]

On 14 October 1747, Rear-Admiral Edward Hawke won the most brilliant naval action of the war, the Second Battle of Cape Finisterre. Concerned to reopen their trade with the West Indies, eight of the line from the Brest fleet, under the Marquis de L'Etanduère, sailed to protect a large convoy, only to be intercepted by Hawke with fourteen more lightly gunned ships of the line. The British benefited from having taken the initiative, and from abandoning the rigid tactics of the line in order to direct heavier concentrations of gunfire on individual French ships. Six of the French ships were forced to surrender and the French also lost 4000 sailors, a crucial limitation of their maritime strength.[42] This victory led Newcastle to reflect: 'All difficulties that could be apprehended in Parliament will by this be removed, the pride of France a little humbled, and I hope our allies so far encouraged, that your Royal Highness will find them willing and able to exert themselves for their own safety and sup-port.' The Duke was also confident that the victory would disappoint Jacobite hopes of a possible invasion.[43] The French fleet could no longer escort major convoys bound for French colonies, and this destroyed the logic of the French imperial system.

British victory at sea transformed the invasion threats of 1744–5 and the danger of the loss of Cape Breton in 1746 into a completely different political, strategic and diplomatic situation. The angry debates over naval policy that had characterised the earlier years of the war ended, so that John, 4th Earl of Sandwich, could write in November 1747: 'it is plain that our fleet has honour and great support'.[44]

The navy ended the war in a rich glow of success, at the same time as the disadvantages of alliance politics and a continental military commitment were abundantly brought home by the French advance into the United Provinces (Netherlands). Newcastle wrote after another naval success in early 1748: 'though we have our mortifications, the enemy have theirs also. Their trade is absolutely ruined for the present.'[45] French wine, for example, became very scarce in Berlin in 1748. The British pressure on Bourbon trade was worldwide. On 20 June 1743, on his circumnavigation of the world, George Anson captured the treasure-laden Manila galleon, *Nuestra Señora de Covadonga*, off the Philippines. Warships based at English Harbour, Antigua, a naval base developed from 1728, successfully blockaded Martinique in 1746–7, and the following winter Commodore George Pocock captured 30 merchantmen in the West Indies.

Privateering, the licensed seizure by private individuals of enemy merchantmen, which was not declared illegal until 1856, entailed a fusion of patriotism and profit: indeed more than 6600 prizes were taken by the British in 1702–83, nearly half by privateers.[46] The prospect of privateering profits was important in mobilising support for imperial warfare within the British colonial mercantile community. Spanish colonial trade was hit from 1739. It was also necessary to protect British trade against Bourbon privateers: it was hit in the 1740s, both by the Spaniards and by the French. The agricultural staple trades of the Carolinas, the Chesapeake and, especially, the Caribbean sustained serious losses, and in 1747–8 Bourbon privateers off the Delaware capes brought Philadelphia's trade to a halt.[47]

The contrast between the private enterprise that could produce so many privateers, and the state warfare that made such little difference to the disposition of Caribbean territories in the 1740s, was marked, but Britain was more successful than its rivals in using trade for warfare.

War in 1739–48 showed that the British navy was an effective fighting force and administrative body, and this effectiveness was true not only in European, but, also, in transoceanic waters. In the West Indies, British failures, as in the large-scale amphibious expedition against Cartagena in 1741, were not primarily due to administrative deficiencies, although victualling faced problems. The difficulties of operating in the West Indies were not new: the main change that the war introduced was in the size of the naval forces deployed in the Caribbean, and thus in the quantity of supplies required. The Admiralty's failure to keep the fleet in the Caribbean adequately manned was a reflection of the degree to which it had not yet solved the problem of manning in general, although this manning situation was exacerbated by the effects of disease. The Sick and Hurt Board supplied all the medicines it was asked to, the Admiralty consented to the building of a new hospital, and the sick were given the best treatment that the medical knowledge of the day allowed, even though the nature of the diseases was not understood. Although convoying was poorly organised, the men on the spot were usually able to make good the administrative deficiencies that were revealed. More generally, British ships in the West Indies were able to fulfil their operational role, the decisive test of a naval administration.[48]

Furthermore, the improvement of naval bases in Jamaica and Antigua had provided an infrastructure for large amphibious operations as well as help in policing the seas. The facilities for refitting and repair provided by naval bases were important to sustaining naval strength, which was a difficult task, not least as a consequence of the natural decay of what were organic working parts. The longevity of most ships of the line was about 12–17 years, longevity defined as the time between launch and the need for at least middling repair, although a complex combination of factors, beginning first with the cutting of the timber, its storage, the mode of construction, weather conditions, the service of the ship, and its care while in reserve, determined the longevity of a ship and the amount of repair that it was likely to need.

In 1749, as a result of long war service, including damaging operations in the Caribbean, the battle fleet in good condition had been greatly reduced, and the dockyards could not cope with requirements for repair and replacement. This problem was overcome in the early 1750s, not least through using the private sector to build new ships. In the long term, improved infrastructure and better naval construction lessened the problems of cyclical decay.[49]

There was no adequate permanent force of naval personnel. Naval efficiency was measured in the ability to create fighting teams for existing ships once mobilisation was ordered. The permanent navy consisted of ships and officers, with relatively few sailors. The formation of a reserve of seamen was proposed without result: the Register Act of 1696, which provided for a voluntary register of seamen, had proved unworkable and was repealed in 1710. Subsequent proposals for legislative action met resistance. Although the enlistment of volunteers was important, and in mid-century landsmen, nearly all of whom were volunteers, composed close to one-third of the navy's wartime strength, the navy continued to be dependent on impressments by the press gang. By law, this method applied only to professional seamen, but it was both abused and arbitrary. More seriously, the system was only partially successful.[50] On many occasions, naval preparations and operations were handicapped by a lack of sailors. Possibly, however, there was no better option, in the absence of any training structure for the navy, and given the difficulty of making recruitment attractive when length of service was until the end of the war.

Naval power and British policy, 1749–55

As with the Anglo-French alliance of 1716–31, the potential of British naval power after the War of Austrian Succession was largely a matter of great-power diplomacy. The deterioration in Franco-Spanish relations that led to the Austro-Spanish Treaty of Aranjuez of 1752 was the single most important factor behind British naval success in the subsequent Seven Years' War (1756–63) in which Spain remained neutral until 1762. Thus the arithmetic of naval confrontation that had in the previous war limited

British flexibility was vitally altered, a change that helps to explain France's subsequent determination to win Spanish assistance in the War of American Independence. The British government offered naval assistance to the new Austro-Spanish alignment, the Earl of Holdernesse, Secretary of State for the Southern Department, writing: 'The very notion of His Majesty's supporting this great alliance with his maritime force gives the greatest weight and sanction to it.'[51] However, the alliance cannot be ascribed to British diplomacy.

The bulk of British diplomatic attention in 1749–53 was devoted to attempts to improve the so-called Old Alliance with Austria and the United Provinces and, in particular, to secure the Imperial succession for the son of Maria Theresa, the future Joseph II. This was to be done by settling differences over the Austrian Netherlands, and by creating an alliance system that would comprise most of the German states and restrain Prussian aggression against Austria and Hanover. Naval power was essentially immaterial to this diplomatic strategy, especially because Austrian defensive and offensive interests in Italy, which had played such a major role in Anglo-Austrian relations in the 1700s and 1710s and during the periods of effective alliance between 1731 and 1733 and 1742 and 1748, and which could be assisted by a British fleet in the Mediterranean, had been settled by the reconciliation with Spain. Nevertheless, the British government believed that the strength of the fleet influenced the continental powers, a view that was to be habitually taken by Britain as the leading naval power and is, of course, a continued refrain of navalists. In 1753, Newcastle wrote to Robert Keith, the envoy at Vienna:

> His Majesty's fleet (though at a very great expence), is in a better condition, than it ever was known to be, in time of peace: and the great effect, which the superiority of the King's navy, the last war, had towards obtaining the peace; shows how necessary and effectual, the keeping up that fleet may be for the preservation of it.

Keith dutifully replied that the Austrian Chancellor, Count Kaunitz, 'was very glad to hear, that the King's Royal Navy is in such a condition, as to promise us a superiority at sea in all events. He knows of what consequence our naval force is; how much it contributed to our obtaining the last peace; and how

necessary and essential the keeping up our fleet is for the preservation of it.'[52] In practice, the powers of central and eastern
Europe (Austria, Prussia and Russia) were less impressed by or
interested in British naval power and, indeed, a failure to consider the views of other powers sufficiently has weakened modern discussion of British naval capability.

Naval power was clearly important in the Baltic and this had
allowed Britain to play a major role in Baltic diplomacy, especially in the Dano-Swedish conflicts in 1658 and 1700, as well
as in the last stage of the Great Northern War in 1715–21, and
in 1726–7. In 1716, there had been a prospect of British naval
support for a Russian–Danish invasion of Sweden. In 1747, the
Russians had pressed for naval assistance against Sweden, Lord
Hyndford reporting that if Britain would 'send a squadron of
ships into the Baltic', Russia would 'attack Sweden on the side
of Finland'. In a reference to the possibility of using naval action
against privateers in order to cover a political commitment, as
had indeed happened against Sweden in 1715–16 during the
Great Northern War, Hyndford continued that the dispatch
of French privateers to the Baltic would provide a pretext.
Hyndford later wrote, 'I believe this court has so great a mind to
drive the successor and all his French adherents out of Sweden,
that, if the king could spare but five or six ships of war for the
Baltic to sustain the Russians, the Empress would undertake the
thing of herself.'[53]

The limitations of British naval power as a diplomatic tool
in the Baltic, however, had been exposed when Peter the Great
had refused to back down in the face of threats of naval attack in
1720, and were to be again in 1791, and it is difficult to believe
that Russia decided not to attack Sweden in 1747 because
Britain would not supply a few warships. In the case of the Holy
Roman Empire (Germany), which became the focus of diplomatic activity and speculation in 1750 after the ending of the
Baltic crisis, British naval power was of little value. In 1753, the
Prussian envoy in Paris pointed out to Frederick the Great that
he had no reason to fear a British maritime war, and he referred,
instead, to the vulnerability to land attack of the Electorate of
Hanover, the German possession of the dynasty ruling Britain.[54]
This contrast posted a central question mark against British diplomatic and military plans.

In its German diplomacy, Britain, indeed, relied not on offers or threats of naval power, but on financial inducements and talk of shared interests. Militarily, British ministers and diplomats referred to the support of Austria and Russia, specifically to the possibility of those powers attacking Frederick if he invaded Hanover. There was no role for naval power comparable, for example, to its importance in sustaining Anglo-Piedmontese co-operation for much of the first half of the century.[55]

Although British ministers, nevertheless, remained convinced of the importance of naval power, they were frequently accused of failing to take adequate steps to counter Bourbon colonial and naval moves, and, indeed, both France and Spain greatly increased the size of their fleet after the War of the Austrian Succession, as they were also to do after the Seven Years' War. The Opposition used this changing situation as evidence of an alleged governmental failure to protect national interests, complementing criticism of an excessive concern for continental diplomacy. The opposition newspaper assault used arguments about naval power and, in doing so, shaped them. The *Remembrancer* of 9 September 1749 claimed: 'we have exhausted ourselves completely, in a cause, that of all the powers in Europe, we were the last, and least, concerned in. The balance of power at land was the bubble we fought for; whereas the commerce and navigation of the world, and the sovereignty of the ocean, ought to have been the principal objects of their attention.' Such language was also used by opposition politicians, Admiral Vernon writing in 1749 to Sir Francis Dashwood, a fellow MP:

> I look on the fate of this country to be drawing to a speedy period whenever France shall attain to a superior maritime power to Britain ... whenever they think themselves so, the first blow they will strike, will be to strip us, of every one of our sugar colonies ... and the natural consequence of that will be that you will by the same blow, lose all your American colonies as to their dependence on Britain.[56]

Whatever opposition criticisms, the ministry in fact kept a close eye on French naval developments, and they were the prime target of British espionage.[57] Prefiguring the situation in the 1790s, 1880s and 1930s, there was an awareness that British naval power might not be equal to all the demands that might be placed upon it. However, Newcastle wrote in 1753 to Joseph Yorke, envoy in The Hague: 'the King will not suffer anything to be done, that may tend to secure France, in case of war, against the superiority of His Majesty's fleet, in any part of the world'.[58]

The Seven Years' War, 1756–63

Britain ended up fighting the Seven Years' War without the support of her former allies and with only one significant ally, Prussia. This diplomatic failure helped to free naval strategy from alliance politics, although there was pressure for the commitment of naval forces to the Baltic, a point pressed hard by Frederick the Great, who anticipated that it would help him with Russia and Sweden, both at war with Prussia, but not Britain. Frederick's demand was supported by Cumberland, who wrote to Holdernesse, one of the Secretaries for State, in 1757:

> I am sorry to say that ... I see three great such fleets sent to sea (viz the Western squadron, that of the Mediterranean, as well as Holburne's reinforced to North America) which, according to the best account sent from France, will nowhere meet with any kind of opposition from their naval force; a very small diminution from those three great fleets, would have formed such a squadron, as might ... have restored His Majesty's weight in the North [northern Europe], where it is but too apparent, that the scale of France, at present preponderates.

Holdernesse's answer, however, made clear that diplomatic obligations had to take second place to naval priorities, while also drawing attention to the key issue of the number of sailors, and Holdernesse reflected the arithmetic of matching French naval strength in particular areas, an arithmetic that was to break down in 1781, with fatal consequences for the British war effort in North America:

> The utility of sending a strong squadron to the Baltic becomes every day more apparent; but I cannot pretend to say there is any great prospect that such an additional number of men, as this service would require, are to be found; although if we credit some fresh advice from Toulon, there are but eight ships of the line in that harbour fit for the sea, since the departure of the four,

supposed to be gone to America; in which case the [British] force
destined for the Mediterranean might be diminished.[59]

This analysis was a long way from the Wars of the Spanish
and Austrian Successions and the War of the Quadruple Alliance
(1718–20), when the British navy had had an important politico-
strategic commitment, namely the control of the Western Mediterranean in order to further the plans of allies in Italy and, in the
case of the War of the Spanish Succession, Spain. The absence
of any such commitment during the Seven Years' War helped to
release British naval power to concentrate on the challenge of
France, and discussion of naval capability and policy was therefore conducted in terms of what Britain could achieve through
the use of naval power against France. The Continental dimension was almost entirely absent. Whereas, in the 1720s, statesmen
had discussed whether British naval power could affect actions
by Austria and Russia that essentially owed nothing to maritime
considerations, in contrast, during the Seven Years' War, the central question was one of the direct impact of naval power. Instead
of assessing whether the bombardment of Naples or Riga might
influence policy, it was possible to discuss the actual implications
of seizing particular French colonies. It was not surprising that this
shift towards operational possibilities encouraged a more optimistic assessment of the nature and potential of British naval power.

It was not simply that British navy and amphibious operations
were more successful in the Seven Years' War than in the previous conflict, but also that their activities and triumphs could
be seen clearly as designed to further what were particularly
regarded as British objectives, a key issue when naval power was
discussed in the increasingly influential public sphere.[60] The contrast between the popularity of naval operations off Canada during the Seven Years' War and operations in Mediterranean waters
during the War of the Austrian Succession was clear, and it was
not only relative success that played a role. In the Seven Years'
War, it was the European operations, especially when unsuccessful or only partially successful, that enjoyed limited popularity in
Britain. In contrast, colonial operations were generally seen as
obviously serving national interests.

It was important, to this end, that in these operations Britain
did not need to consult the views of allies. She had last had to do

so in the colonial sphere in the Wars of the Spanish Succession and Quadruple Alliance, but, thereafter, the damaging accusations of surrender to the views of allies or the Hanoverian interests of the monarch, that so often compromised the public reputation of European operations, were absent. This situation was very significant in enhancing political and popular support for British naval activity both then and subsequently, for example in the naval war with Italy in 1940. The American navy was to benefit from being seen to fight a war not dependent on allies during the conflict with Japan in 1941-5, in contrast to the more contentious nature of strategy against Germany.

Thus, between 1688 and 1763, there was a major shift in British naval commitments that reflected diplomatic and strategic exigencies, and, in turn, affected the political context that helped to shape expectations concerning naval power. The move away from Europe created a different political context for the use of naval power, one that altered the politico-naval capabilities and weaknesses of the Royal Navy. The navy had always been helped in its public and political reputation by the minor degree to which it required the support of allies, a marked contrast to the army. The growing weakness of Dutch naval power furthered this process. By the Seven Years' War, this trend was complete, and naval action could be envisaged simply in an Anglo-Bourbon context, as also in the plans to support transoceanic pretensions after the conflict. The navy could be regarded as truly British, not only in its composition, but also in its objectives. If the possible use of naval power would have been no more able to prevent the First Partition of Poland by Austria, Prussia and Russia (1772), nor to intimidate Russia during the Ochakov Crisis (1791), than it had been able to persuade Peter the Great to restore some of his conquests from Sweden, the navy could, nevertheless, be seen clearly as a force designed and commonly used to support what were generally seen as the national goals: the security of Britain and her colonies, and maritime hegemony.

The political context explains the willingness of the British political nation to spend substantial sums in order to gain and maintain naval superiority, whereas in France and Spain there were no comparable ideologies and constituencies of support. This willingness accounts for British expenditure on new vessels and on maintenance, dockyards and equipment; indeed a continuous pattern of support that facilitated improvements in operational practice and tactical effectiveness. The political context also explains the objectives that the navy was set.

Britain's global triumphs rested on naval power. By 1762 the navy had about 300 ships and 84,000 men, a size that reflected political support, the growth of the mercantile marine, population, economy and public finances, as well as a heavy shipbuilding programme during the Seven Years' War. The size of the mercantile marine ensured that Britain had a greater reservoir of trained seamen than France and could therefore deploy more warships; there was also good naval leadership, although the Navy Board of the 1750s did not always welcome innovation. An experienced admiral, George, Lord Anson, was First Lord of the Admiralty in 1751–62, while admirals such as Boscawen, Hawke, Pocock and Rodney were bold and effective commanders. The superiority of French ships was outweighed by better British shiphandling.

The war at sea

Once at war, Britain needed to destroy her opponents' fleets, as both France and Spain were increasing their naval strength. Together, they launched warships with a total displacement of around 250,000 tons in 1746–55, while Britain launched only 90,000, losing its previous superiority over the combined Bourbon powers. Fortunately for Britain, Spain did not join the war until 1762 and, by then, France had been defeated at sea, losing about 50,000 tons of warships to British captures. Thanks to captures and shipbuilding, the British navy in 1760 had a displacement tonnage of about 375,000, at that point the largest in the world. Nevertheless, the potential strength of her opponents' united naval power, combined with the danger of invasion, made it necessary for the British to blockade the principal French bases, especially Brest. Fortunately, improvements in revictualling at sea and the development of watering facilities at Torbay made this possible.[61]

Initially, the naval war went badly for Britain. In 1755, Boscawen had failed to destroy the French fleet taking reinforcements to Canada. Causing greater humiliation, in 1756, the French had successfully invaded Britain's Mediterranean colony of Minorca, while most of the British fleet was in home waters, prepared to resist a feared French invasion of England. England thus served like a moored convoy that admirals had to seek to defend, although, unlike a convoy, the impact was strategic rather than tactical. Due to concern about naval strength in home waters,[62] only a small squadron of ten ships of the line under Byng was sent to the Mediterranean. Reinforced by three ships from Gibraltar, Byng attacked a French fleet of comparable size under La Galissonière 30 miles south-east of Minorca on 20 May. The battle was indecisive and the French withdrew; Byng neither pressed home his attack nor pursued the French. Instead, he withdrew to Gibraltar, the besieged British garrison at Fort St Philip on Minorca surrendered, and, in the ensuing political furore, the government incurred much criticism and Byng was court-martialled and shot.[63] Such punishments were believed to be an effective way to inculcate bold leadership.

In 1757, a planned British attack on Louisbourg in Cape Breton Island was abandoned and an expedition against the French port of Rochefort failed, but French trade was under increasing pressure from British warships, both in European waters and further afield. For example, in the Gulf of Mexico most ships bound for New Orleans were captured, and this weakened the French colony of Louisiana, not least by increasing discontent among the Native Americans, who could be given fewer trade goods as inducements to maintain their support.

In 1758, the ability of the British navy to act both as an offensive operational force and as a restraint on French trade was fully demonstrated. Louisbourg fell to an amphibious expedition, while Commodore Charles Holmes sailed up the unbuoyed channel of the River Ems, and, by cutting the supplies of the French garrison of Emden, led to their withdrawal, which provided the British with a landing port in Continental Europe. Holmes thereafter supported the deployment of British troops in Germany. French commerce dried up by the end of 1758, while the rise of captures by the British navy was indicative of its superiority in most Western waters.

Individual French warships proved vulnerable to the increasingly insistent British naval pressure in European water, and the cumulative effect weakened the French. The large number of warships captured by Britain and incorporated into her navy played a major role in affecting the balance of naval strength. This incorporation aided the process by which the British changed the nature of their navy, copying the large Bourbon two-deckers. These were more manoeuvrable than the small three-decker 80- and 90-gun ships that had been so important earlier in the century. British shipbuilding policy was radically reviewed after 1744, with much more emphasis on large two-deckers and single-decked frigates. Battery height was the decisive element in this. Small three-deckers were often unable to use their lower cannon in offensive actions from a windward position because the battery came too close to the water. The same problem occurred with small two-deckers, although they were useful as defensive convoy escorts as they had much firepower in relation to their size. The new ships were better sailers and better fighters, both manoeuvrable and capable of holding their own in the punishing artillery duels of the line-of-battle engagements that the British preferred to conduct at close range, in contrast to the French preference for long-range fire.[64]

The crucial mid-century naval victories occurred in 1759. The French prepared a knockout blow, an invasion of Britain by 100,000 troops. Had even only part of the French force landed, it would still have posed serious problems for the British, but the division of the French navy between the ports of Brest and Toulon made it difficult to concentrate the necessary covering force, and the blockading British squadrons sought to maintain the division, while attempts were also made to disrupt invasion preparations especially by blockading the invasion port of Le Havre. Although the Toulon fleet, under La Clue, managed to leave first the harbour and then the Mediterranean, it was defeated by the pursuing British under Boscawen near Lagos on the Portuguese coast on 18–19 August. Stubborn resistance by the rearmost French warship, the *Centaure*, held off the British while La Clue sailed the rest of his fleet into neutral waters, but, on the following day, Boscawen violated Portuguese neutrality and launched a successful attack. Mortally wounded, La Clue ran his vessel ashore and burnt it to prevent British capture, and the outnumbered French lost a total of five ships, three captured and two destroyed. The remainder of La Clue's fleet was then blockaded in the River Tagus.

Bad weather forced Hawke, the chief exponent of close block-
age, to lift his blockade of Brest in November 1759 and to take
shelter in Torbay, but the French fleet under Conflans failed in its
attempt to reach Scotland via the west coast of Ireland. Conflans
could not sail direct for Scotland. He had first to meet transports
from Bordeaux and Nantes at Morbihan, and this led to a fatal
delay. As a result, Conflans was trapped by Hawke while still off
the Breton coast. He took refuge in Quiberon Bay, counting on
its shoaly waters and strong swell to deter Hawke's ships. The
British had scant knowledge of the Bay's rocks. Nevertheless,
on 20 November, Hawke made a bold attack. With topsails set,
despite the ferocity of the wind, which was blowing at nearly
forty knots, his ships sailed into the confined space of the bay,
overhauled the French rear division and forced a general action.
British gunnery and seamanship proved superior in this confused
action and seven French ships of the line were captured, sunk or
wrecked. Like Jutland (1916), this was a battle that could have
decided the fate of the war had the British lost.

All possibility of a French invasion of Britain was shattered by
these two decisive victories. Quiberon Bay gets all the credit, but
the Battle of Lagos in 1759 was a huge relief to politicians and
naval officers alike: they knew that the invasion had become that
much more difficult. After Hawke's victory, much of the Brest
fleet took refuge in the River Vilaine, further up Quiberon Bay,
and stayed there for the remainder of the war,[65] while political
and financial support for the navy ebbed in France.[66] The aftermath resembled that of Barfleur in 1692.

The British, who did not have comparable financial problems,
were left to take the initiative at sea. Thus, the French navy did
not disrupt the attack on the island of Belle Isle off Brittany in
1761 nor the dispatch of troops to Portugal in 1762, despite the
fact that both enterprises were vulnerable to naval forces based in
Brittany. A squadron under Keppel covered the Belle Isle expedition, while in 1762 a fleet based at Gibraltar under Saunders
discouraged a junction between Bourbon naval forces in the
Atlantic and the Mediterranean. More generally, British warships
were increasingly successful both in limiting French privateering
and in damaging French trade.

Victory at sea, combined with successful amphibious operations
which proved a major force multiplier for an otherwise relatively

small army,[67] altered the strategic situation. The Bourbons were still able to launch a massive programme of naval rearmament after the war ended in 1763, but British colonial conquests during the war ensured that the geopolitics and infrastructure of power were different. With Canada conquered from France in 1758–60, and Florida acquired from Spain in 1763, North America now appeared to be securely British. When, in 1770–1, there was the prospect of war with the Bourbons over the Falkland Islands, there was little need for Britain to consider the security of North America; the situation was totally different to that of 1754–6.

There were to be new strategic challenges in the two decades after 1763 – the rebuilding of the Bourbon fleets, a Russian-led League of Northern European powers in the Baltic, the combination of France and Mysore in southern India, and, most obviously, rebellion in the Thirteen Colonies in North America from 1775 – but in 1763 the situation appeared promising. Whereas, in the 1690s, the British had had to rely on Dutch support to achieve a naval edge over the French, and that only with difficulty, in the Seven Years' War Britain, alone on the oceans, had defeated France and Spain.

British naval success was not due to superior weaponry. Neither the ships nor their equipment were substantially different from those of the Bourbons, although the British had more dry docks and deep-sea sailors. Instead, the crucial factors were, first, a level of continuous high commitment and expenditure that helped to ensure that a high level of both was regarded as normal and necessary and that naval strength never collapsed; secondly, the inculcation of an ethos and policy that combined the strategic and operational offensive with tactical aggression; and, thirdly, within the constraints of naval warfare and technology, an effective use of the warships of the period.[68] British naval commanders generally took the initiative and were therefore best placed to obtain propitious circumstances. At a gut level, the British fought to win, and not just to survive for another day, and this quality was apparent in the victories that gave them the commanding position in the European world.

4 1775–1815

Discussion about military change and, more specifically, concerning modern and/or total warfare in the period 1775–1815, focuses on land conflict in the Western world, particularly the armies of the American and French Revolutions and of Napoleon, and, in contrast, generally ignores or underrates the importance of naval developments. This approach is unfortunate as, on the world scale, it was as naval powers with an amphibious capability that the Western states were particularly important and effective. Indeed, as throughout the period covered by this book, there was a Western naval exceptionalism that rewards attention. Moreover, victories, the deeds of a few hours, however much they represented the toil of decades, blazed the way for a world that was not only to be dominated by the West, but also by a particular set of Western values.

Non-Western navies

If Western powers shared land capability with non-Western counterparts, the situation was different at sea. It was not that the Westerners alone had naval forces. Other states also did so, including North African powers, the Ottoman (Turkish) empire, Kamehameha I of Hawaii, and a number of others, although the literature devoted to them is limited, and certainly far far less than that on Western navies. It would be seriously mistaken to lump non-Western navies all together, as there were major differences in fighting styles and environments, as was also the case for armies. For example, the Ottomans were capable of fleet engagements, while, in contrast, the North African powers – Morocco, Algiers, Tunis and Tripoli – essentially deployed privateering forces appropriate for commerce raiding. The Ottomans and the North Africans used the same maritime technology as Western Europeans, although galleys became less important in the Mediterranean and, in 1748, France abolished its galley fleet, which had been regarded as very important in the seventeenth century.

Unlike in the Mediterranean, however, most non-Western naval forces were not deep-sea. Instead, particularly along the coasts of Africa, South-East Asia and the East Indies, there were polities that controlled flotillas operating in inshore, estuarine, deltaic and riverine waters.[1] These boats were shallow in draught, and therefore enjoyed a local range denied to Western warships. They were also quick, manoeuvrable, beachable and inexpensive. Their crews usually fought with missile weapons, which, in the eighteenth century, increasingly meant muskets, and some canoes also carried cannon. Similar technology was also employed in the Pacific, and along the coasts of New Zealand and Pacific North America. Missile weapons could be used prior to, or in lieu of boarding. As with land warfare in some non-Western societies, and in marked contrast to the situation in the West, the divide between conflict between humans and the hunting of animals, especially whales and seals, was not too great at this level of weapon technology and military organisation.

At the same time, non-Western naval and amphibious forces were not only hunters or raiders, but could achieve operational goals, as was seen in conflict between the New Zealand Maori in the early nineteenth century, and, even more clearly, in the earlier unification of the Hawaiian archipelago. By 1789, Kamehameha I was using a swivel gun secured to a platform on the hulls of a big double canoe. Soon after, he had a large double canoe mounting two cannon and rigged like a Western schooner. Such boats helped him as he expanded his power across the archipelago. Kamehameha won dominance of the island of Hawaii in 1791, and of the islands of Maui and Oahu in 1795. In 1796 and 1809, the difficult waters between Oahu and Kauai, and outbreaks of disease, ended his plans to invade Kauai, but, in 1810, Kaumualii, the ruler of the islands of Kauai and Niihau, agreed to serve as a client king.[2]

Operational goals drew on an impressive capacity for troop transport and amphibious operations. When Captain James Cook, British naval officer and famed explorer, visited the Pacific island of Tahiti for the second time in 1774, its fleet was preparing for a punishment expedition against the neighbouring island of Moorea. Cook and the painter William Hodges took great interest in these war preparations, as did the general public when the painting *The War Boats of the Island of Otaheite [Tahiti]* was exhibited in London in 1777. Cook estimated that the expedition involved 4000 men. Cook's three voyages to the Pacific, which were supported by the Admiralty, were also highly impressive examples of naval organisation, albeit to different ends.

None of the non-Western capability stands comparison with Western navies, but, instead of considering a single standard of capability, it is necessary to note the diversity of goals and the variety of best practice. For example, the North African, Omani and Maratha ships were commerce raiders whose emphasis was on speed and manoeuvrability,[3] whereas the heavy, slow, big ships of the line of Western navies were designed for battle and emphasised battering power, although such a comparison, in turn, should note the considerable variety in the specifications and goals of these ships of the line.[4] Furthermore, there were other types of ships in the Western navies that were not ships of the line and which were specifically designed for fast, manoeuvrable, inshore work, for example the cutters used to help customs services in the incessant war against smugglers. This was a war that prefigured the current one against drug smugglers, although the latter involves a more extensive naval presence, and greater and more distant force projection, not least thanks to the supporting use of air power.

The strength of Western battle fleets was already apparent in the early sixteenth century, with successive Portuguese victories over Indian, Egyptian and Ottoman fleets in the Indian Ocean, and the balance of battle advantage remained with the West, and increasingly so in the eighteenth-century conflict with the Ottomans in the Mediterranean and, later, Black Sea. It would be mistaken to see this advantage simply in terms of firepower. The most dramatic Western naval victory over non-Western forces in the period 1650–1815, the battle of Cesmé in the Aegean off Chios in 1770, was primarily due to the effective Russian use of fireships against the closely moored Ottoman fleet; both the method and the result were highly unusual. About 11,000 Ottomans were killed, although the Russians totally failed in their attempt to exploit the situation by driving the Ottomans from the Aegean islands.

Further afield, naval forces also enforced Western interests. In 1725, when French merchants were expelled from their base at Mahé on the west coast of India, a squadron was sent from Pondicherry, the main French position in India. It forced the return of the merchants and secured new commercial benefits. Moves against French trade at the coffee port of Mocha in Yemen similarly led to the dispatch of a squadron from Pondicherry in October 1736. Arriving off Mocha the following January, the French bombarded and seized the port, disembarking troops, thereby restoring their commercial privileges. Pondicherry, however, was to prove vulnerable to British attack in successive wars, surviving attack in 1748 in the War of the Austrian Succession, but being captured in 1760, 1778, 1793 and 1803, in the Seven Years', American Independence, French Revolutionary and Napoleonic Wars, before being restored in each subsequent peace.

In part because the Western powers devoted so much of their effort to fighting each other, there was no focus on naval action with non-Westerners. The situation did not change until after the Napoleonic Wars, when, with Britain clearly dominant at sea, Western powers ceased their high-intensity naval conflicts/ confrontations, and managed differences, for example over the fate of the Spanish empire in the 1810s without conflict. Instead, there were now dramatic clashes with non-Western powers, including the successful British attack on Algiers (1816), the Anglo-French-Russian destruction of the Ottoman/Egyptian fleet at Cape Navarino off Greece (1827), the British action against Mehmet Ali of Egypt (1839–40), Anglo-Chinese conflict in the First Opium War (1839–42), and the Russian destruction of the Ottoman fleet at Sinope in the Black Sea (1853). Also in the eighteenth century, there was no anticipation of the enhanced Western capability for inshore and riverine power projection that was to follow from the mid-nineteenth century.

Such an increase in relative Western capability was not to occur until the application of steam power, and, despite the use of stationary steam engines for industrial processes in the eighteenth century, this application bore little relationship to Western naval conflict in the period 1775–1815. In 1813, the American Robert Fulton drew up plans for a powerful steam-propelled frigate, significantly named *Demologos* ('Voice of the People', launched in October 1814), but such developments still lay in the future.[5]

The absence of large-scale deep-sea naval conflict not involving Western fleets in the period 1600–1880 draws attention to Western exceptionalism and to the interacting roles of military goals, strategic cultures and interest groups. There were no inherent reasons why major non-Western powers, especially those of East Asia, should not deploy substantial fleets, and some had done so in the past. That they no longer did so is a subject that by its nature is difficult to probe. Aside from the conceptual problem of assessing why something did not occur, there are major difficulties in researching the subject.

It is instructive, however, to consider the emphasis in recent study on Western naval developments on the co-operation of states and mercantile élites,[6] and, in particular, on the openness of the first to advice from the latter, and on an ability to derive mutual profit from naval requirements and financial resources. Oceanic naval power depended on a maritime economy to supply resources in depth: in other words, demand from governments alone would not generate sustainable maritime infrastructure. This infrastructure required both an effective governmental machinery and a strong maritime economy, and that combination was not only quite rare but could also be put under great pressure in war, as France discovered in repeated conflicts with Britain.[7]

In contrast to Western capability, the situation was different in the rest of Eurasia because, although Asian merchants remained important in long-distance trade,[8] the mercantile élites were generally separated from rulers by ethnic or religious divides. Linked to this, the relationship between port cities and states was often uneasy, and was nothing like that represented by the role of London in British policy. Jews, Greeks and Armenians did not have close relations with the Ottomans, while China after the Manchu conquest in the mid-seventeenth century was very much dominated by an élite whose values were not maritime. The Manchus overcame the attempt of the Ming loyalist Zheng Chenggong to use naval strength as the basis for political power, although the potential of this course was shown in his conquest of Taiwan from the Dutch in 1661.[9] The same emphasis on landed values was true of the Mughals in India, and of the rulers who succeeded the Safavids in Persia from the 1720s.

Close attention reveals, however, that, whatever the political and governmental system outside the West, there was generally more accommodation, compromise and pressures from short-term exigencies than concern with formal structures might suggest. This situation certainly left plentiful 'spaces' for maritime activity, but, as the USA also showed, such maritime activity was not synonymous with naval strength; and certainly of the battle-fleet type, with its focus on ship-killing, rather than the self-financing commerce raiding that it was easier to pursue in such 'spaces' and which did not require a supporting governmental infrastructure. The USA lacked a battle-fleet until the 1850s, when the launching of seven very large frigates armed with large-calibre shell guns helped ensure that by 1860 the American navy was the fourth largest in the world.

The decision to create such navies throws light on the strategic culture of individual states, while the organisation of such forces was a formidable task. Many states lacked the requisite stability for such state naval power, although England, which had such power in the 1650s, was scarcely stable. Moreover, government by ruler-generals tended to accentuate the focus on land forces and campaigning, as was amply seen in eighteenth-century Burma, Persia and Siam, and again with Napoleon; although both Oliver Cromwell in England in the 1650s and Peter the Great in Russia in the 1700s–1720s backed strong navies.

Japan and China had greater governmental continuity than Burma, Persia and Siam, but this continuity did not lead to a focus on naval forces. Japan was very much an insular state, and, if the term strategic culture means much, then it certainly pertains to the inward-looking governing élite. As a sign of widespread conservatism, most political, economic, cultural and intellectual efforts in Japan were directed at the preservation and strengthening of established arrangements, although, by the end of the eighteenth century, there was greater interest in new political, economic and cultural forms.[10]

In China, the formidable bureaucratic culture – a legacy of the Chinese past maintained by the Manchu rulers – was not open to mercantile influences, and certainly not in comparison to Western Europe. Furthermore, policy goals (themselves set in the context of socio-political assumptions and strategic cultures) did not lend themselves to naval development. Having, in the 1750s, vanquished the Zunghars of Xinkiang, a serious steppe challenge from the 1680s, and then occupied Kashgar, China did not move into a military quiescence comparable to Japan. Instead, there were a series of wars, unsuccessful against Burma in 1765–9 and Tongking (northern Vietnam) in 1788–9, and successful against Nepal in 1792. None of these conflicts, however, required long-range naval activity: Burma was attacked overland, and not, as it was to be by Britain in 1824–6, partly by sea.

With its settlement colonies on its landward frontiers,[11] China's ambitions focused on near-China, and not on distant seas. Its international relations were based on Chinese hegemony, and the offer of tributes by neighbours sufficed. Taiwan had been brought under control in 1683; there was no drive to conquer Japan, as the Mongols, once they had conquered China, had unsuccessfully sought to do in the thirteenth century; and the frontier with Russia fixed in 1689 and 1729, which excluded Russia from the Amur valley, was seen as acceptable. Neither China nor Japan challenged Russia's eighteenth-century expansion across the North Pacific into the Aleutian Islands and Alaska.

Vietnamese, Siamese and Burmese actions and ambitions similarly focused on landward activities, and, despite the earlier interests of the Maratha Angria family[12] and, to a lesser extent, Haidar Ali and Tipu Sultan, rulers of Mysore, this was also true of Indian counterparts. Indian naval strength anyway was cut short by British action – against the Angrias in 1755–6 and against Mysore in 1783. Persian rulers claimed hegemony over the Persian Gulf, and Nadir Shah sent a force to Oman,[13] but Persian warfare focused on conflict on landward frontiers to east, north and west: with Indian rulers, the Uzbeks, Russia and the Ottomans. Regional naval forces in Asia, such as those of the Buginese state of Bone in modern Indonesia, or the Illanos of the Sulu Islands, whose heavily armed galleys attacked warships of the Dutch East India Company, were only of local significance. Nevertheless, this continual use of galleys, which was also to be seen under Gia-long of Vietnam (r. 1806–20), who constructed square-rigged galleys, indicated the appropriate character of these vessels, notably for in-shore operations, and, more generally, the continuity of military challenges and circumstances.

In so far as the development of 'modern' naval power by non-Western powers constituted a naval revolution, it needs to be dated to the late nineteenth century, most notably with Japan; although, in the late seventeenth century, the Ottomans abandoned their traditional dependence on galleys and built a new fleet of sail-powered galleons which carried more cannon. As a result, the Ottomans developed an amphibious capability that was very useful for the conquest of the Morea (Peloponnese) from Venice in 1715. The Ottoman fleet also defeated the Venetians off Chios in 1695 and checked a largely Venetian fleet off Cerigo in 1718, both important to the Ottoman control of the Aegean, and each contrasting with Russian success there against the Ottomans in 1770. The Ottomans subsequently continued their borrowing, employing French experts on ship construction in the mid-1780s, although they were defeated by the Russians in the Black Sea, at the battles of the Dnieper (1788) and Tendra (1790). However, no comparable response to Western naval power occurred in the Orient until the late-nineteenth century.

The USA

Even in the case of the New World, where European control (by Britain, France, Spain and Portugal) largely collapsed in 1775–1826, naval power in terms of significant specialised fleets did not develop until the second half of the nineteenth century. The new states, instead, focused their military activity on armies. This focus reflected the extent to which strongly held ideas about the desirability of a militia basis for military power proved far more conducive to land than sea capability, while considerable reliance was placed on the support of European navies or unofficial support: by the Americans on France in 1778–83, and by the Latin Americans, in the following century, on British support against the possibilities of Spanish reconquest and French intervention.[14]

In the USA, the Department of the Navy was established in 1798, and the governing Federalists built up a navy, first to fight the Barbary States and then to engage France in the 'Quasi War' of 1798–1800. The French sank or captured over 300 American merchantmen in response to the American role in maintaining British trade routes: France did not accept that neutral ships should carry British goods. Clashes between warships from the summer of 1798 were largely won by the Americans.[15]

In the USA, the Federalists' plan to build up the navy was stopped, however, when Thomas Jefferson and the Democratic Republicans gained power after the election of 1800. Jefferson favoured coastal gunboats, rather than the more expensive frigates with their oceanic range built in the 1790s. As a reminder of the political basis of strategic culture, the emphasis on gunboats conformed to the militia tradition of American republicanism, and the militia could use gunboats to defend the coastal fortifications being built. Based on New Orleans, American gunboats operated against French and Spanish privateers off the Mississippi Delta in 1806–10, while others played a valuable role against Britain in the war of 1812–15.[16]

Nevertheless, although, thanks to the expansion of their merchant marine, the Americans had an abundance of trained seamen to man their fleets, and the most powerful frigates of the age, which they were also adept at handling in ship-to-ship actions, they had no ships of the line, and their total navy at the outset of the War of 1812 comprised only 17 ships. They thus lacked the capacity for fleet action. This emphasis reflected the force structure and doctrine developed under Jefferson's agrarian republicanism and was very different in its military results to the large battle fleets created and sustained by the mercantile republics of the United Provinces and Commonwealth England in the seventeenth century.

European navies

The focus in naval power was therefore resolutely Western, and more particularly European. Although Western warships (and merchantmen) found it difficult to operate in tropical estuary, delta and river waters,[17] there was no naval balance, nor any frontier of capability and control between Western and non-Western powers on the oceans of the world. The absence of any challenge to Western naval power on the oceans was dramatically demonstrated in the 1770s, 1780s and 1790s, as Western warships, under commanders such as Cook, Vancouver, La Pérouse and Malaspina, explored the waters and shores of the Pacific, charting, (re-)naming and claiming the coasts of the world, and established Western trading bases and colonies in Australasia and along the west coast of North America (the latter process had started earlier).[18] There was still much of the world's land surface where Western military strength and models were unknown, but the warships that showed their flags and ran out their guns around the globe were the forceful edge of a Western integration of the world.

There was also an important build-up of naval strength and expansion of capability within the existing technological constraints. There was, for example, a major Western naval race in the 1780s as there had been also in the second half of the seventeenth century. In the 1780s, Britain, France and Spain all launched a formidable amount of tonnage, Spain devoting over 20 per cent of governmental expenditure that decade to the navy.[19] These huge naval forces dwarfed those of non-Western powers far more decisively than they had when Christopher Columbus and Vasco da Gama sailed forth in the 1490s. Some other powers also greatly expanded their navies in the 1780s. Russia and the Dutch became the fourth and fifth largest naval powers in the world, while Denmark, Sweden, Naples, Portugal and the Ottomans also all increased the size of their navies. The total displacement of European navies rose from 750,000 tons in 1770 to one million tons by 1780, and 1.7 million tons in 1790.[20] This increase was the background to the naval conflict of the French Revolutionary and Napoleonic Wars, and established the challenge facing the British if they were to maintain naval primacy.

Infrastructure

Alongside new shipping, there was the continual effort required to maintain and repair ships, an effort that in part stemmed from the vulnerability of ships' organic properties, especially wood and canvas. As the specifications of warships changed relatively little, ships could be kept in the line for decades as long as they were kept seaworthy. Programmes of naval construction, repair and enhancement registered not only the growing resources of Western governments but also the capability of their military-industrial complexes, and the ability of their administrative systems to plan and implement changes. Fleets of warships were powerful and sophisticated military systems, sustained by mighty industrial and logistical resources based in dockyards that were among the largest industrial plants, employers of labour, and groups of buildings in the world, for example Portsmouth, Plymouth, Brest, Toulon, Ferrol, Cadiz and Karlskrona. The last was a more southerly Swedish naval base, built in 1683, and, by 1700, the third most populous town in the country.[21]

These dockyards posed major logistical problems, and were supported by massive storehouses, such as the vast Lands Zeemagazijn in Amsterdam, which was destroyed by fire in 1791, as well as manufacturing to support the workforce, such as bakeries and distilleries, as at Karlskrona. Naval dockyards were also among the most important, large and lavish buildings in Britain. Christopher Wren's naval hospital at Greenwich, finished in 1752, was one of the most impressive buildings in the entire country, while the 1095 foot-long ropery opened at Portsmouth in 1776 may well have been the largest building in the world at the time. Naval bases required considerable investment, as did the search for timber and other naval stores.[22]

Developments in government policy and strategic intent led to new naval facilities. The major expansion of Russian naval power under Peter the Great (r. 1689–1725) was linked to the foundation of St Petersburg as capital, 'window to the west', and port on Russia's newly conquered Baltic coastline. In 1703, Peter himself laid the foundation stone of the Peter-Paul Fortress there. The following year, he founded the Admiralty shipyard on the bank of the River Neva opposite the fortress, and in 1706 its first warship was launched. A naval academy followed in 1715. Furthermore, as soon as the Russians had seized a Black Sea coastline and the Crimea in 1783, they began to develop bases there, particularly at Kherson, Odessa and Sevastopol. These bases threatened a direct attack on the Ottoman capital, Constantinople, providing the Russians with a strategy different to that of a land advance across the eastern Balkans. As a result, Sevastopol was to play a key role in Allied goals during the Crimean War (1854–6). In an indicative display of power, Catherine II took the visiting Joseph II of Austria to visit Sevastopol in 1787.

The establishment of military-industrial complexes also demonstrated a more widespread capacity to stimulate change. Improved infrastructure and better naval construction lessened the problems of decay caused by the use of what were organic working parts made from wood, hemp and flax.[23] There were also numerous innovations, which were put to good use. As an instance of the importance of incremental improvements, British cannon fire proved particularly effective in the major victory over the French off the Îles des Saintes on 12 April 1782. These improvements, including in flintlocks, tin tubes, flannel cartridges, wedges to absorb recoil, and steel compression springs, increased the ease of serving cannon, of firing them instantaneously, and the possible angles of training.

Battle

Moreover, the location of that battle, south of Guadeloupe in the West Indies, was a testimony to the importance of trans-oceanic operations: in 1759, in contrast, the key naval battles of the Anglo-French section of the Seven Years' War, Lagos (off Portugal) and Quiberon Bay had been fought in European waters, as the central issue was the threat of a French invasion to Britain, which appeared to be the sole way to counter Britain's trans-oceanic operations, as well as its crucial role in supporting opposition to French interests in Germany.[24] Similarly, the major naval battles in the Dutch, Nine Years', Spanish Succession, Quadruple Alliance and Austrian Succession wars had all been in European waters: Beachy Head (1690) and Barfleur (1692) arose over the threat of French invasion of Britain, while Malaga (1704), Cape Passaro (1718), Toulon (1744) and Minorca (1756) reflected the attempt to use naval force in order to affect Mediterranean amphibious operations, and the two battles off Cape Finisterre (both 1747) were related to commerce interception.

Battle alone was not the key: strategic advantage without battle was demonstrated in 1745–6 when the British navy joined the weather in dissuading the French from invading Britain in support of the Jacobites. In response to the latter, the British navy also covered the supply of advancing forces in eastern Scotland in 1746. On other occasions, such roles led to battles, as in 1716 at Dynekilen, where the Danish squadron defeated a Swedish supply fleet, ending Charles XII's attempt to capture the fortress of Fredriksen that year. Powers that were at peace could also use naval demonstrations in order to further their views, as when France sent squadrons to the Baltic in 1739 and to the Caribbean in 1742.

Improved capability

During the eighteenth century, improvements in seaworthiness, stemming in part from the abandonment of earlier top-heavy and clumsy ship designs, increased the capability of warships, both to take part in all-weather blockades and to operate across the oceans. The European emphasis on maximising firepower in the late seventeenth century had led to a development of three-decker capability. In the early eighteenth century, the focus, instead, was on stability, range and versatility, which led to a move toward two-deckers; but three-deckers became important anew for the bruising naval confrontations of the late-eighteenth century.

During the War of American Independence (1775–83), the British navy responded both by arranging a major programme of construction, including the use of private shipbuilders to enhance capacity, and by technological advances. Copper-sheathing reduced the difficulties caused to wooden hulls by barnacles, weeds and the teredo worm, and the consequent loss of speed, and also made refits easier. This sheathing was pressed forward from February 1779 by Sir Charles Middleton, Comptroller of the Navy from 1778 to 1790. In 1780, 42 ships of the line were given copper sheathing. Politicians noted a sense of new potential, Charles, 2nd Marquess of Rockingham claiming in 1781: 'The copper bottoms occasioning our ships to sail so much better enables us either to go and attack if we should see an inferior fleet or to decline the attempt if we should see a superior fleet.' The value of copper sheathing can be questioned, but the administrative achievement it represented was considerable,[25] and this achievement encouraged the assumption that similar changes should be possible.

The introduction of the carronade, a new, light, short-barrelled gun that was very effective at close quarters, adopted by Britain in 1779, was also important: it proved potent at the Battle of the Saintes in 1782, where copper-sheathing also helped the British; the French, in contrast, had neither. After the War of American Independence, the French adopted recent British naval innovations, such as copper-sheathing. As an aspect of organisational method designed to maintain capability, such standardisation, furthermore, was increasingly apparent prior to the changes brought in the late nineteenth century by the universal adoption of steam power and armour plating: indeed, in 1786, the French adopted standard ship designs for their fleet.

More generally, progress in metallurgy improved British gunnery towards the end of the eighteenth century. In turn, the need for cannon helped drive the growth of the iron industry. Britain had an advantage in technology in the shape of more powerful guns, as well as benefiting greatly from superior seamanship and well-drilled gun crews. The impact of British naval gunfire on enemy hulls and crews markedly increased during the war period 1793–1815, with enemy ships reduced to wrecks in a comparatively short time.[26]

Improvements in aspects of naval capability and activity in part reflected the strength of the learning process in which experience and ideas were systematised, analysed and applied. This process was helped greatly by the active culture of print, which provided opportunities for the dissemination of ideas. That profit could be earned by publications reflected the strength of interest in the subject. Works included John Ardesoif's *An Introduction to Marine Fortification and Gunnery* (1772).

The incremental process of naval improvement continued in the last decades of sail, but, nevertheless, with the hindsight provided by consideration of subsequent technological developments, it is possible to see the period in terms of the use of yet greater resources of people, *matériel* and funds to pursue familiar military courses, a comment also true for much of the warfare on land. The American and French Revolutions, moreover, did not bring changes in naval warfare comparable to those on land.

Instead, the long-term growing stress on naval firepower continued to affect fleet structures. Whereas in 1720 there were only two warships displacing more than 3000 tons, by 1815 nearly a fifth of the naval strength above 500 tons was in this category. In 1800–15, ships of 2500–3000 tons also achieved greater importance in Western naval capability, whereas those of 2000–2500 and 1500–2000 tons declined in number. These bigger ships were able to carry heavier guns. Whereas the average ship of the line in 1720 had 60 guns, and was armed with 12- and 24-pounders, that of 1815 had 74 guns, with 32- and 36-pounders on the lower deck. Nevertheless, this greater firepower, both on individual ships and in aggregate terms, did not lead to dramatic changes in naval warfare.[27]

There were other improvements in naval capability. Better signalling in the period of the 1790s–1810s helped considerably to enhance the potential for tactical control. The quest for improvement ensured the development of the profession of naval engineering which combined a general mathematical culture, able to understand technical issues, with the study of the old craft rules for building ships in order to enhance best practice.[28] This commitment to improved naval engineering ensured that wooden warships were far from unchanging. In particular, the invention of a system of ship construction using diagonal bracing in order to strengthen hulls and to prevent the arching of keels was to increase the resilience of ships, and thus their sea- and battle-worthiness, and to permit the building of longer two-deckers armed with 80 or 90 guns.

These improvements helped make earlier ships appear redundant, certainly for the line of battle, but, although Robert Seppings, Surveyor of the [British] Navy from 1813 to 1832, experimented in the 1800s at Plymouth and Chatham, the first ship built entirely on this principle, the *Howe*, was not launched until 1815. Diagonal framing contributed to the increase in the power of wooden warships after the Napoleonic Wars and was mainly significant after the introduction of steam made it important to build longer ships. More mundanely, but also as part of a general process of improvement, there were earlier developments in fittings, for example new patterns of anchors and the first chain cable, as well as iron water-tanks in place of wooden casks.[29]

Alongside incremental improvements, progress did not constitute a steady chronological continuum. Instead, the entire business of being at sea and fighting at sea fluctuated for a number of reasons, not least of which was the impact of peace, when most of the lessons learnt in the last war were usually forgotten, albeit briefly. Furthermore, the lack of a structured and rigorous system of officer training in the skills of command led to a wide variation in command competence and method through-out the period: the situation indeed was still bad for the British at Trafalgar in 1805. There were many ups and downs within a slow trajectory of improvement.[30]

As a more impressive display of effectiveness, Westerners also took their naval military-industrial capability abroad, developing major shipyards at colonial bases, such as Bombay and Halifax, Nova Scotia for the British, and Havana, where the Spaniards made good use of tropical hardwoods, producing particularly good ships, including several of their larger warships which fought at Trafalgar. These bases were important in helping to make empires systems of power, and also played a key role in local economies. Halifax naval yard, founded in 1758, was the largest industrial centre in British North America after the War of American Independence.[31] In the West Indies, the British had two naval bases on Jamaica – Port Royal and Port Antonio – as well as English Harbour on Antigua, begun in 1728 and still impressive today. Port Royal was able to careen the larger ships of the line sent there.

Moreover, the growing British naval and mercantile presence in the Indian Ocean owed much to shipyards in India, where merchantmen averaging 600–800 tonnes and capable of carry-ing very large cargoes were constructed, as well as naval vessels, including several ships of the line. Batavia (Djakarta) was the key naval base for the Dutch in the region, and Port Louis on Mauritius for the French.

The far-flung capability stemming from naval power had been demonstrated in 1762, when British expeditions captured Havana and Manila, prefiguring the American achievement (also at the expense of Spain) in 1898. Such capability was shown anew in 1780 when France sent expeditions to India and North America. Although no other region of the world could match this naval capability, the limited availability of Western bases, as well as logistical problems, disease and climate, substantially cir-cumscribed Western power projection outside European waters, certainly by the standards of the late nineteenth century.

Naval operations outside Europe, especially in the Indian Ocean and the Caribbean, but not only there, as the disastrous French expedition to North American waters in 1746 showed, remained greatly conditioned by, or at least affected by, climate and disease. Despite improvements in some spheres, in the British case by the Sick and Hurt Board, the general conditions of service at sea remained bleak. Aside from cramped living conditions and poor sanitation, food supplies could be inadequate and inappropriate, with a lack of fresh food, fruit and vegetables, and thus of vitamin C. The cumulative impact was both to make naval service unattractive and to lead to heavy losses among those already in service, with Spanish naval manpower, for example, affected by repeated epidemics of yellow fever.

The War of American Independence, 1775–83

Yet, whereas British naval administration was good enough to ensure that warships fulfilled their operational role on distant stations, the British navy, notwithstanding the use of Halifax, Bermuda and Jamaica, lacked the requisite support bases to mount an effective blockade of the east-coast of North America, either in 1775–83 or in 1812–15, although it could inflict considerable damage on the American economy.[32] Indeed the course of the War of American Independence (1775–83) indicated the limitations of naval and amphibious power. The campaigns that led to the British relief of Quebec in 1776 and their capture of New York (1776), Philadelphia (1777), Savannah (1778) and Charleston (1780), and to the Franco-American concentration against the British in Yorktown in 1781, each reflected, at least in part, the amphibious capability stemming from naval strength and drawing on a development of relevant doctrine.[33] Nevertheless, in every case, the exploitation of this capability was dependent on the campaigning on land. More generally, British naval strength could not ensure a decisive victory over the main American field army.[34]

This factor, and the consequences of French entry into the war in 1778, were important to the course of the war; whereas American experimentation with new naval technology in the shape of the submarine had no effect. The ideas were genuinely revolutionary, but successful execution was a different matter. David Bushnell's *Turtle* was first employed against the *Eagle* in New York harbour on 6 September 1776, but Bushnell encountered serious problems with navigating in the face of the currents and could not attach the explosive charge to the ship. The second attempt, against the *Phoenix* on 5 October 1776, also failed. George Washington pointed out the difficulty of operating the machine satisfactorily, and it is not surprising that Bushnell received scant support from the hard-pressed government.

French entry into the war in 1778, followed by that of Spain in 1779 and the Dutch in 1780, totally altered the maritime situation, leading to a worldwide naval conflict, at once more extensive and in some spheres, such as the vigorous Anglo-French struggle in the Bay of Bengal, more intensive than previous maritime wars between Western powers. The determination of the French government to maintain access to the key fishing grounds off Newfoundland, and thus to support a fishing industry that was an important reservoir of sailors for the navy, had been important to their peace negotiations with Britain at the close of the Seven Years' War, and, after that, the French navy had been built up anew, in part as a result of a patriotic subscription.[35]

In the early 1770s, the French fleet deteriorated, primarily as a result of the unhelpful administrative changes of Bourgeois de Boynes, Minister of Marine 1771–4, and, to a lesser extent, due to the fiscal stringency of these years, but, by 1780, thanks to shipbuilding since 1763, France and Spain had a combined quantitative superiority over Britain of about 25 per cent. Partly as a result, Britain gained control of neither European nor American waters, and therefore was unable to repeat its success in the Seven Years' War of 1756–63. Instead, British warships had to be redeployed in response to the integration of the American conflict into a wider struggle, in which the naval balance in American waters was interrelated with that in European and, more obviously, Caribbean waters.

The War of American Independence posed serious problems of naval strategy for Britain, France and Spain, some of them new, although, in response, there was no revolution in strategy. For Britain, aside from the logistical nightmare posed by supplying the forces on the other side of the Atlantic, the issue of numbers of warships interacted with disputes over strategy. In particular, the desirability of blockading French ports, for which there were arguably too few British ships, clashed with the prudent argument of John, 4th Earl of Sandwich, the First Lord of the Admiralty, that naval strength should be concentrated in home waters, not only to deter invasion, but also to permit a serious challenge to the main French fleet, which was based nearby at Brest, and thus to gain a position of naval dominance. This goal would be compromised by dispersing much of the fleet among distant stations, where it could support amphibious operations and protect trade, but could not materially affect the struggle for naval dominance.

Due to the state of communications technology, a situation that was to be transformed by the telegraph in the nineteenth century, but that was not to change radically until the use of radio in the early twentieth century, the commanders of those distant stations were difficult to control effectively. These commanders jealously guarded their autonomy and resources, producing an inflexibility that was ill-suited to the need to react to French initiatives.[36]

The concentration of naval strength in home waters, however, ensured that France's Mediterranean naval base, Toulon, was not blockaded, and in 1778 the Toulon fleet was able to sail to American waters and threaten the British position in New York. The arrival of the French warships was the first warning that the British garrison had of the outbreak of war, but the French failed to press home their surprise.

Despite grave strategic and organisational problems, the French were more successful at sea than in the Seven Years' War, in part thanks to the British delay in mobilising and in part to determined and effective French leadership.[37] Indeed the role of the latter emerges clearly in the French war effort. There is a ready contrast between the able and energetic Admiral Pierre André Suffren, who proved a persistent, redoubtable and brave opponent to the British in the Bay of Bengal and off Sri Lanka in 1782–3, and d'Orvilliers, the commander of the attempt to invade England in 1779. This attempt was thwarted by disease and poor organisation, rather than by British naval action.

The battles of the period indicated the difficulty of achieving a sweeping naval victory, which, in successive wars, the British were not to gain until 1747, 1759, 1782, 1798 and 1805. Lacking, by modern standards, deep keels, sailing vessels suffered from limited seaworthiness, while the operational problems of working sailing ships for combat were very different from those that steam-powered vessels were to encounter. The optimal conditions for sailing ships were to come from windward in a force 4–6 wind across a sea that was relatively flat; it was more difficult to range guns in a swell. Limitations on manoeuvrability ensured that ships were deployed in line in order to maximise their firepower, and skill, in handling ships in line or in battle, entailed balancing the wind between the sails of the three masts in order to achieve control over manoeuvrability and speed.[38] Line tactics and fighting instructions were designed to encourage an organisational cohesion that permitted more effective firepower, mutual support and flexibility in the uncertainty of battle.

Tactical practice, however, conformed to theory (usually geometrical[39]) even less at sea than on land, due in part to the impact of weather and wind on manoeuvrability. The nature of conflict at sea, not least the unwieldy nature of the line, made it difficult to maintain cohesion once ships became closely engaged, and, although experience, standardisation and design improvements enhanced performance, there were still significant limitations.[40] The report on the indecisive battle with the French Brest fleet off Ushant on 27 July 1778 by John Blankett indicated the dependence on wind direction:

> the forcing a fleet to action, equal in force, and with the advantage of the wind must always be done with great risk, and our fleet was not equal to that manoeuvre, but chance, which determines many events, put it out of the Admiral's power to choose his disposition ... the truth is, unless two fleets of equal force are equally determined for battle, whoever attacks must do it with infinite risk, but a fleet to leeward attacking one to windward is a dangerous manoeuvre indeed.[41]

The indecisive character of this battle ensured that Britain faced French intervention in the War of American Independence in a difficult situation. Conversely, victory that day would have limited the possibilities of French attack on the British empire, and would have increased French dependence on Spain.

Three years later, Graves failed to defeat the French off the Virginia Capes, an indecisive battle in terms of the damage inflicted with no ships sunk, but, as it prevented British relief of Earl Cornwallis's besieged army at Yorktown, an important success for the French. The impact of Cornwallis's subsequent surrender on British political opinion ensured that the campaign had a strategic impact. The ministry of Lord North fell, to be replaced by one pledged to negotiate peace. Yet, this can only be seen as a result of naval action if it is appreciated that this action could not force this result: instead news of the conflict interacted with political tensions in Britain.

The French Revolutionary and Napoleonic Wars

Britain and France came close to renewed conflict in the Dutch Crisis of 1787 and, this time with Spain on France's side, in the Nootka Sound Crisis of 1790. Each crisis witnessed major and competitive naval preparations, the course of which demonstrated resolve and strength. The two powers did not fight again, however, until 1793, by which time the leadership and administration of the French fleet had been badly affected by the collapse of royal authority in the French Revolution and the resulting political and administrative disruption. The impact was more serious than in the case of the army. Aside from a breakdown in relations between officers and men, there was factionalism within the officer corps, and the contrary demands of politicians in Paris and the ports. In 1793, the British were invited into Toulon by French Royalists, before being driven out again by Revolutionary forces benefiting from the well-sited cannon of Napoleon, then a young artillery officer. Disaffection within the French navy was more serious than in its British counterpart during the naval mutinies of 1797; a counterpart to the contrast between the serious German naval mutinies in 1918 and the far less grave British naval disaffection the following year.[42]

The British enjoyed far more sweeping naval victories in fleet actions in the 1790s and 1800s than in the War of American Independence, particularly the Glorious First of June over France (1794), St Vincent over Spain (1797), the Nile over France (1798) and Trafalgar over France and Spain (1805).[43] This success reflected fighting ability within a defined military system, rather than a quantum leap forward. Well-drilled gun crews, superior seamanship, bold leadership and effective command were key. Indeed, George III in 1797 had 'confidence in naval skill and British valour to supply want of numbers. I am too true

an Englishman to have ever adopted the more modern and igno-
ble mode of expecting equal numbers on all occasions.'[44]

Thanks to its naval strength, Britain was also able during the
French Revolutionary and Napoleonic Wars to maintain an effective convoy system that helped it increase its proportion of world
mercantile shipping, and also to deny access to world markets
to France and its allies. More generally, the strength and nature
of British naval power and maritime resources enabled Britain
to resist Napoleon's attempt to isolate it commercially from the
Continent from 1806. Naval strength also supported the British
campaigns in Portugal and Spain,[45] not least by providing the
guarantee of withdrawal for British forces, for example from
Corunna in 1809 and Lisbon in 1810–11; the first was used,
while the second proved unnecessary.

The navy yet again was crucial to amphibious operations,
leading to the capture of French and allied overseas bases, which
further lessened their ability to challenge the British: Cape
Town fell in 1806 (it had been captured in 1796 and restored in
1802), Martinique in 1809, Réunion and Mauritius in 1810 and
Batavia (Djakarta) in 1811. In 1808, Napoleon planned to take
over the Spanish overseas empire, not only in the New World
but also the Philippines. These hopes were thwarted by Spanish
resistance, but would, anyway, have been inhibited by British
naval power, just as the French attempt to regain Haiti from its
rebellious black population had been in 1803.

The War of 1812–15

British naval strength was also crucial in the War of 1812–15 with
the USA. At sea, the British, whose focus during this conflict
still remained the war with France, suffered initially from over-
confidence, inaccurate gunnery, and ships that were simply less
powerful and less well-prepared than those of their opponents.
However, aside from three frigates lost in ship-to-ship clashes in
1812, the British losses were all of smaller vessels, and British naval
effectiveness improved during the war, both in Atlantic waters and
on the Great Lakes. To operate at all in North America, the British
were dependent both on routes across the Atlantic and on an ability to act in coastal waters. Naval blockade, which became effective

from 1813, hit the American economy as well as American naval operations, British amphibious forces were able to capture Washington and threaten Baltimore, and it was possible to send reinforcements to Canada in order to resist successfully American attacks that were poorly led and uncoordinated. The importance to the campaigning of naval operations on the Great Lakes and Lake Champlain, not least of American victories on Lakes Erie and Champlain in 1813 and 1814, respectively, demonstrated the significance of inland waterways and related conflict.

British naval power

British naval power rested on a sophisticated and well-financed (each readily apparent in a comparative context) administrative structure. The large British fleet drew on the manpower of a substantial, indeed world-leading, mercantile marine and fishing fleet and, although there were never enough sailors, war trained the landsmen drafted into naval service.[46] Moreover, the relationship between the merchant and royal navies ensured that the navy was more integrated into the domestic economy than the army. British naval power also rested on an ability to win engagements that reflected widely diffused qualities of seamanship and gunnery, a skilled and determined corps of captains, and able leadership. This able leadership was true not only of command at sea, as with Nelson's innovative tactics, but also of effective institutional leadership that developed organisational efficiency, seen for example in the rebuilding of the fleet after the War of American Independence.[47]

Although the image of naval warfare was defined in different ways and contested politically,[48] Britain had a more meritocratic, and more ostentatiously meritocratic, promotion system and more unified naval tradition than those of France; as well as a greater commitment of national resources to naval rather than land warfare, a political choice that reflected the major role of trade and also the national self-image. The French, in contrast, lacked an effective chain of naval command, and trade was less important to their government and their political culture than that of Britain. The same was also true of Spain and Russia.

In turn, British capability rested on the unique Western experience of creating a global network of empire and trade, which was based on a distinctive type of interaction between economy, technology and state formation, and on the specific strength of the liberal political systems, pre-eminently those of Britain and the Netherlands. These systems were notably successful in eliciting the co-operation of their own and, also, other capitalists, producing a symbiosis of government and the private sector that proved both effective and, especially, valuable for developing naval strength. China, Korea and Japan could build large and many ships and manufacture guns, their states were relatively centralised, and their economies and levels of culture were not clearly weaker than those of contemporary Western states. However, in contrast to Western powers, there was hardly any interaction in these three states between economy, technology and state formation, aimed at creating maritime effectiveness.

The potential of Western naval power was still far less than it was to be by 1920. First submarines and, subsequently, aircraft carriers led to a transformation in the relationship between warships and the environment in which they operated. The latter changed the way in which naval forces could press on land powers, as well, more specifically, as their ability to mount successful amphibious assaults. This ability was to be continued with submarine-launched cruise missiles. In contrast, naval power during the French Revolutionary and Napoleonic Wars did not have comparable impact. Successive naval victories protected Britain from invasion and enabled her to risk amphibious operations, but neither these victories, nor indeed such operations, even if successful, could greatly influence, let alone determine, the course of conflict on land. After Trafalgar (1805), in which 19 French and Spanish ships of the line were captured or destroyed, the British enjoyed a clear superiority in ships of the line, but Napoleon's victories over Austria, Prussia and Russia in 1805–7 ensured that the War of the Third Coalition ended with France in a far stronger position in Europe than at the start of the conflict.

More generally, whatever the success of their operations in Iberia, the British could not overthrow Napoleon without the help of powerful land allies. This situation repeated the British failure to coerce Russia into returning conquests from Sweden and the Ottomans, in 1720–1 and 1791, respectively. Russia, significantly, concentrated attention on its army, rather than on the navy on which Peter the Great (r. 1689–1725) and Catherine the Great (r. 1762–96) had lavished so much attention. In place of

Russian amphibious forces in Holland and the Mediterranean in the 1790s came a focus in 1813–14 on operations from Poland into Germany and then France. Nevertheless, the Russians used naval power to dominate Finland which they conquered from Sweden in 1808.

British victories in battle certainly had an operational and a strategic impact as far as the war at sea was concerned, because they greatly altered the balance of naval power. The first British naval victory of the French Revolutionary War, the Glorious First of June in 1794, helped deter France from plans drawn up a year earlier to build up a major fleet, reduced the French naval threat in British home waters, and therefore helped free more of the British navy for operations further afield, particularly in both the Mediterranean and the Caribbean. The fate of battle partly explains the contrast between the first two years of this war, in which France lost 22 ships, and the first four years in the Anglo-French stage of the War of American Independence, in which France only lost four warships.[49]

In 1798, Nelson's total victory over a French fleet in the Battle of the Nile (Aboukir Bay), followed by the British capture of Seringapatam in Mysore in 1799 and the killing there of Tipu Sultan, and by Britain's victory over the French army in Egypt in 1801,[50] made it clear that France would not be able to project her power successfully along the Egypt–India axis. War with Britain also prevented France from enjoying the full benefits of the European hegemony she seized. The British had grasped the controlling maritime position, only to see it collapse in 1795–6, when the French forced the Dutch and Spain into alliance and gained the benefit of their fleets, leading the British to evacuate the Mediterranean. Thanks, however, to British naval victories in 1797–1805, the colonial empires of France's European allies were outside her (and their) control, and the resources that Napoleon deployed could not be used to project French power overseas. This was a failure that was not inherent in France's position, but one that reflected the relatively low priority of maritime as opposed to continental activities for France, and, even more, the successes of the British navy.

Yet, British victory at sea could not prevent the French from trying to build up their navy, not least to rebuild it after defeat at Trafalgar in 1805. This response was more generally true of numerous naval defeats, such as that of the Ottomans after Lepanto, the Spaniards after the Armada, and the Japanese after Midway in 1571, 1588 and 1942, respectively. Major fleet defeats, however, could be important in forcing a shift in strategy, as after Barfleur. At the same time, battles have to be put in comparative context, as other naval operations could have an equivalent or even greater impact, for example sustained British excellence in amphibious operations in the Seven Years' and Napoleonic Wars or anti-submarine operations in the two world wars.

By 1809, thanks to the French build-up, the Toulon fleet was nearly as large as the British blockaders. French naval strength, however, had been badly battered by heavy losses of sailors, dead or captured, in successive defeats, and in 1808 Napoleon also lost the support of the Spanish navy when he invaded Spain. The role of the international context was underlined in 1812–14, when Britain's military capability was effective in the crucial period of Napoleonic decline as part of an international league in which the major blows against France were struck on land, and by Britain's allies. The victory by Austrian, Prussian and Russian forces at Leipzig (1813), and not Trafalgar, was the battle that spelled the end for Napoleon.

Furthermore, as a reminder of British limitations, some British amphibious expeditions, such as those against both Buenos Aires and Egypt in 1807, were eventually unsuccessful, in the former case leading to the surrender of the British force attacking the city. The same year, the Ottomans refused to yield to British naval intimidation when a fleet forced the Dardanelles. Amphibious operations in Western waters could also be unsuccessful, as with the Walcheren expedition of 1809, a mismanaged and disease-hit large-scale British attempt to seize control of the port of Antwerp, and thus hinder Napoleon's attempt to rebuild his navy after Trafalgar. The effort devoted to this expedition reflected the importance attached to the goal.

Blockade

Naval battles between Britain and France and her allies – Spain, the Dutch and the Danes – tend to dominate attention, but the strength and weaknesses of naval power also emerge clearly from a consideration of other aspects of naval activity. Blockade, a combination of naval strength, economic intelligence, financial pressure and diplomatic negotiation, was particularly important, with British squadrons policing the seas of Europe and, to a lesser extent, in so far as they could, the oceans of the world. An ability to wreck the foreign trade of rivals could damage their navies, depriving them of timber and naval stores, as that of Spain was in the 1800s. This ability could also cripple their imperial system; greatly hamper their economy, as happened to the French at Britain's hands in 1747–8 and to the economy of Napoleonic-controlled Europe;[51] and hit popular support. For example, living standards in Norway were hit hard by the blockade in 1807–14 which weakened support there for rule by France's ally Denmark.

Even if it was not possible to inflict this degree of damage, higher insurance premiums, danger money for sailors, and the need to resort to convoys and other defensive measures could push up the cost of trade. George III wrote in 1795 'of the necessity of keeping constantly detached squadrons to keep the Channel, the Bay of Biscay, and the North Sea clear of the enemy's ships; had that measure been uniformly adopted by the Admiralty I am certain by this time the trade of France would have been totally annihilated'.[52] As a strategic response, Napoleon built, from 1800, the Sempione arterial road from France to Italy, so as to bypass the British coastal blockade.

There were different types of blockade, which serves as a reminder for the continual need to define terms and to watch against the habit when employing concepts, for example power projection or littoral warfare and descriptions, such as submarine warfare, of running together what is often, at best, a range of activities and, at worse, contradictory goals. Close blockade was designed to stop an enemy naval force emerging, while open blockade was intended to catch an enemy naval force emerging, and maritime blockade to stop maritime commerce and to have a direct economic impact on the opponent's society, an aspect that can be related to notions of total war.

These different forms of blockade had variable success rates, although blockading anywhere is very difficult. The history of British blockading squadrons, moreover, was often that of storms and of disappointed hopes of engaging the French. Blockading squadrons could be driven off station by wind and weather,[53] and blockading Toulon was particularly difficult.[54] The small watching squadron off Toulon was blown off station when the French sailed for Egypt in May 1798.

The exposure of British warships to the constant battering of wind and wave also placed a major strain on an increasingly ageing fleet, which served as a stark warning of the more general process by which war compromised effectiveness, a process which made it difficult to realise plans and to maintain pre-war impressions of proficiency. The British Channel fleet, for example, was dispersed by a strong gale on 3 January 1804, and the blockade of the French port of Le Havre was lifted. The weather claimed and damaged more British ships than the French: out of the 317 British warships lost in 1803–15, 223 were wrecked or foundered, including, in 1811, the St George, a 98-gunner, with the loss of all bar twelve of the crew of 850, when it was driven onto the Danish coast in a storm. Tropical stations could be particularly dangerous, and in 1807 Admiral Trowbridge and *Blenheim* disappeared in a storm in the Indian Ocean off Madagascar.

Fog was also a problem, particularly for blockaders. It could cover French movements, as when the Brest fleet sailed in April 1798, and, once a fleet had sailed, it was impossible to know where it had gone: in this case, the British were unsure whether the French would head for Ireland or the Mediterranean, in both of which they were vulnerable. In January 1808, the French Rochefort squadron evaded the British blockaders in bad weather and poor visibility, and then sailed to Toulon, making the concentration of French warships there more serious.

The poorly charted nature of inshore waters was a problem that led to ships frequently running aground. It was particularly easy to do so when enforcing blockades, and shoals were also a problem when attacking enemy warships sheltering in coastal waters. Once aground, ships were vulnerable to attack and to the weather.

Wind-powered warships were dependent both tactically and operationally on the weather, and this dependence was therefore important to naval capability and the understanding of naval power. Ships could only sail up to a certain angle to the wind. Too much or insufficient wind were serious problems.

Reliance on the wind alone made inshore naval operations very chancy, which underlined the continued value of galleys, notably in the rocky waters of the Gulf of Finland. French ships could only leave their major Atlantic port – Brest – with an easterly wind. Due to the prevailing westerly and south-westerly winds, this wind was not all that prevalent, but that also created difficulties for the British blockaders who were continually blown towards the treacherous coast of Brittany, which made their life very dangerous and a misery. British blockading skills changed over time. They were really very good off Brest by the end of the Napoleonic Wars, but ships could still escape even then. A key British goal was to stop food and naval stores from getting to Brest, which was more easily achieved. Thus, blockade was as much to do with preventing goods from getting in as much as stopping ships leaving. This was especially important for Brest because of its atrocious landward communications: everything had to come by sea.

There were also serious limitations in the surveillance, and command and control capabilities of naval power. These made it very difficult to 'see' in tactical and operational terms or control waters in any strategic sense, and certainly limited the value of any blockade. It was generally possible for a lookout to see only about 15 miles from the top of the main mast in fine weather. However, fleets used a series of frigates stationed just over the horizon, and they signalled using their sails, which were much bigger than flags, and, because the masts were so tall, could be seen at some distance over the horizon. This relay system was particularly important for blockading British fleets: there would be an inshore squadron of highly manoeuvrable ships (which were unlikely to get caught against the lee shore) that physically watched the French in Brest and Toulon, or the Spaniards in Cadiz, and they then signalled, using a relay of frigates, to the main fleet which was located a few miles off in greater safety.

Surveillance capability was surprisingly sophisticated: by simply 'looking' at a ship, its nationality, strength, skill, manpower, capability and performance could all be determined. Yet, the possibilities brought by improved means of surveillance and command and control in the early twentieth century, for example air power, radio and radar, were not only to transform the situation but also to ensure that the language of control of that and subsequent periods provides a misleading impression when applied to the Age of Nelson.

Britain's maritime position

More generally, operational limitations were tested by skill and developments. For example, specialised sailing ships, in particular bomb ketches, were designed with coastal operations in shallow waters foremost in mind.[55] It is also possible to adduce examples of successful campaigns in precisely such waters, for example the British navy's Chesapeake campaign of 1814. Yet, as a reminder of the ambiguous nature of success, the ability to project power, and indeed to land troops, who defeated an American force at Bladensburg and burned down the public buildings in Washington, as well as subsequently threatening Baltimore, did not bring a settlement of the war on Britain's terms substantially closer, and certainly inflamed American views. The use of the new rocket-firing ships to bombard Fort McHenry outside Baltimore proved singularly unsuccessful and helped provide the Americans with a lasting symbol of fortitude celebrated in the anthem 'The Star-Spangled Banner'.

Despite its difficulties, British naval power permitted a great increase in maritime strength, and this was important to the global protection and expansion of her trade. For example, British commercial penetration of South and South-East Asia and the Far East was aided by naval strength: occupation, as of the Dutch colony of Java in 1811–16, was important to this process and in the subsequent settlement the British gained control of Singapore, which they were to build up as a major trading centre.

More generally, her dominant maritime position served to ensure that Britain took the leading role in exploration, trade and the assembling of knowledge about the world, including the charting of all its waters. This role left its mark on the imperial capital, where there was a major expansion in shipping and docks, important developments in the commercial infrastructure of the Empire. Elsewhere in Britain, war with France led to an expansion of shipbuilding, both for the navy and for trade. The strength of the British maritime economy explains Napoleon's attempts to stop British trade with continental Europe, and also his encouragement of British smugglers in order to increase the flight of gold from Britain. In turn, British naval power was involved in the struggle with smuggling.

Naval power was a condition as well as a product of economic growth. As the Industrial Revolution was crucial to British and, subsequently, global modernisation, so the ability of the British navy to operate effectively, within existing constraints, in order to foster British trade was highly significant in fostering British economic growth. This Industrial Revolution was to have fundamental implications for the ability, in the nineteenth and early twentieth centuries, to develop and sustain new-model navies with totally different tactical, operational and, eventually, strategic capabilities to those hitherto. Yet, if a technology-driven account of military strength and change is employed, then the naval capability of the Age of Nelson certainly does not deserve discussion in terms of naval revolution.

Indeed, the case of the submarine demonstrated that an awareness of the difficulties posed by introducing new developments helped ensure a reluctance in adopting them. Following on from Bushnell's lead, another American, Robert Fulton, produced a submarine in 1797, but found neither France nor Britain greatly interested in its acquisition. His experiments for the French in 1800–1 included the testing of a system of compressed air in a portable container and the successful destruction of a moored vessel by an underwater explosion. Fulton also proposed the use of steamships for an invasion of England, but, in 1803, the French Academy of Sciences rejected the idea. Moreover, in Britain, in 1804–6, Fulton worked on mines. They were used, with scant effect, for an attack on French shipping in Boulogne in 1804, but, in trials in 1805, he became the first to sink a large ship with a mine.

British interest in radical new technology, however, declined after Trafalgar, when Britain's naval position seemed comparatively safe; while Fulton was held back in his experiments with torpedoes from 1807 by his failure to devise an effective firing device. During the Anglo-American war of 1812–15, Fulton played a role in unsuccessful American experiments with a submarine, mines and underwater guns. He was not alone. In 1807–10, Ivan Fistum, a Russian, made advances in electrical detonation and the use of floating mines for harbour defences, while in 1809 Napoleon authorised a French company to build a submarine.[56] The bases for submarine warfare, including effective systems for underwater propulsion and storing air, however, were not yet present.

Defining naval strength and modernity

Despite both the pressures of war and a general process of search for improvement, a focus on technological transformation is of limited value for this period. The scant usefulness of contemporary advances in (hot-air) balloons and rockets for conflict at sea as well as on land in the wars of 1792–1815 is indicative. Instead of a focus on technology, it is more helpful to consider multi-definitional approaches to capability, effectiveness and development. Within that context, a key element was the ability to operate at reasonable effectiveness within existing constraints. This effectiveness was, and is, easier to obtain in contexts in which there are not radical shifts in technological potential, in other words, periods such as 1660–1815; as opposed, for example, to the First World War. As far as the former period is considered, the key element in successfully operating at such effectiveness tended, indeed, to be institutional, a product of administrative skill, financial strength, and governmental stability and support.

All three criteria found Britain at an advantage, before, during and after the French Revolution. It would indeed be possible to argue that the British navy of the period 1793–1815 was so much ahead of all other navies that it could be described as a modern navy, while other navies still were early modern. However, such vocabulary introduces a problematic teleology and linear approach to the past that need to be critically considered in terms of the variety of goals arising from, and reflected in, contemporary strategic cultures, as well as the related concept of fitness for purpose in terms of specific and differing force structures and investment patterns. Navies might be, at once, fit for purpose and yet far from the cutting edge in terms of contemporary views of modernity; a point that remains pertinent.

To return to the concept of the British navy as modern, it was not warship technology that was different (British warships for most of the period were on the average older than those of the

French), but the cumulative nature of British advances in gun-casting, gunnery methods (flintlocks), food supply and methods for storing food on ships, naval medicine and surgery, and the quality of sails and ropes. These advances were all considerable in 1793–1815, while they were largely absent in other navies which, to some extent, actually went backwards and became deskilled. The other navies were certainly very different in scale to that of Britain. By 1812, the victualling system of the British navy was feeding 140,000 men daily, aside from the numerous prisoners of war that helped ensure the weakness of the French navy. This victualling system was an aspect of a formidable British organi-sational capability[57] that serves as a reminder of the limitations of thinking of change primarily in terms of weapons technology, with the general emphasis, in such an approach, accordingly for navies on the period 1500–1670 (including the first two Anglo-Dutch Wars) and, subsequently, on the Age of Steam.

Furthermore, prior to the Age of Steam, the British navy was able to achieve the contemporary goals of naval power and to fulfil the assumptions of British strategic culture. As yet, the abil-ity to act against a continental state that was to stem from air power and, subsequently, missiles was not conceivable, no more than the shifts that were to arise from steam power, shell guns and iron ships, or, subsequently, radio. These paradigm shifts in capability were to be revolutionary as far as ship killing, ship control, and power projection were concerned, and, indeed, in 1806 Fulton argued that 'It does not require much depth of thought to trace that science by discovering gunpowder changed the whole art of war by land and sea; and by future combination may sweep military marines from the ocean.'[58]

During the Napoleonic Wars, Britain's maritime strength and its ability to thwart French invasion were sustained in the face of major difficulties. As a result, there was no naval parity sub-sequently in the nineteenth century, but, instead, a British naval hegemony. This hegemony rested on an industrial strength and a strategic culture that together ensured that shifts in techno-logical potential occurred within the existing hierarchy of naval power, rather than overthrowing it. This situation remained true even of the major challenge to Britain in the 1900s and 1910s from Germany, a leading industrial power willing to invest in naval strength. The subsequent shift from British to American naval hegemony, one accomplished by 1945, was achieved without conflict between Britain and the USA and, indeed, while the two were allies; and even Germany and Japan in co-operation in 1941–5 were not able to thwart this transformation. In terms of the standard linear approach, naval (and indeed imperial) rivalry between Britain and France from 1689 to 1815, as well as their subsequent competition short of war, can be seen as part of a sequence of challenges in and to the use of naval power, and not as a limited form of warfare that subsequently became total or more total. Indeed, the length of large-scale, deep-sea naval conflict between Britain and France during the French Revolutionary and Napoleonic Wars has never been matched since.

5 1815–1914

The nineteenth century was an age of British naval dominance, yet also a period in which there were moves towards a challenge to Western naval superiority. Indeed, in 1905, the Japanese dramatically defeated the Russian navy. Yet, unlike the Oriental warships that competed in the same waters in the 1590s, the Japanese victor was organised on the Western model and, indeed, had been trained and equipped by the British. As another key instance of continuity, although naval technologies changed dramatically over the nineteenth century, especially those of propulsion, firepower and armour, the essentials of the Western naval model did not alter. The reliance throughout was on specialised warships, instead of armed merchantmen (although there was a place for the latter and for armed liners in naval plans); and the stress was on permanent naval forces, and not on units raised for particular conflicts. As another important element of continuity, navies depended on a sophisticated infrastructure of bases and supply systems and were the product of an advanced military-industrial system.

This situation had already been the case in the Age of Sail, and notably so for the British Royal Navy, but, if anything, the relationship became even stronger in light of the developments in battleship specifications in the 1860s–1900s. Technological advances therefore could only become operative as a result of production structures and naval systems, and these, in turn, were dependent on economic and political parameters.

Throughout the period covered in this chapter, Britain had the largest and most successful navy in the world. As with the Age of Sail, this success was not due to any special superiority in British warships or guns, for, although there could be particular advantages, the Royal Navy was very similar to its opponents in the weaponry it employed, a similarity that did not change with the pace of technological change. Instead, the greater effectiveness of the Royal Navy was largely due to its capacity to build and maintain more ships and different types of ship, as well as its extensive and effective administrative infrastructure, the global range of its bases, the strength of public finances, and good naval leadership. Britain could also build ships more quickly than its rivals, and had important technological leads in metallurgy and hydrodynamics, while the Admiralty was the largest patron of science in Britain, with naval activity being both subject and means of research.[1] The British, moreover, had a meritocratic promotion system and a stronger naval tradition than that of France, the second naval power for most of the period.

This naval tradition was linked to the greater proportion of national resources devoted in Britain to naval as opposed to land capability, a political choice that reflected the key role of overseas trade, an unprecedented expansion of overseas empire, and the fact that, as an island, as well as an empire dependent on maritime links and vulnerable to attack, the sea was Britain's front line in a war. The Royal Navy also benefited from the quality and size of Britain's merchant marine and the number of shipbuilding firms.

The national self-image was also highly relevant and remained so. In contrast with Britain, trade was less important to the government and political culture of France, and to those of the world's two leading land powers, China and Russia. Both geopolitical circumstances and political culture were important, with the British able to afford to prioritise the navy above the army.

1815–50

Thanks to its naval resources and organisation, Britain had turned tactical triumphs and operational successes to strategic advantage during the Napoleonic Wars. Napoleon's very surrender to a British warship in 1815 and his dispatch on another to the remote South Atlantic island colony of St Helena were clear indications of the role of the navy. So, more practically, in the Waterloo campaign, was the British ability to deploy troops direct from Halifax and New Orleans to Belgium. The inevitable dominance of the British navy led Napoleon, who was anyway short of troops, to recruit sailors from the French navy into his army in 1815. Napoleon's regime was also put under pressure by naval demonstrations off French ports, and the British navy played a major role in the restoration of Bourbon authority in Marseilles, Toulon and Bordeaux.

Moreover, successive victories in the Napoleonic Wars, especially Trafalgar, conditioned British and foreign expectations, both then and subsequently, about the nature of naval power and of Britain's maritime role. A confidence in naval power was readily manifested. In May 1815, a squadron of British warships entered the Bay of Naples and threatened to bombard the city unless it surrendered within 48 hours, and this duly occurred, helping to ensure the overthrow of Murat's regime and thus to bring stability to Italy and end the prospect of a diversion in favour of Napoleon. At the same time, Murat's earlier defeat by the Austrians at Tolentino and the advance of an Austrian army on Naples were also important.

Within Britain, an impression of naval power was propagated in terms of the national destiny. The image of naval strength was kept alive in British culture through the arts, especially paintings and on the stage.[2] This depiction looked towards later works such as Gilbert and Sullivan's operetta *HMS Pinafore* (1878). Indeed, in 1940, the attack on the Italian fleet was originally planned for Trafalgar Day, 21 October.

Throughout much of the nineteenth century, foreign expectations and fears about British power allowed Britain to get grudging unofficial recognition of the Pax Britannica, the doctrine of the Royal Navy keeping the peace of the seas for all to benefit, and thus underpinning the world order. These assumptions, however, were, at least in part, misleading. The number of British ships of the line considered fit for service was actually lower than the supposed number of warships. Moreover, as the level of naval threat was diminished, the size of the navy fell rapidly from 1815, in part because some wartime launchings had been of ships rapidly built from unseasoned wood, and they swiftly deteriorated. The same problem greatly affected the French navy.

Post-war retrenchment was also important. In Britain, this retrenchment reflected the legacy of unprecedented levels of wartime expenditure and post-war debt, as well as political pressures including the ending of income tax in 1816. Costs and manpower were cut by keeping most of the ships of the line in reserve. Yet, this reserve – 84 ships of the line in 1817 – was the deterrent on which British naval strength rested. Moreover, the use of seasoned timber ensured that the new ships were more long-lasting than many built in the wartime rush. The British deterrent was also about the massive naval infrastructure behind the number of ships. Manpower was reduced, but was geared up to mobilise very quickly. In many respects, the numerous empty receiving ships that littered British harbours were as indicative of British capability as the warships in ordinary themselves.

Strategic requirements also played a role in retrenchment. The British felt no need to maintain their wartime rate of construction or maintenance because, unlike after the Seven Years' War (1756–63), the Bourbons (of France and Spain) did not launch a major programme of naval construction after 1815. Instead, the French government, for which the army was far more important, not least to secure internal order, decided to concentrate, at sea, on frigates and, in the event of another war, to attack British trade.

Until the revival of French naval strength from the mid-1820s, the British Admiralty saw the American fleet as its most likely rival. Yet, despite expansion from 1815 that reflected the prestige gained in the War of 1812–15, as well as the role of its naval power in supporting commercial and diplomatic goals, for example an expedition against Algiers in 1815,[3] the American navy remained small. Also, Anglo-American rivalry was limited as the two powers implicitly co-operated on crucial issues, especially in opposing Spanish control in Latin America. Furthermore, neither attempted to win colonies there, and Britain and the USA collaborated to suppress the slave trade and piracy. The latter tasks ensured frequent action, as in the American attacks on Cuban pirate bases in 1821.

Action against pirates and slavers was the cutting edge of the process by which maritime action and force were brought under the control of sovereign states and their navies. The extension of the laws and fiscal authority of governments to cover maritime activity was an aspect of this activity, and was related to the allocation of coastal regions and waters among particular countries as authority was clarified and solidified. Dealing with pirates was an aspect of a more general hostile response to adventurers, enterprising individuals operating outside the ambit of the state, such as American filibusterers. William Walker, who sought to take control of Nicaragua and Honduras, was thwarted by the American and British navies in 1857–60. Filibustering was now only acceptable at the behest of governments.

The Spaniards, after 1815, had tried to build up a fleet to support their efforts to restore power in Latin America, not least by buying Russian warships in 1818–19, but the Wars of Liberation in Latin America did not lead to conflict between the major naval powers. Spain and Britain avoided war with each other, and the Spanish fleet, which was far smaller than that of Britain, declined greatly in the 1820s and 1830s. These Wars of Liberation, however, did involve local naval conflict. The new Chilean republic created a navy that, in 1818, captured a Spanish frigate and transport fleet bringing reinforcements. Thereafter, the Chilean fleet blockaded and attacked Spanish-held Peru, playing a crucial role in the successful Chilean invasion of 1820–1, and prefiguring the situation during the War of the Pacific in 1879–83 in which naval success enabled Chile to invade Peru. The Chilean navy drew heavily on British and American manpower and leadership, both of which were available owing to demobilisation in 1815.[4]

The success of the Brazilian rebels against Portugal in conquering the northern provinces as well as the coastal cities south of Rio owed much to the successful use of naval force: like the Chileans, the Brazilians hired British officers and men who were available thanks to post-war demobilisation. In 1823, the Portuguese were forced to leave Salvador da Bahia, and the Brazilian squadron also captured Maranhão (São Luis), Belém do Pará and Montevideo. In the case of the last, the squadron supported a siege by Brazilian land forces. Portugal became a significantly weaker naval power as a result of its failure to retain Brazil.

Naval power was also important in the politics of the newly independent state. In 1824, for example, a rising in the province of Pernambuco was suppressed after the port of Recife had been blockaded into surrender by the Brazilian navy. In the struggle between Brazil and Argentina over control of Uruguay in 1825–30, both sides sought to employ economic warfare, the more powerful Brazilian navy blockading Buenos Aires, while Argentinian privateers attacked Brazilian trade.

In the post-Napoleonic period, Western navies were involved in operations against non-Western powers and, in some cases, overpowered them. A bombardment of Algiers by a British fleet (supported by a Dutch frigate squadron) in 1816 led to an agreement to end the taking of Christian slaves, in a nineteenth-century example of the navy giving force to what was termed in the 1990s and 2000s both ethical foreign policy and the Clash of Civilisations. In 1815, an American squadron had forced Algiers to pay compensation for attacks on American shipping. The threat of renewed naval bombardment led Husain III, the Dey of Algiers, to capitulate to British demands in 1824, although the Algerine capitulations were largely bogus, which undercut the extent of the naval successes.

Three years later, thanks largely to overwhelming British firepower at almost point-blank range, an Anglo-French-Russian fleet under Sir Edward Codrington destroyed the Ottoman and Egyptian fleets at the battle of Navarino Bay, a key event in the struggle for Greek independence. This battle was the last great one of the Age of Fighting Sail. It was one in which the Western fatalities were far lower than those of their opponents: 177 to about 17,000.

Steam power

Because of the absence of naval conflict between Western powers in the decades after 1815, these decades have received less attention from naval historians than the previous four decades. The major theme in writing on the years after 1815 has been on technological change, and on developments looking towards future capability, in particular the application of steam power. The steam engine, developed in Britain in the eighteenth century, was harnessed to the cause of marine propulsion. Steam power eventually replaced dependence on the wind, making journey times more predictable and quicker, although it also made the availability of coal and the ability to carry sufficient coal key issues.

Change was not immediate. Ship designers still believed in the steadying-power of canvas to prevent the ship from rolling too heavily. The prevention of rolling was particularly important for paddle ships, in order to keep their paddles in the water. Early steamships, moreover, suffered from slow speed, a high rate of coal consumption, and the difficulties posed by side and paddle wheels, which included the considerable space they took up and their vulnerability to attack and accident. As a result, steamships could carry few guns. There were also serious problems in producing and maintaining reliable engines.

Thus, the substitution of steam engines for sails in warships did not happen overnight. Instead, the process by which steam technology transformed naval warfare occurred through a series of innovations, each with its own chronology and pattern of diffusion. The paddle wheel and more powerful naval ordnance developed in the 1820s,[5] and the screw propeller (placed at the stern) in the 1840s became a feasible alternative to the paddle wheel. The adoption of the screw propeller made the tactical advantages of steam clear-cut: it was now possible to carry a full broadside armament. The first screw-driven ship of the line, the *Napoléon*, was ordered for the French navy in 1847 and launched in 1850. Investing heavily in new technology and the engineering potential of their economy, the British quickly followed suit in their determination to ensure that the Royal Navy stayed to the fore, heavily outspending the French.[6]

Steam enhanced the tactical and operational possibilities of sea power, as was seen for example in the extensive anti-slavery operations of the British navy. Now able to manoeuvre in calms and to make headway against contrary winds, the independence of individual warships in a fleet action was greatly extended. Moreover, the increased manoeuvrability of ships, not least their capacity to act in the face of adverse winds, made it easier to sound inshore and in hazardous waters, to attack opposing fleets in harbour, and to mount landings. Steamships could work with confidence close inshore. This capability had an impact on piracy, but the fall of tariffs, as free-trade agreements were negotiated, was possibly as important as it reduced the viability of fencing stolen property.

The ability of ships to operate in rivers was also enhanced. Steam indeed was extremely important for inland navigation, and played a major role in enabling the expansion of empires deep into the interior, for example carrying troops into Africa. In the First Anglo-Burmese War of 1824–5, the 60-horsepower engine of the British East India Company's steamer *Diana* allowed her to operate on the swiftly-flowing River Irrawaddy. The *Diana* towed sailing ships and destroyed Burmese war boats. The ship was crucial to the British advance 400 miles upriver, which led the Burmese to negotiate and accept British terms.

Steamships were also better able to cope with bad weather. The *Nemesis*, a British iron steamer that sailed through the winter gales off the Cape of Good Hope to China in 1840, was the first such warship to reach Macao, although two smaller steam warships had crossed the Pacific from Chile the same year. Steamships, however, were also unseaworthy in bad weather, particularly the paddle-steamers. They could hold their own in a gale, if not make some ground to windward, but they were not pleasant to be on. Indeed, most steamships in this period retained their sailing rigs for added comfort because they steadied the ship. Subsequently, the dual propulsion system of sail and steam remained until the 1890s, as an ability to use sail reduced the need to rely on coal supplies and boilers. The last British armoured warships (excluding sloops) with a full-masted rig were laid down in 1881, although the rigs were removed straight after their trials, while the last fully rigged French cruisers were laid down in 1885.

Steam capability changed the geopolitics of naval power, as well as its strategy and operational and tactical geography, leading to new senses of vulnerability and opportunity. In 1849, in a demonstration of the new capability, the French had been able to move 7500 troops and supplies rapidly by steamships across the Mediterranean from Toulon to Civitavecchia, the port for Rome, a deployment that led to the fall of the Roman Republic. Improved logistics was a key advantage brought by steam power. Moreover, a fear of vulnerability to an invasion by French steamships prompted the construction in the 1860s of major coastal defence works on the south coast of England to protect the naval bases, and especially Portsmouth, from an attack from the rear.[7] In 1853–4, as war neared with Russia, Sir James Graham, the First Lord of the Admiralty, was more concerned by the threat from France.[8]

Steam power was not the only technological change transforming naval capability. Indeed, the interlinked nature of change is such that the isolation of individual factors for analysis is problematic. Thus, for example, while steam increased the manoeuvrability of warships along coasts, long-range artillery and the defensive strength of armour plate were also important as they made the warships more effective against coastal forts.

British cannon firing solid shot proved effective against the Ottoman fleet at Navarino Bay in 1827, but naval ordnance was to change radically thanks to the work of the French gunner Colonel Henri-Joseph Paixhans, who used exploding shells, not solid shot. Exploding shells were not new – the French had first taken shell-firing mortars to sea in the 1690s and many people had experimented with shell guns in the eighteenth century. However, the fusing problem was then insuperable. In the early 1820s, Paixhans constructed a cannon and a gun carriage steady enough to cope with the report produced by the explosive charges required to fire large projectiles and to give them a high enough initial speed to pierce the side of a big ship and to explode inside. Now, exploding shells could be fired from the main guns, and not from mortars.

Paixhans's innovations were demonstrated successfully in 1824, and their impact was increased by his publications, including *Nouvelle Force Maritime et Artillerie* (1822). Such publications testified to the extent to which public discussion, even opinion, were seen as playing a role in military decisions. Such debate became a factor in naval policy in liberal states and can be seen as a key aspect of the modern naval age. Paixhans pressed for the combination of his new ordnance with the new steamship technology, and intended that shell-firing paddle steamers should make sailing ships of the line obsolete. Such a quest proved a key element in naval speculation and experimentation as there were repeated efforts to offset and counter the strength of the leading naval power. An awareness of the potential of new developments combined with the culture of print to ensure the rapid dissemination of new ideas.

In 1837, the French established the Paixhans shell gun as a part of every warship's armament, but they found it difficult to manufacture reliable shell-firing guns. As a consequence, the hopes of Paixhans's supporters that new technology would enable France to threaten Britain's naval hegemony proved abortive in the 1820s and 1830s. Moreover, the process by which the comparative advantage of one power was lessened by the diffusion of the new technology it could deploy was shown in this case. The British adopted shell guns as part of their standard armament in 1838, although their limited range encouraged continued reliance on the 32-pounders firing solid shot. In the 1840s, the main criticism of shells was still their inaccuracy at long range.

The new naval capability, nevertheless, was demonstrated in action when a British fleet bombarded Egyptian-held Acre in Palestine in 1840: steamers showed their ability to operate inshore, while a shell caused the explosion of the fortress's main magazine. Two years earlier, the British had used small local gunboats to blockade the Siamese-occupied port of Quedah (Kedah on the coast of modern Malaysia), because the corvette *Hyacinth* was too deep-draught to get close to the coast.

Meanwhile, competition between Western powers helped drive naval activity elsewhere. In particular, British concern about French ambitions registered around the world, leading, for example, to the mapping of the Suez isthmus by the British in 1836, to naval demonstrations off Tunis in 1836 and 1837, to the annexation of New Zealand in 1840, and to the development, from 1846, of a naval base at Labuan off Borneo, in response to the danger that the French, from their base at Danang in Vietnam, would threaten the lucrative commercial route to China.[9]

The 1850s

The development of cannon firing shells posed a terrible threat to wooden ships, as was demonstrated by the leading battle of mid-century. A wooden Ottoman squadron was surprised and destroyed at Sinope on 30 November 1853 by a Russian fleet under Vice-Admiral Pavel Nakhimov. The 8 Russian warships carried in total 38 Paixhans shell-firing guns. Of the 4400 Turks present, 3000 were killed, and 9 of their 10 ships were lost. The battle helped make the name of the shell gun, although it is important not to exaggerate its effectiveness: the Russians took six hours to win, the Ottomans had only frigates and corvettes, and, given the disparity between the two fleets, the same outcome would have been expected with solid shot. Shells, nevertheless, helped lead to armoured warships, ironclads, although there was a gap between shell guns and the response, armour.

The 1850s also saw a major shift to steam in the British and French battle fleets, with the construction of new screw ships of the line and the conversion of other ships. Elsewhere, the pace was slower. By the end of the Crimean War, in 1856, only Russia and Sweden also had screw ships of the line, although Austria, Denmark and Turkey followed later. In that war (1854–6), the British mounted a formidable naval effort, in both the Baltic and the Black Seas, their large Baltic fleet blockading the Russians in St Petersburg. Indeed, the threat to St Petersburg in 1855–6 was an important factor in the end of the war as Britain's ability to threaten coastal attacks helped leverage peace talks and indicated the importance of a potential for harbour attack. As the Russians remained in port, there were no naval battles in the Crimean War, while, similarly, in 1859, the Austrian navy stayed in port and did not engage the more powerful French navy, and the Franco-Prussian war of 1870–1 was a land struggle: the French prepared for an expedition to the Baltic, purchasing British ships to that end, but it was never launched.

The Crimean War demonstrated the global range of naval power and the consequent pressures on planning. Russia's position as a Pacific, as well as Baltic, Black Sea and Arctic power, represented a threat to British trade routes and colonies, and led to attacks on Russian naval bases. Moreover, Rear-Admiral Sir James Stirling, Commander-in-Chief in China and the East Indies, responded to the outbreak of the war by taking steps to secure the Straits of Malacca and Sunda, so that the routes between the Indian Ocean and the South China Sea should be under British control. Stirling's concern about Russian naval strength in the Far East led him to press for the dispatch there of more warships.[10]

The shift to armour in the shape of iron reflected the strength of the British naval system. The first British iron warship, the *Warrior*, laid down in 1859 and completed in 1861 (and still afloat in Portsmouth Harbour today), was iron-hulled, while the French *La Gloire*, laid down in 1858, was simply an ironclad. The French had the infrastructure to build a few big iron ships, but not a new fleet, while the British had been building large iron ships for some time. They had the experience of the merchant marine, of skilled shipbuilding and of ambitious and innovative ship-designers like Isambard Kingdom Brunel on which to draw. Brunel's SS *Great Britain* had been launched as early as

1843. This situation underlined the extent to which naval power rested on a more general shipbuilding capacity as well as a maritime culture that produced sailors. Each of these factors could be remedied in part by purchase from elsewhere, buying ships and hiring sailors, but this method proved less effective (and more costly) than using local resources.

The 1860s

Naval power was demonstrated, but in a different fashion, during the American Civil War (1861–5). Ultimately, the navy of the Union or North became the second largest in the world, with (figures vary) 650–675 warships, including 49 ironclads. Difficulties were encountered in building up naval strength, not least in developing the capacity to roll the necessary iron plating and in building iron ships using the traditional methods of shipbuilding with wood.[11] Nevertheless, the Union's navy was a key strategic asset.

In particular, while permeable by small, fast steamships until late in the conflict, the blockade of the Southern (Confederate) States, organised by the Union's Blockade Board established in 1861, indicated the potency of economic warfare: 295 Confederate steamers and 1189 sailing ships were destroyed or seized. The Confederate States of America issued letters of marque to a number of privateers in 1861, but the effort failed because of the difficulty (even early on) of bringing a prize home safely through the Union blockade to a Confederate port. As a result, the supporting structure of prize courts (itself an outmoded form of naval war) never developed, and Southern maritime entrepreneurs turned almost exclusively to blockade-running to make their fortunes. Effective disruption of Union commerce came at the hands of raiders, such as the *Alabama* and the *Shenandoah*, which were commissioned in the Confederate navy, rather than by privateers.

The blockade drew on American experience against Mexico in the successful war of 1846–8, and was the last major blockade before, successively, torpedo boats, submarines and air power changed the parameters for blockade and sea denial in general. The Union blockade also helped limit Confederate efforts to build up their own fleet. Even before the blockade became effective, they had made insufficient efforts to import rolled iron and machinery,[12] which was serious because they were so short of iron that they had to pull up railway track.

The Union's early strategy included an important amphibious dimension, useful in leading to the capture, in 1862, of New Orleans, the largest city (and port) in the Confederacy, and also in tying up large numbers of Confederate troops in coastal defence. However, without army support, naval attack could prove unsuccessful, as Union warships discovered at Charleston in 1863. Moreover, in what proved a recurrent pattern for amphibious operations, advancing from coastal positions into the interior proved less effective for the Union than amphibious attacks on coastal positions.

Yet, although victory was won on land, the Union's seaborne and riverine campaigns were more than incidental to the war's outcome.[13] The early coastal operations greatly contributed to the effectiveness of the blockade, while the 'brown-water' (inland) navy played a key role in the success of Union operations in the Mississippi basin, both severing the Confederacy and securing the Midwest for the Union. The army was committed to the building of ironclads for their operations in the West.[14]

Faced with an industrial backwardness that made competition in shipbuilding implausible, the Confederacy sought to offset Union superiority by using mines and submarines. Most of the naval conflict involved clashes between Union warships and Confederate shore defences, or between individual ships, most famously the *Monitor* and the *Virginia* in Hampton Roads in 1862.[15] The dispersed nature of the Confederate fleet, and the Southern interest in blockade-running and commerce-raiding, ensured that larger actions were uncommon. Indeed, more generally, the extent to which steam power and iron ships might have changed the nature of naval warfare by 1865 was unclear owing to the paucity of naval battles over the previous decade; although, as at Sevastopol, mines and static defences did suggest that coastal assaults could be checked at minimal cost.

The largest naval clash in the 1860s occurred not off North America but in the Adriatic, at the Battle of Lissa on 20 July 1866, as an episode in the war between Italy and Austria that occurred as a result of the conflict between the latter and

Prussia. This battle reflected Italian ambitions, because, despite talk of threatening the flank of the Italian army, the Austrian navy remained on the defensive. Alongside conquering Venetia, the Italian government was also interested in seizing the territories of Istria and Dalmatia on the other side of the Adriatic. It first planned to seize the island of Lissa, but its fleet was attacked by a smaller and less heavily-armed Austrian fleet under Baron Wilhelm von Tegetthoff, who tried to compensate for these weaknesses by ramming the Italian warships. Some commentators erroneously saw this method of attack as a key lesson of the battle. The battle, the first between fleets of ironclads (seven Austrian versus twelve Italian) became a confused mêlée of ship-to-ship actions in which Italian unpreparedness and lack of command skills played a role in leading to their heavier losses.[16]

Although navies did not deliver knock-out blows in the mid-century wars, naval potential was both demonstrated and developed. For example, the French capture of Mexican ports, such as Vera Cruz and Acapulco, made possible their intervention in Mexico in 1862–7. Yet that episode also highlighted the contrast between output, in the shape of force projection, and outcome, in the shape of subsequent control over the interior. The French were able to operate into the interior and to capture major cities, notably Mexico City and Puebla, but they could not end resistance and, in the end, were obliged to abandon their protégé, the Emperor Maximilian. This decision was taken largely for reasons of power politics, specifically the threat to French power posed by Prussia's total victory over Austria in 1866, as well as pressure for French evacuation from the USA which was newly strong after the Union's victory in the Civil War. Thus, there were no specific naval reasons for French failure. On the other hand, this failure did serve as a potent qualification of the advantages brought by power projection. So also, albeit to a lesser extent, did the tough Indian resistance to British forces during the Indian Mutiny of 1859–9.

The threat of French naval power encouraged heavy British investment in the navy, and the two powers took part in an ironclad naval race in 1859–65 that was won by Britain with its greater resources and commitment. Alongside the combination of the screw propeller and armour, there were also improvements in armament. Ericsson and Coles simultaneously invented turrets, similar in concept but quite different in design. Neither led directly to the modern gun turret, but Coles did incorporate the roller patch, which was a key element in modern big-gun mountings. The revolving turret began with the American *Monitor* in 1862, and the practice of locating heavy guns in an armoured casemate with the British *Research* in 1864. The American Civil War saw important innovative work on submarines, notably with the Confederate *Hunley* which sank the *Housatonic* off Charleston in 1864; while the modern self-propelled torpedo originated with the development by Robert Whitehead in 1864 of the Austrian idea of a submerged torpedo driven by compressed air with an explosive charge at the head. Although the essentials of naval power, such as the relationship between economic strength and naval power, were not changing, the means of maritime force were being transformed.

Moreover, states rapidly borrowed each other's best practice in an effort to reduce the threat posed by others. Thus, Russia invested, during the Crimean War, in screw-propelled gunboats, and, from 1861, in ironclads.[17] In the American Civil War, the Union developed ironclads in order to be able to resist the danger of British intervention on behalf of the Confederacy, and lessened Britain's political leverage in the struggle by so doing.[18] Poorer states, such as Portugal, clung to sail and wood for longer, but there was pressure for change across the West and also from powers affected by Western pressure.

The 1870s–80s

Radical technological developments, however, ensured that a high degree of uncertainty grew up about the likely nature of naval combat, about the strengths and weaknesses of the new ship types, and about what effect all this might have on the organisation of fleets, tactics, strategy and maritime dominance. With their options increased by technological change, states watched the naval developments of each other keenly, and worried about the best places to put their money. Proven reliability clashed with the adoption of technological innovation.

Britain retained a clear dominance, underpinning its central role in global commerce and communications. The seizure of

Cyprus (1878), Egypt (1882), and other territories strengthened Britain's naval position, but Britain's naval dominance was not without serious problems. If put to the test, the Royal Navy was not up to Britain's global commitments, although such an assessment was only pertinent if the commitments were all tested at the same time; and, in practice, the ability to do anything, anywhere, was an excessively high bar, and remains so far as current assessments of the USA are concerned.

No individual rival could threaten Britain, although the defence of India against Russian threats, which led in 1885 to the Penjdeh Crisis over Russian pressure on Afghanistan's northern frontier, was linked to concern about the Mediterranean, for Russian and French naval power (from Sevastopol in the Black Sea and Toulon respectively) would have to be repelled there. In 1878, in the face of Russian expansionism at the expense of the Ottoman Empire, the Admiralty could not guarantee to force the Dardanelles en route to Constantinople, but, in the event, the fleet did pass through them. The 1877–8 Anglo-Russian crisis indicated the potential capability, range, and, yet also, vulnerability of naval power. Indian army units were swiftly sent by Britain to Malta via the Suez Canal, which had been opened in 1869, while, in turn, the Russians planned commerce-raiding in the Atlantic and Indian Oceans, and attacks on the ports of the British empire such as Sydney.[19] Russia backed a Greater Bulgaria in order to gain access to the Mediterranean through a Russian presence on the Aegean, but British pressure thwarted this ambition.

Meanwhile, the size and cost of major warships increased significantly. The tension between armour and armament, weight and manoeuvrability, not least the mutually interacting need for more effective guns and stronger armour, led to changes in armour and hull materials. Wooden-hulled ironclads were quickly superseded in the 1860s. The wrought-iron navy was followed in the late 1870s, after experimentation with iron and wood armour, by one using compound armour plate: the iron and steel navy. There were also moves towards the first all-steel battleships in the 1870s. Ship designers faced the problem of juggling the three desirable, but mutually antagonistic qualities required of a steady weapons platform: speed, armament and armour. One could only be enhanced at the expense of the others because of the weight problem, although replacing iron with steel was understood as the solution pretty early on. Ship design also had to adapt to important changes in armament.

In place of warships designed to fire broadsides, came guns mounted in centreline turrets, which were able to fire end-on, as well as to turn. Moreover, firing armour-piercing explosive shells, guns became more effective. These were ships clearly designed for battle and, from the 1880s, it became common for them to be called battleships, ships that were defined by their function. However, it required much less effort to sink a steel battleship with high-explosive armour-piercing shells than a wooden ship of the line with cannon. Guns also became more rapid-firing, as breech-loaders replaced muzzle-loading guns, which took a long time to load with large shells. Rifled artillery, percussion detonators and high explosives, especially cordite and melmite in the 1880s and 1890s, altered the ratio between naval bombardment and coastal fortifications.

Some commentators, however, wondered in the 1880s if battleships had a future in the face of torpedoes, the development of which attracted numerous inventors.[20] Moreover, the Swedish-American inventor and consulting engineer John Ericsson (1803–89), who had played a key role in the development of ironclad monitors, was far more interested in the 1870s and 1880s in underwater weapons and effective torpedo-carrying warships, building the *Destroyer*, an armoured prototype of the latter, in about 1880.[21] As the British navy was not yet willing to abandon the practice of close blockade, it was felt necessary in the exercises of 1885 to plan for the establishment of a defensible advance base, so as to reduce vulnerability to torpedo attack.

Concern about torpedoes, which seemed to some to be the weapon of the future, was but part of a wider sense of uncertainty about the role of large warships, and the battleship critics were right, just very early: it was not underwater weapons that were to doom the battleship but, in the 1940s, air attack. The apparent threat from torpedo boats helped ensure that in the 1880s battleship-building (except in Italy) slowed down rather drastically. No one quite knew what to do about torpedo boats.

While an emphasis on battleships remained strong among British naval professionals, a group that lacked formal doctrinal training,[22] the situation was different in France. Faced with political concern with the German army and the heavy costs of the French response on land, Admiral Théophile Aube (navy minister in 1886–7) and the French *Jeune École* provided an ideology for opponents of battleships that gained at least some support in every navy. They pressed for the less expensive option of unarmoured light cruisers, which would use less coal and be faster and more manoeuvrable than battleships, and able to protect sea lanes, to advance imperial expansion, and to attack the commerce of opponents. Arguing that the self-propelled torpedo made close blockades too risky, the *Jeune École* believed that their cruisers would be able to launch a war on enemy trade that would be more potent because it would be a form of total war in which 'everything is ... legitimate'.[23]

In line with the contemporary preference for the offensive, which indeed made sense in terms of developing naval technology, Aube also favoured the torpedo boat, and claimed that it nullified the power of the British battleship and could break any British blockade. Torpedo boats helped naval firepower in ensuring French victory over a Chinese squadron at Fuzhou in 1884 when six Chinese cruisers were sunk. These ideas also had an impact outside France. By 1888, with the active backing of Leo, Graf von Carprivi, Chief of the Admiralty from 1883 to 1888, and under the dynamic leadership of Alfred Tirpitz (later von Tirpitz), appointed Director of Torpedo Development in 1878, Germany had commissioned 72 torpedo boats and developed the manufacture of good torpedoes.[24] Although, after 1905, Tirpitz himself was opposed to submarines, in part because he wished to focus expenditure on battleships, the emphasis on torpedoes looked towards later German interest in the submarine, although torpedo boats were too limited to pose a comparable challenge, because they were too vulnerable and also unviable as independent seagoing warships.[25]

Doctrine was linked to strategic need, and thus geopolitics, with the development of global trade and Western colonial empires leading to an emphasis on naval power, and to the related 'relays', especially naval bases and coaling depots, such that speed was converted into action at the will of the centre.[26] The extension of the network of British coaling stations ensured that their steam-powered armoured warships could be used in deep waters across the world, an extension advocated in 1881–2 in reports produced by the Carnarvon Commission. In 1885, during the Penjdeh Crisis, the Royal Navy was placed on full alert and plans for attacks included a bombardment of Kronstadt, Russia's Baltic naval base, and amphibious operations against Batum on the Black Sea and Vladivostok, the latter to be preceded by the establishment of a base in Korea.

More generally, in the 1880s, a decade in which public discussion of naval issues increased in Britain, British naval expenditure was close to the combined figure of the next two high-spending powers, France and Russia. While there was no other individual navy able to pose a fundamental challenge to Britain's naval position,[27] the creation of a Franco-Russian alliance in the 1890s posed what seemed to be a clear threat, although the effectiveness of this alliance was exaggerated. This apparent threat led to an interest in naval history, as past conflict with France now appeared far more relevant in Britain.

There was an irony in French naval building in response to British action, in turn generating new British construction. In the Fashoda Crisis of 1898 over competing interests in Sudan, the British sent the Channel fleet to Gibraltar in order to put pressure on the French position in the Mediterranean. In turn, the Germans built up their fleet in part in response to British naval strength and partly as a result of German impotence in southern Africa prior to and at the time of the Boer War. Indeed, from 1897, Britain kept a naval force in Delagoa Bay larger than that of any other power. This force ensured an ability to prevent supplies from reaching Transvaal via the neutral Portuguese colony of Mozambique.

Other powers also extended their naval reach. In 1899, with new commitments across the Pacific, the American navy established coal depots at strategic ports round the world. The previous year, the Americans had destroyed Spanish squadrons off Santiago in Cuba and in Manila Bay. The seven Spanish ships destroyed by the American cruiser squadron under George Dewey in Manila Bay cost the Americans only seven wounded, although, without troops, Dewey was unable to capture Manila and had to wait for the army's arrival. Dewey's victory makes naval success seem easy, but it was hard going because the gunnery was so uncertain. Only a small percentage of shells found their targets, which was an aspect of the problems with new technology also seen with torpedoes. Nevertheless, the American fleet played a major role in isolating Spanish forces both in the Philippines and in the West Indies. Complete victory over the Spanish fleet off Santiago in Cuba on 3 July gave vital leeway in Cuba to the poorly-trained American army, and encouraged the Spanish commander in Santiago to surrender. The operational advantage provided by naval strength was demonstrated on 21 July when an American squadron captured Bahia de Nipe on the north coast of Cuba, destroying the Spanish warship guarding the port and providing a new sphere of operations for the army. Naval force was also crucial in the capture of Puerto Rico, enabling successive bombardment, blockade and invasion.

The war encouraged American investment in the navy and the dispatch of a fleet, the Great White Fleet, to show the flag by sailing round the world. The debates in the early national period over the value of long-range naval power had been definitely settled in favour of navalism.[28] The navy also enabled the USA to project its power in Latin America. For example, warships carried a Marine expeditionary force to ensure a peaceful (though coerced) election in the Panama Canal Zone in 1908, represented the USA at the inauguration of the new Cuban President in 1909, and landed Marines in Cuba in 1912. In 1913, a policy of keeping three or four battleships in Mexican waters was followed as a means of defending American interests in Mexico. The navy supported the landing of Marines at Veracruz in 1914 and also the occupation of the Dominican Republic in 1916.

Meanwhile, German interest in cruisers increased in the 1880s as their overseas empire developed from 1884 in Africa and the Pacific, and there were new maritime routes to defend. In German naval thought, there was also an emphasis on commerce-raiding. In 1897, a German squadron seized Kiao-chou and forced the Chinese to grant a 99-year lease on the base.[29]

At the same time, transoceanic imperial expansion and security were important as a cause of naval activity, not only for the leading powers, particularly Britain and France and the new imperial powers, Germany, the USA and Japan, but also for lesser ones such as Portugal. The 'white man's burden' could be used to justify naval expenditure in support of colonial policing, for example against pirates, slavers and smugglers, although much of the gunboat activity was by relatively small ships, such as the British schooners on the coast of British Columbia which overawed Native Americans.[30] Operations against pirates on the Malayan coast enabled the British to extend their influence way beyond their Straits Settlements – Penang, Singapore and Malacca – and, combined with these positions, gave Britain the dominant position on the route between the Indian Ocean and the Far East.

Such activity is a reminder of the extent to which navies were the sharp end of aggressive foreign and imperial policies. Western publics saw this in rather blinkered terms, which encouraged the British, in particular, in their cosy assumptions about naval power as exemplary. Yet, alongside the pirates and slavers who were pursued, came, for example, art and other treasures seized by sailors, as well as other forms of disruption stemming from the use of naval power. This use was also unwelcome to other states, as with the Zamponi affair of 1870 when the employment of a British gunboat to control a Sardinian vendetta led to a diplomatic dispute with Italy.

Towards the dreadnought

A reaction against battleships affected some naval thinkers in the 1880s, but there was a shift back to them in the 1890s. In part, this return reflected growing awareness of the potential of defences against torpedoes, specifically torpedo nets, and thick belt armour around the waterline. Electric searchlights (electricity was used on warships from the 1870s) were seen as important in detecting torpedo boats, while quick-firing medium-calibre guns could provide a secondary armament for use against them. Tactics also changed in response to the threat from torpedoes. Moreover, there were concerns about the level of the seaworthiness of torpedo boats, and the reliability of torpedoes, which, indeed, remained an issue well into the Second World War. Even in Japan's decisive victory over a Russian fleet at Tsushima in 1905, the torpedoes were only used to finish off already disabled Russian warships. Finally, there was the development of the, originally specialist, torpedo boat destroyer, or all-purpose 'destroyer', as it later became.

Thus, tactically, the ability to destroy battleships was neutralised to a considerable extent. Earlier, this ability had never equated with 'command of the sea' in so far as that was a helpful concept. Torpedo boats offered the prospect of sea denial in narrow waters (and, indeed, from the 1890s curtailed British naval interest in littoral warfare), but did not threaten oceanic communications nor 'command of the sea'. Moreover, the advent of smokeless powder eliminated the artificial 'fog of war' that the *Jeune École* tacticians had optimistically assumed would provide cover for their torpedo boat attacks against larger warships.

In part, changes in warship capability were crucial to the shift back to battleships, changes that helped give a dynamic quality to the British annual naval manoeuvres which began in 1885. Despite the earlier appearance of steam, iron armour, and breech-loading guns, the true ocean-going (all-steam) battleship did not really emerge until the 1890s. The invention of the barbette was significant. It was a fixed armoured trunk or tube protecting the gun mounting, which revolved within it, and, in the original version, fired over the rim. Later, a light gunhouse was added, revolving with the mounting, to form the beginning of the modern armoured gun turret, which rests on the fixed barbette.

This system was important to the development of ocean-going battleships, as opposed to coastal ones, as it allowed guns to be mounted in central locations on deck without compromising the stability of the ship. As a result, the very low freeboard of the earlier ships – like the coastal monitors – was no longer necessary. With a higher freeboard, the warship could travel anywhere in the world. Thus, the key shift was being able to mount the new heavy guns high enough out of the water to enable a ship to go to sea rather than being a sort of armoured raft that was useless in anything but a flat calm. The key movers in the invention of the barbette were French and they were usually slightly ahead of the British in many key aspects of technical developments in this period, in particular regarding breech-loading guns, although France did not have an infrastructure to implement innovations comparable to that of Britain.

As instances of the rapid rate of change, the marine turbine engine had been invented by Sir Charles Parsons in 1884, the new water-tube boiler technology of the early 1880s was introduced in larger ships, while nickel-steel armoured warships were developed in the 1890s after trials in America in 1890 had shown that carbon-treated nickel-steel was more effective in resisting fire than compound armour. The eight 14,150-ton British battleships of the *Royal Sovereign* class, laid down under the Naval Defence Act of 1889, the largest yet built, were, thanks to better engines, capable of 18 knots, a speed seen as a response to the threat from torpedo boats. As a result of the Act, British naval estimates rose from £11 million in 1883 to £18.7 million in 1896, while the number of British battleships rose from 38 in 1883 to 62 in service or construction in 1897, a product of an uneasy relationship between strength and insecurity. Convoy no longer seemed the viable way to protect trade, not least because merchant steamers were now as fast as warships, and a large navy able to carry the war to the enemy by close blockade and attacks on enemy warships in ports was regarded as the best way to win at sea and thus to avoid the need for a large army or for alliances. This requirement entailed a large peacetime navy capable of fast mobilisation so that the opposing fleet would be confined to port. The origins of the Naval Defence Act can be traced to the Near East Crisis of 1878.[31]

Nickel-steel was improved in 1892 when the German Krupp works introduced a process of 'gas cementing', which gave additional protection without added weight, encouraging the construction of bigger ships, a process that required a sophisticated shipbuilding industry and much expenditure. This protection was a necessary response to the development of chrome steel shells and armour-piercing shell caps, while the latter had increased the effectiveness of major pieces of naval ordnance, and this effectiveness provided a greater role for large ships able to carry such guns. Advances in machine tools, metallurgy and explosives ensured that more accurate guns, capable of far longer ranges and supported by better explosives, could be produced, while hydraulic motors enabled guns to be turned or elevated mechanically. The net effect of technological change was a frequent retooling in order to retain competitive advantage, and, from the 1820s, warships became obsolete more rapidly than in the past.

Although sailing rig had been a complex technology, the sophisticated equipment of the late nineteenth century led to a need for better, or at least differently, trained officers and sailors, and, therefore, to the creation of new colleges and training methods. There was also a professionalisation of naval construction, with an emphasis on scientific methods of design and construction that rested on careful mathematical calculations and detailed problems, rather than on intuition and half-hull models,[32] although it is necessary not to denigrate eighteenth-century ship-building, as the science and mathematics had been understood for some time. In the nineteenth century, this professionalisation was matched by close relations between navies and large industrial concerns.

In part, the shift to the battleship was reflected by, and was a reflection of, the most influential writer on naval power, Alfred Thayer Mahan (1840–1914), who lectured at the new American Naval War College at Newport, Rhode Island. Emphasising the importance of command of the sea, he saw the destruction of the opponent's battle fleet as the means to achieve this goal, and treated commerce-raiding as less important. In terms of force structure, the Mahanian approach led to a stress on battleships, not cruisers. The idea of command of the sea was also ventilated in Britain, not least with the book of that title published in 1894 by the influential journalist Spenser Wilkinson and with Admiral Philip Colomb's *Naval Warfare: Its Ruling Principles and Practice Historically Treated* (1891). There was a parallel between the benefits supposed to stem from command of the sea and those that were being allegedly gained from the scramble for empire.

Nevertheless, major differences in strategic culture and tasking affected powers that had access to similar weaponry. Thus, Britain had to protect maritime routes that provided her with food and raw materials, while challengers, particularly France in the late nineteenth century, Germany in both world wars, and the Soviet Union during the Cold War, sought a doctrine, force structure, strategy and operational practice that could contest these routes. Differences in strategic culture and tasking lent point to the discussion of sea power, and indeed to its ideological character, and this discussion was made dynamic by new potentials and capabilities. Thus, naval capability indicated the dynamic relationship between doctrine based on established practice, and thus, in part, historical analysis and example, and the pressures for change stemming from new technology.

The nineteenth-century practice of validation by historical example was important to the habit of looking for continuities in naval power and of searching the past to understand the present.[33] Mahan was influenced by the German historian Theodor Mommsen (1817–1903), who, in his *History of Rome*, presented Roman naval power as playing a crucial role against Carthage in the Second Punic War. Reading this in Lima in 1884, while on naval duty protecting American interests, Mahan was struck by 'how different things might have been could Hannibal have invaded Italy by sea ... instead of by the long land route; or could he, after arrival, have been in free communication [with Carthage] by land'.[34] Mahan and Theodore Roosevelt both wrote histories of the naval aspects of the Anglo-American War of 1812, and Mahan's influence on American policy owed something to his friendship with Roosevelt, who was Assistant Naval Secretary during the 1898 war with Spain, and later President.[35]

In turn, in *Some Principles of Maritime Strategy* (1911),[36] the British writer Julian Corbett (1854–1922) provided a nuanced account of naval power with an emphasis on combined operations. He also demonstrated the historical validity of his approach in his *England in the Seven Years' War* (1907). In offering influential accounts of naval history, Mahan and Corbett were both also writing about present policy, as well as seeking to relate strategy to power. Mahan's focus, seen with his *The Interest of America in Sea Power, Present and Future* (1897), was on how the USA should draw on the example of Britain to use naval capability best in order to become a great power. In contrast, Corbett's stress was on the way in which Britain should employ its naval strength to preserve its global interests. To Corbett, Britain's interests were not best served by a large-scale land commitment in Europe.[37]

The notion of decisive victory leading to a command of the sea that could be employed to strategic effect was an account of how to win war that did not require the acquiescence of the defeated. In short, a potential was asserted (or to its protagonists) grasped, one that was, in practice, to be more elusive for many victors on land. The will to believe in victory was important to the analysis. Combined with the creation of naval planning staffs, an emphasis on control of the sea encouraged the development of strategic naval plans, with Germany's first war plan against Britain drafted in 1897, followed, in 1900, with an implausible plan for an attack on the USA.[38]

Mahan's views were widely disseminated, and contributed considerably to a tendency to see the number of battleships as a measure of power and thus a definition of status as a great power.[39] The governmental and popular manifestation of these processes included extensive celebration of warship launches, as well as the development of naval leagues: popular movements for stronger navies that were usually pushed by governments, special interests and committed publicists. The vast crowds that attended launches, particularly in Britain and Germany, were joined by those who read about them in the illustrated press or watched early films.

This process was significant to the creation of mass constituencies for naval power, and these were seen as important, given the need to vote substantial sums through representative bodies. Thus, the process by which shared interests underlay naval power was reconceptualised for a new democratic, or at least populist, age. The implications of this for naval strategy were unclear, but there were expectations that in any war the drama of the launch of large warships (and the dominant theme was one of scale) would be replicated in naval conflict. The status of size has a modern equivalent with the cult of the aircraft carrier, a cult which sits alongside (and possibly in part conditions) rational discussion of the merits of these warships.

An emphasis in the 1890s both on naval strength, and on battleships as its measure, extended to the non-Western world, which contrasted with the situation there 50 years earlier when neither China nor Japan had pursued such a goal. Mahan's *The Influence of Sea Power upon History* (1890) was translated into Japanese (as well as German) in 1896. Although the Japanese translation significantly altered the original, it was symptomatic of the extent to which non-Western powers looked to the West. This process was most apparent towards the close of the nineteenth century, but was already in evidence earlier, with foreign shipbuilders playing the key role when the Istanbul arsenal was reorganised on Western lines under the direction of a French naval architect who entered Ottoman service in 1793.[40]

King Kalākaua of Hawaii commissioned and fitted out a sometime guano trader as a warship, the *Ka'imloa*. Intended as a training vessel for the fledgling Hawaiian navy, this was equipped with four brass cannon and two Gatling guns. The captain was

British and the standing regulations for the British navy were adopted for its Hawaiian counterpart, which was designed to give effect to the plan for a Pacific confederation of Hawaii, Samoa, Tonga and the Cook Islands, intended to prevent Western annexations; to that end, the ship was sent to Samoa in 1887. Germany saw this as interference in its plans and German warships shadowed the *Ka'imcloa* but, faced by serious indiscipline among the crew, the Hawaiian vessel was recalled and mothballed.[41]

In the late-nineteenth century, Japan and Turkey (the Ottoman Empire) turned to Britain for naval advice. William Armstrong (1810–1900), the British armaments king, who built warships on the River Tyne, entertained foreign rulers seeking arms deals, including Nasir-ud-Din, the Shah of Persia, in 1889 and Rama V, King of Siam (Thailand) in 1897. A similar process could be seen within the West, with the shipbuilding states dominating a system that others could only enter on their terms, albeit that competition between the major states also played a role. Despite competition from France, Germany and the USA, Britain remained the major supplier of warships to other powers.

A non-Western power, Japan, made the most dramatic use of naval power, first, and successfully, against China in 1894–5, and more spectacularly in the Russo-Japanese War (1904–5), in the battles of the Yellow Sea (1904) and Tsushima (1905). Big Japanese 12-inch guns inflicted the damage, and at Tsushima, the Japanese, whose ships were newer and faster, only lost three torpedo boats. Of the seven Russian ships in the original Port Arthur squadron, one was sunk by a mine, one escaped to a neutral port after the battle of the Yellow Sea, and the remaining five were sunk at Port Arthur, although four were salvaged and repaired by the Japanese. Of the ten Russian battleships at Tsushima, six were sunk and four taken. Just as with American naval victories over Spain in 1898, but more spectacularly, Tsushima appeared to vindicate Mahanian ideas: a high-sea encounter would occur, it could be a decisive battle, and the result would then affect the fate of nations.

In practical terms, however, Japanese success in the war, a success that left Japan dominant in Manchuria and able to annex Korea, was not simply due to victory at sea, and Tsushima, and the subsequent cult of the Japanese commander, Togo, proved misleading when it was employed to argue that a sweeping victory in battle would result in success in war, an attitude that helped lead the Japanese to the attack on America at Pearl Harbor in 1941. In 1905, other factors for Japanese success included the fiscal pressures affecting Russia, as well as the internal opposition that in part was stirred up by the Japanese secret service, while the Russians were also under severe pressure in the land war in Manchuria. As a reminder, however, of the problems of extrapolating success from naval victory, Japan itself faced serious difficulties, both in financing the war and in the campaigning on land in Manchuria, and was unable to force the Russians to the negotiating table. Tsushima prevented Russia from mounting naval attacks on Japan and on Japanese supply routes to Korea, but it could not ensure victory in the war.

Tsushima, nevertheless, helped make the Japanese navy popular, linking it with views on the national destiny, as well as encouraging politicians to associate themselves with the navy, which, in turn, helped secure its expansion. In 1907, the idea of a ratio in Japanese fleet size vis-à-vis that of the USA was advanced, an idea that was to be influential until the Second World War.[42]

The Yellow Sea and Tsushima led many commentators and planners to conclude (correctly) that, due to new advances in range-finding and gun-sighting, future battleship engagements would be fought at great distance (and thus outside the range of torpedoes),[43] reinforcing the case for the heavily-armoured, all-big-gun battleships. This case was to be embodied by the British warship *Dreadnought*, designed before Tsushima but validated by it and launched in 1906, which, with its ten 12-inch guns paired in five turrets, was the first of a new class of all-big-gun battleships. It was the first capital ship in the world to be powered by the marine turbine engine and was completed in one year with some judicious spin about exactly when her keel was laid and how long she took to fit out. She also used guns and mountings originally ordered for other vessels.

This spin was intended to produce a propaganda coup that was designed to demonstrate the futility of matching Britain in a naval race. The effect was heightened by the secrecy of the design and of other aspects of the project. This effort reflected the belief in a 'silver bullet' or technological trump card which forced other players out by slowly bankrupting them. Thus, the public image of naval capability and proficiency, an image that helped foster popular support, was matched by a determination to use the news in order to create an impression of power. This use helped feed the increase in printed discussion of naval issues in Britain from 1904–5.

The role of perception was institutionalised by the presence of naval attachés that reported on developments. The attachés were the legitimate end of information-gathering processes that became increasingly systematic, in part because of the possibility that other states could alter their relative position by new developments.

Whatever the spin, no battleship of the size of *Dreadnought* had ever been built so quickly, and her construction reflected the industrial and organisational efficiency of British shipbuilding. This was an efficiency linked to the well-organised responsive discipline that characterised the Royal Navy as a system of command and coordination. At the same time, the rising cost of battleships and cruisers posed a major financial burden for Britain, while the new class made the Royal Navy's numerical superiority in first-class capital ships disappear: with their pre-dreadnoughts obsolete, this superiority had to be rebuilt.

Competitive emulation between navies set the pace. The dreadnought was faster and more heavily gunned than any other battleship then sailing, and made the earlier arithmetic of relative naval capability redundant. This redundancy encouraged the Germans to respond, although their *Nassau* class, laid down from 1907, put more of a stress on protection than armaments and did not use turbines. At the same time, the need to respond put major pressure on the Reichstag's support for naval plans. The bigger British second-generation dreadnoughts put even greater pressure on this support.

The British won the naval race, as they had also beaten the French in the mid-nineteenth century. The German navy, the sixth largest navy in the world in 1888, was the second in 1914, and from 1900 the British Admiralty was aware that Germany's naval building programme might become Britain's foremost maritime threat,[44] although, at this stage, there was still concern about France and Russia. The British were willing to pay to win the new battleship race, as well as to invest in fast, but lighter-armed, warships, the well-armed cruisers later called battle-cruisers, which, in part, were designed to meet the threat to trade from Germany's fast armed ocean liners.[45] These battle-cruisers may have been the initial British preference for new war-ships, and were, for a while, intended to be the capital ship of the future; but, by 1912, the rapid expansion of the German battle fleet, combined with improved relations with France from 1904, had led to a British operational and tactical emphasis on how best to win a battleship struggle with Germany in the North Sea. Moreover, British strategic concerns elsewhere were greatly lessened by alliance with Japan from 1902, as well as by the conclusion in 1908 by the Committee of Imperial Defence and the Foreign Office that the possibility of war with the USA was remote. Against Germany, the British emphasis was on a blockade, both as a means of economic warfare, and also as a means to force the German fleet to sea. It has been argued that the preferred British tactic was a major 'pulse of firepower',[46] which required battleships, although this interpretation has been challenged.

In Germany, in contrast to Britain, the naval race was overly tied to the ambitions, interests and ideology of its protagonist, Admiral Alfred von Tirpitz (State Secretary of the Imperial Naval Office from 1897 to 1916). He was supported by the anglophobic Emperor Wilhelm II, who was greatly impressed by Mahan's work; but the policy failed to command support across the political horizon, with the Social Democratic Party (which did well in the January 1912 Reichstag elections) being par-ticularly opposed, not least because the Tirpitz Plan challenged their interpretation of the role of the Reichstag: as far as some of the other politicians were concerned, however, Tirpitz co-opted, rather than challenged, the Reichstag. The combination of unexpected (although predictable) British resolve in opposing the German naval build-up and the passage of French legislation designed to strengthen the army caused momentum within the German military/political leadership and the dominant parties in the Reichstag to swing back in favour of the army, as reflected in the successful German Army Bill of 1913, which was, in effect, a unilateral German declaration of naval arms limitation, albeit at a very high level of annual construction.[47] The concern of Theobald von Bethmann Hollweg, who became Chancellor in 1909, about naval costs was matched by the army's emphasis on the needs of a two-front war on land.

Moreover, Tirpitz's tactical, operational and strategic assumptions and planning were greatly flawed, and this vitiated his achievements in training and procurement.[48] German battleships may have been technologically better than their British counterparts, but tests on German ships after the First World War did not suggest this to British designers. Germany also faced serious strategic problems in establishing itself as a seapower, not least those posed by distance from the Atlantic and the intervening position of the British navy.

More generally, the wisdom of German policy can be tested. It helped cement Britain's position in the anti-German camp, a situation that otherwise would not have been obvious. Given the popular nature of British commitment to naval power, German policy can be seen as particularly provocative, and thus foolish. The idea of a world war with Britain based on a supposed German naval destiny was tangential froth to the key priority of overcoming the two-front challenge to Germany posed by the Franco-Russian alliance. British entry on the side of that alliance into any war would scarcely be to Germany's advantage, and indeed, this proved to be the case in the First World War.

The assessment of this apparently irrational German policy is more generally important to the discussion of naval power. First, it is not necessarily helpful to separate supposedly irrational and rational policies, not least because that creates the impression that the ideological factors that contributed to the first should not have a role in naval policy and, moreover, that such factors do not play a role in rational policies. Neither proposition is well-founded. Instead, procurement policies, doctrine and strategy all reflect particular values that need to be discussed in terms of ideology.

This was the case, for example, in the build-up of American naval power from the 1890s, with East-Coast industrial interests, notably Pennsylvania shipyards and steelworks, linked to politicians and commentators keen not only to present America as a great power but also as able to take a central role in global power politics. These were views that would have been anathema to Jeffersonian Democrats in the early decades of the century. Launched in 1884, the *Dolphin* was the first American steel warship to circumnavigate the world, although she was only a dispatch boat. As President, Benjamin Harrison (1889–93) was a supporter of the naval build-up, as, later, was Theodore Roosevelt (1901–9). As a reminder of the centrality of politics and the contentious and nonlinear character of strategic cultures, such views would have been far more sympathetically received by the Federalists, who were more strongly committed to the development of American naval power than their rivals, the Jeffersonians.

The interaction of ideologies of naval power with political strategies and sociocultural assumptions has not traditionally been a field of consistent interest, especially in popular work, which is a problem as this situation leaves some discussion of policy rather poorly rooted. The popular conviction that naval power is a key and unproblematic component of identity and strategic interest can thus seem self-evident, especially where there is a tendency to underplay the role of the armed forces in politics, and of politics in the armed forces.

The argument throughout this book, however, is that such a view is inaccurate and therefore that popular works on naval history that present narratives and analyses in terms of battle and technology, with contention essentially limited to competing personalities, are wanting. The space available in this book, as well as the research that is readily accessible, do not permit a consistent discussion of this theme, but it should be regarded as relevant throughout. For example, the competition between army and navy priorities in Germany can be seen elsewhere, and indeed they spilled over in some states, especially Brazil and Chile in the 1890s, into opposing interventions in domestic politics. Such competition also existed in other states, albeit frequently more covertly, and drew on the extent to which there was no 'true' basis for the respective allocation of funds and other priorities. Instead, they emerged through the contention over national interests and how best to pursue them.

Governmental, political and civilian tensions in Germany over naval expenditure were seen elsewhere as military procurement posed severe budgetary problems. Thus, in Russia, the Duma (Parliament) acted to try to secure civilian control of the military, while the Japanese navy linked itself to the Seiyukai party which opposed oligarchic rivals linked to the army.[49] France, however, focused on competition with Germany on land, especially as a consequence of improved relations with Britain from 1904.

As a result, France, by 1914, had dropped from second to fifth among the world's navies, although, in the wake of the launch of the *Dreadnought*, the French shifted to battleships from enthusiasm for the ships advocated by the *Jeune École*. These battleships seemed necessary because, with Britain confronting Germany, France needed to be able to resist any moves by Germany's allies, Austria and Italy, both of which had increased their navies. France's colonial competition with Italy in North Africa was a factor, as was the need to protect the key Algiers–Marseilles route, a route that would be used in the event of war in order to move troops to France.

Lesser powers also developed and used their navies, and could be at the forefront of naval technology, notably with the Austrians and the torpedo. In 1900–1, Austria, which had the eighth largest navy in the world in 1914, one based in the Adriatic, sent a squadron to Chinese waters as part of the international response to the Boxer Rising. As a reminder of the diversity of naval power and tasks, Austrian gunboats on the Danube and Sava rivers were to make some of the first naval moves of the First World War, in their case against Serbia.

Lesser powers also used the fleets they built up. In 1912–13, in the First Balkan War, the Greek navy, which had been developed with French expertise, loans and warships from the 1880s, cut Turkish communications in the Aegean and covered amphibious attacks that resulted in the capture of islands including Lemnos, Chios and Samos.[50] Less spectacularly, the Bulgarian navy cut Turkish communications in the Black Sea, which increased the pressure on the Turks in the Balkans.

Politics was a key theme in naval developments. This theme was a matter not only of finance, a central element in procurement and one that influenced British developments,[51] but also in doctrine, another crucial element in procurement, and in tasking. At the same time, although politics was both intertwined with naval developments and a prism through which they can be understood, there were other sources of action. A crucial one was the application of knowledge, and its importance to contemporaries was enhanced by the sense that technological change was both normative and crucial to capability. This application of knowledge was affected and limited by institutional pressures, but it is also impressive to see the extent to which ideas and prototypes were tested. Indeed, the open willingness to experiment led to the major confusion in the 1870s over best practice in warship design. This willingness was very different to earlier generations that had been criticised (often unfairly) for conservatism, and was not what might have been expected from large institutions like navies. For example, the British Admiralty made major advances in the collection and processing of information, so as to be able to provide coherent control of naval resources.[52]

Furthermore, major changes, such as the introduction of naval aviation, occurred as a result of experimentation or were linked to it. For example, the testing of engines by the American navy in 1866 and from 1898 led, in 1913, to the adoption of a policy of only building ships with oil-firing steam engines.[53] American interest was not so much technical as to escape dependence on coal. The justification for the new American battle fleet rested on the threat from Japan, but, although the USA produced coal in West Virginia and Kentucky, its fleet could not cross the Pacific without British coal, which was scarcely likely to be on offer to fight a British ally. The steam merchant ships under the American flag lacked the necessary colliers and the network of bunkering coal merchants round the world was under British control, as were many of the colliers. Britain and Japan were allies from 1902. As a result, the Russian fleet that sailed from the Baltic to fight Japan in 1905 had to rely on German coal and colliers which were only able to fulfil the task with some difficulty. The Royal Navy also followed a course towards oil-firing steam-engines, because of the enormous technical advantages of oil, while by 1912 the Royal Navy had begun to install geared turbines in its destroyers.

The navies that entered the First World War did so as rapidly-changing bodies, at least technologically, although not necessarily tactically or operationally. The war, however, was to expose the difficulty of predicting developments and thus the limitations of much pre-war planning and speculation.

6 1914–45

The First World War

The battle of Jutland of 31 May–1 June 1916 between the main British and German fleets was not to be the Trafalgar or, as it was then seen, sweeping victory hoped for by naval planners. Indeed, there was no decisive clash between the British and German fleets in the First World War (1914–18). Similarly, there was no decisive battle in that conflict in the Adriatic between the Austrians and the Italians or, further east, involving the Turks. However, the lack of a decisive naval battle, and the extent to which the decision to put an army of unprecedented size into the field proved a major change in the British way of warfare,[1] did not mean that naval power was unimportant in that war. Instead, thanks to the navy, the British retained control of their home waters and were, therefore, able to avoid blockade and invasion, to maintain a flow of men and munitions to their army in France unmolested, to retain trade links that permitted the mobilisation of British resources, and to blockade Germany.[2] However, the very serious impact of the British blockade, which indeed violated the norms of commercial warfare, was lessened by Germany's continental position and her ability to obtain most of the resources she required from within Europe.

In the opening months of the war, there were two surface actions in the North Sea, the key area of conflict between the British and German surface fleets, but neither saw a clash between capital ships. In the battle of Heligoland Bight on 28 August 1914, British battle-cruisers played the decisive role in an engagement that started as a clash between British and German squadrons of light cruisers and destroyers. The Germans lost three light cruisers and one destroyer, while, although one British light cruiser and two destroyers were badly damaged, the fact that none was lost helped ensure that the battle was presented as a striking victory; it certainly gave the British a powerful psychological advantage, which was underlined on 17 October 1914 when, in the Battle of Texel, four German destroyers were sunk.

In 1914, the loss of ships to German submarines and mines cost the British more men and major ships than the Germans lost in battle, but the impact of these losses was less dramatic in terms of the sense of relative advantage. Indeed, submarines and mines appeared to be the means to snipe at the British naval advantage, rather than an effective counter to it.

At the Battle of Dogger Bank, on 24 January 1915, British and German capital ships clashed for the first time, as battle-cruisers engaged in a pursuit action in which the retreating Germans lost an armoured cruiser but British gunnery suffered from poor fire control. The German plan was to fall upon part of the British Grand Fleet with their entire High Seas fleet, but that miscarried in the sortie that ended at Dogger Bank, in three other sorties in early 1916 that did not result in a battle, and in the Jutland operation itself. At Jutland, the British, suffering from problems with fire control, inadequate armour protection, the unsafe handling of powder, poor signalling and inadequate training, for example in destroyer torpedo attacks, lost more ships and men than the Germans: 14 ships, including 3 battle-cruisers to 11, including one battle-cruiser, and 6097 to 2551 men. Nevertheless, the German fleet had been badly damaged in the big-gun exchange[3] and their confidence had been hit hard: 'more important was the spectre of irresistible coercive power which mere glimpses of the Grand Fleet had left in the minds and memories of German officers'. Thereafter in the war, the German High Seas Fleet sailed beyond the defensive minefields of the Heligoland Bight on only three occasions, and, on each occasion, it took care to avoid conflict with the British Grand Fleet.[4]

It is easy to derive a picture of relative naval capability from the result of engagements, but it is also necessary to make due allowance for other factors, not least command decisions. Thus, the caution of Admiral Sir John Jellicoe, the commander of the Grand Fleet at Jutland, possibly denied the British the victory they might have obtained had the bolder Admiral Sir David Beatty, commander of the battle-cruiser squadron, been in overall command, although Jellicoe, who was in command of a larger fleet than his German opponent, did not need to win this battle, only not to lose it: it was famously remarked that he could have lost the war in an afternoon. Informed contemporaries felt that the quality of command was important. Thus, Earl Kitchener, the Secretary of State for War, observed in 1915: 'In the solution of the Dardanelles much I fear depends on the Navy. If we only had Beatty out there I should feel very much happier.'[5]

Shipbuilding alliances were also important. Because the Germans finished not one of the dreadnoughts or battle-cruisers they laid down during the war, compared with the five battle-cruisers laid down and completed by Britain, the Germans did not have the margin of safety of a shipbuilding programme to fall back upon. Nor did they have the prospect of support from the warships of new allies that the British gained with the entry of Italy (1915) and, even more, the USA (1917). The strategic advantages of the Allies nullified the capability the Germans derived from their submarines: fewer Allied warships were sunk than were added to the combined total.

Geography was also a key factor, with the Germans bottled up in the North Sea by Britain's location athwart their routes to the oceans. The British position was anchored on Scapa Flow in the Orkneys, but, in 1909, a new base at Rosyth on the Firth of Forth had been begun. It was designed to help the Grand Fleet contest the North Sea, and included three dry docks able to take dreadnoughts. The lack of a comparable base further south on the east coast, however, was a major problem, both in protecting the coastline from attack and in responding rapidly to German naval moves.

Britain's supply system, that of a country that could not feed itself, an imperial economy which relied on trade, and a military system that required troop movements within the empire, was challenged by German surface raiders, but these were hunted down in the early stages of the war. The East Asiatic Squadron under Vice-Admiral Maximilian Graf von Spee was the leading German naval force outside Europe at the outset of the war. It sailed to Chile, where a weaker British force was defeated off Coronel on 1 November with the loss of two cruisers. Spee then sailed on to attack the Falkland Islands, a British colony and naval base, but Sir John Fisher, the First Sea Lord, had sent two battle-cruisers there to hunt down Spee, and he was defeated on

8 December, although only after a prolonged chase which practically exhausted the magazines of the battle-cruisers. The autobiographical records of sailors indicate the strength of patriotism. Henry Welch of the *Kent* reported vividly on the sinking of the German *Nürnberg* in the Battle of the Falkland Islands:

> ... we have avenged the *Monmouth*. I really believe it was in the *Nürnberg's* power to have saved many of the *Monmouth's* crew. Instead, she simply shelled her until the last part was visible above water. Noble work of which the German nation should feel proud. Thank God I am British.[6]

Thereafter, the Germans only had individual warships at large and these were eventually hunted down, although not before the *Emden* had inflicted some damage (and more disruption) on shipping in the Indian Ocean and had shelled Madras. The *Emden* was lost to the combination of naval fire and a reef in the Cocos Islands on 9 November 1914, and the threat from German surface raiders was essentially restricted to the opening months of the war. Indeed, Allied success in blockading the North Sea, the English Channel and the Adriatic, and in capturing Germany's overseas colonies, ensured that, after the initial stages of the war, and, despite the use of submarines, the range of German naval operations was smaller than those of American and French privateers when attacking British trade between 1775 and 1815.

Submarine warfare

Britain's economy was challenged more seriously by submarines than by surface ships, and the submarines were also a major threat to warships. Indeed, the British Grand Fleet was obliged to withdraw from the North Sea and from its base of Scapa Flow in 1914 to new bases on the north-west coast of Scotland owing to the threat of submarine attack: it did not return to Scapa Flow until 1915, when its defences had been strengthened. There had been considerable speculation prior to the war about the likely impact of submarines, but scant experience on which to base discussion. In 1901, H.O. Arnold-Foster, Parliamentary Secretary to the

Admiralty, was interested in how best to counter submarines:

> the submarine is, in fact, the true reply to the submarine ... That provided we are as well equipped in the matter of submarines as our neighbours, the introduction of this new weapon, so far from being a disadvantage to us, will strengthen our position. We have no desire to invade any other country: it is important that we ourselves should not be invaded. If the submarine proves as formidable as some authorities think is likely to be the case, the bombardment of our ports, and the landing of troops on our shores will become absolutely impossible. The same reasoning applies to every part of our empire which is approachable by water only.

The following year, Fisher, then Second Sea Lord, saw submarines as an instance of the competitive enhancement of weaponry, for example the introduction of both wireless and the gyroscope, in which he felt Britain had been falling behind:

> The great principle to be invariably followed by us is that no naval weapon of any description must be adopted by foreign navies, without exhaustive trials of it on our part, to ascertain its capabilities and possibilities in a future naval war, and to make provision accordingly. We cannot afford to leave anything to be a matter of opinion which affects, in the slightest degree, the fighting efficiency of the fleet.[7]

Submarines had not featured prominently in naval operations over the previous decade, for example in the Russo-Japanese (1904–5) or Balkan (1912–13) Wars. Indeed, their potential had been greatly underestimated by most commanders.[8] Tirpitz, the head of the German navy, was a late convert to submarines. Nevertheless, Fisher was concerned about the vulnerability of battleships to torpedoes, and this led him to emphasise flotilla defences for home waters. Britain, which had only launched its first submarine in 1901, had the largest number – 89 – at the outbreak of the First World War, but had devoted insufficient thought to the defence of warships and merchantmen against submarines.

The Germans stepped up submarine production once war had begun, but relatively few were ordered, and most were delivered behind schedule, in part because of problems with organising and supplying construction, but largely because of a lack of commitment from within the navy to submarine warfare, a preference, instead, for surface warships, and, crucially, a longstanding concentration of industrial resources on the army,[9] a pattern that was to be repeated in the Second World War. As a result, although submarines swiftly affected the conduct of operations, the Germans had insufficient submarines to match their aspirations. Concern about submarines, nevertheless, led Jellicoe in 1915 to observe: 'I am most absolutely adverse to moving the Battle Fleet without a full destroyer screen.'[10]

Submarines, moreover, benefited from an increase in their range, seaworthiness, speed and comfort, from improvements in the accuracy, range and speed of torpedoes, which, by 1914, could travel 7000 yards at 45 knots, and from the limited effectiveness of anti-submarine weaponry. These improvements reflected the possibilities for warmaking of a modern industrial society. In October 1916, Jellicoe wrote that the greater size and range of submarines and their increased use of the torpedo, so that they did not need to come to the surface, meant that the submarine menace was getting worse.[11]

Submarines came to play a major role in naval planning, both operationally, in terms of trying to deny bodies of water to opponents, and tactically, with the hope that, in engagements, opposing warships could be drawn across submarine lines, a tactic attempted by the Germans in 1916. Arthur Balfour, the First Lord of the Admiralty, wrote in November 1916: 'the submarine has already profoundly modified naval tactics ... It was a very evil day for this country when this engine of naval warfare was discovered.'[12]

On 4 July 1916, recognising that Jutland had left the British still dominant in the North Sea, the German commander there, Vice-Admiral Reinhard Scheer, suggested to Wilhelm II that Germany could only win at sea by means of using submarines. During the war, indeed, the Germans sunk 11.9 million tons of Allied shipping at the cost of 199 submarines. Most of this was commercial shipping, as the *guerre de course* was the submarines' most productive *métier*, and not attacks on warships. By attacking merchant shipping, the Germans were demonstrating that the sea, far from being a source of protection for Britain, was in fact a barrier to safe re-supply. In 1915, the Germans launched unrestricted submarine warfare – attacking all shipping and sinking without warning – only for this to be stopped as likely to provoke American intervention.

A continuing desire to deliver a knockout blow, nevertheless, led, on 2 February 1917, to the resumption of such warfare; but doing so helped bring the USA into the war on 6 April. Alongside Germany's crass wartime diplomacy, her actions, especially the unrestricted submarine warfare that sank American ships (and also violated international law), led to a major shift in attitudes in which Americans became persuaded of the dangerous consequences of German strength and ambitions, but also did so in a highly moralised form that encouraged large-scale commitment. Brazil, which also suffered from the unrestricted submarine warfare, declared war on Germany in October 1917.

Operating by the well-established prize rules was restricted warfare, and without regard to these rules, unrestricted warfare. The prize rules were essentially to stop suspected vessels, search them for contraband, and, if contraband was found, to take them into port where the ship could be condemned by a court as a prize. If it was impossible to get the vessel into port, the prize rules stipulated that it was to be scuttled after provision had been made for the crew and passengers by allowing them into the lifeboats or holding them on board. Unrestricted submarine warfare was part of a deliberate campaign to starve Britain into submission, and a reflection of the failure of the Germans to win victory at Jutland. The objective was total war, even if the Germans lacked the submarine fleet to achieve this objective. In the spring of 1917, British leaders, including Jellicoe, were pessimistic about the chances of success against the submarines. Indeed, the initial rate of Allied losses was sufficiently high to threaten defeat. Serious losses were inflicted on Allied, particularly British, commerce, in large part due to British inexperience in confronting submarine attacks. The limited effectiveness of anti-submarine weaponry was also an issue. Depth charges were effective only if they exploded close to the hull.

This situation was serious because, in 1914, neither Britain nor France had an industrial system to match that of Germany, which had forged ahead of Britain in iron and steel production. The Allies were dependent on the USA for machine tools, mass-production plants, and much else, including the parts of shells. American industrial output was equivalent to that of the whole of Europe by 1914, and the British ability to keep Atlantic sea-lanes open ensured that America made a key contribution before its formal entry into the war. Transoceanic trade and naval dominance also allowed the British and French to draw on the resources of their empires.

Submarines, in turn, were a new type of old challenge, the commerce-raider, and, in some respects, were less of a challenge because the latter had benefited from France's many anchorages, while the Germans had only limited access to the high seas, not only because they had fewer anchorages but also as Britain could try to block the English Channel and the North Sea through anti-submarine measures, particularly minefields. Nevertheless, the submarines were a serious challenge.

In the event, product substitution and enhanced agricultural production helped Britain survive the onslaught. The British did not sue for peace on 1 August 1917, as it had been claimed they would. Moreover, the introduction, by the British in May 1917, of a system of escorted convoys cut shipping losses dramatically and led to an increase in the sinking of German submarines. Convoys might appear such an obvious solution that it is surprising they were not adopted earlier, but there were counter-arguments, including the number of escorts required, the delays that would be forced on shipping, and the possibility that convoys would simply offer a bigger target. They were also resisted by the Admiralty for some time as not sufficiently in touch with the bold 'Nelson touch'. Although in the first four months of the unrestricted submarine attack, the British lost an average of 630,000 tons, only 393 of the 95,000 ships that were to be convoyed across the Atlantic were sunk.[13]

Moreover, convoys facilitated the transport of over two million American troops to Europe aboard thousands of ships, with the loss of just three transports (one of which managed to limp to Brest after being torpedoed) and 68 soldiers drowned. This achievement was very significant for the pressure building up against Germany in 1918, especially as many German submarine enthusiasts had assumed that their force would very seriously impede the movement of American troops to Europe.

Convoys reduced the targets for submarines and ensured that, when they found them, the submarines could be attacked by escorts. In providing sufficient numbers of escorts, the British were helped by their wartime shipbuilding programme, which included 56 destroyers and 50 anti-submarine motor launches. Convoys also benefited from the 'shoal' factor: submarines, when they found one, only had time to sink a limited number of ships. In coastal waters, convoys were supported by aircraft and airships, and this support forced the submarines to remain submerged, where they were much slower.

More generally, the complex relationships between tactics, technology, manufacturing and operational experience was shown in anti-submarine warfare. For example, one of the advantages of aircraft in dealing with submarines is that viewing submerged objects is far easier from above than from sea level. However, aircraft were not yet able to make a fundamental contribution to anti-submarine operations because key specifications they had by the Second World War were lacking during the First, while the anti-submarine weapons dropped by aircraft were fairly unsophisticated compared to those of the Second World War.

Mines

Convoys limited the potency of German attacks, but mines sank more submarines than other weapons. They played an important role in the war, but have been underrated in favour of more spectacular weapons. Mine barrages limited the options for surface and submarine vessels. The Allies laid massive barrages across the English Channel (at Dover), the North Sea (between the Orkneys and Norway) and the Straits of Otranto at the entrance to the Adriatic, in order to limit the operational range of German and Austrian forces. The massive mine barrages reflected industrial capacity and organisational capability. There were important improvements in mine technology during the war, although these are apt to be overlooked. By the end of the war, magnetic mines had been developed and were being laid by the British.

Particular operations were also affected by mines. The British naval attempt to force the Dardanelles en route to Constantinople on 18 May 1915 was stopped by mines, shore batteries and an unwillingness to accept further losses after three battleships were sunk, and three more were badly damaged. The naval experts had been aware of the hazards posed by the mines and shore batteries of the Dardanelles, not least because, before the war, the British naval mission had provided advice on mine-laying, but their caution was thrust aside by Winston Churchill, then First Lord of the Admiralty, who was a keen advocate of the scheme for a naval advance on Constantinople.[14]

The Dardanelles offensive also led to the arrival of German submarines in the Mediterranean. They sank two British battleships in the Dardanelles campaign itself, and went on to attack shipping in the Mediterranean. This threat led to the Allied laying of mines in the Straits of Otranto, in order to keep the hostile submarines in their Adriatic bases. The campaign also led British submarines to pass through the Dardanelles and to operate in the Sea of Marmara.

The failure of the Allied naval assault on the Dardanelles was followed that year by an attempt to gain control of the shores by landing troops, the Gallipoli expedition. The British had been building powered landing-craft from 1914, but most of the troops that went ashore in amphibious operations during the First World War, for example at Gallipoli, were landed from ordinary ships, in other words, steam-driven vessels that could not beach. As a result, troops were often landed into dinghies, a vulnerable situation, or into shallows that were far from shallow. Equipment had to be landed at a port.

Command and control was an area of naval operations that benefited from technological improvement. As on land and in the air, developments with radio made it easier to retain detailed operational control. Directional wireless equipment aided location and navigation, and was employed to hunt German submarines by triangulation, while radio transmissions changed from a spark method to a continuous-wave system. Alongside a focus on dramatically new technology and doctrine, including submarines, radio, aircraft, airships and anti-submarine warfare, it is necessary to note the role of traditional practices, such as blockade, as well as of incremental improvement, less spectacular technology, and manufacturing capacity. This contrast and point is more generally true of developments in naval capability.

A host of naval powers, 1914–18

The struggle between Britain and Germany dominates discussion of the First World War at sea, and the British lost more capital ships than all the other combatants combined, but naval operations involving other powers were also extensive. The decision of Italy to abandon its allies in the Triple Alliance, with whom they had agreed a naval convention in 1913, and, instead, to join Britain and France in 1915, ensured that the Mediterranean was dominated by the Entente powers, with Austria and Turkey unable to contest their dominance. The small German squadron in the Mediterranean in 1914 took shelter with the Turks, while a French squadron at Corfu and most of the Italian fleet at Taranto confined the Austrians to the Adriatic, and prevented them from breaking out into the Mediterranean. Due to hostile submarines, however, the French and Italians withdrew their major ships from the Adriatic.[15]

In the Black Sea, the Russians had more warships than the Turks and, from 1915, blockaded the Bosporus. They also used the navy from 1916 to help operations in the Caucasus.[16] In contrast, in the Baltic, the Russian fleet was weaker than the forces the Germans could deploy if they moved in some of their High Seas Fleet units from the North Sea via the Kiel Canal. This German capability encouraged Russian caution, which was also in keeping with long-established Russian doctrine and with the Russian emphasis in the Baltic on local operations. Defeat by the Japanese at Tsushima in 1905 was scarcely an encouragement for bolder operations. The Russians laid extensive minefields to protect the Gulf of Finland and staged raids into the southern Baltic in order to mine German shipping routes. The Germans, in turn, laid mines, but also staged the most successful amphibious operation of the war in European waters (and their only operation) when they conquered Russia's Baltic islands in 1917, a success helped by the disruptive impact of the March Revolution on Russian forces.[17]

The Japanese, who fought on the Allied side, used their navy in their successful attacks on Germany's Chinese base of Tsingtao in 1914 and on German bases in the Pacific, escorted British convoys from Australia, hunted German surface raiders, and in 1917 sent warships to assist the Allies in the Mediterranean.

'Over There', the recruitment poster drawn in 1917 by Albert Sterner for the American navy, pointed the way for America's battleships. When war with Germany was declared in that year, the American navy had no appropriate war plan for the Atlantic, a key symptom of a more generally poorly-prepared force, which, in particular, lacked experience in anti-submarine warfare. Moreover, the major shipbuilding programme authorised in 1916 had yet to come to fruition. Nevertheless, American entry into the war was crucial. The USA was not only the world's largest economy, but also had the third largest navy after Britain and Germany.

The Americans deployed their fleet to help protect communication routes across the Atlantic, and their escort vessels contributed to the effectiveness of convoying, although the major battleships they had built were not used in battle. The key American naval contribution was in destroyers, fast enough to track submarines and to keep them submerged. From May 1917, American warships contributed to anti-submarine patrols in European waters. To assist convoying in the Mediterranean, American warships were based in Gibraltar and Japanese ones in Malta.[18] Five American dreadnoughts joined the British Grand Fleet in December 1917, four sailing with it on 24 April 1918 when it failed to intercept an ultimately unsuccessful German sortie into the North Sea. These battleships made any idea of a decisive German naval sortie less credible, and the German surface fleet languished while their crews became seriously discontented, leading to their mutiny at the close of the war.[19]

The First World War also looked to the future in demonstrating that the rise of American naval power was pertinent not just for weak states, like Spain in 1898, but also for great-power naval relations. Moreover, geopolitical shifts enhanced America's naval potential. This was the case not only of the country's growing prominence in East Asia/Western Pacific, an area of increasing international prominence, but also of the opening of the Panama Canal in 1914 which transformed the strategic place of the Caribbean in naval plans and greatly increased the flexibility of the American navy by making it easier to move warships between the Atlantic and the Pacific.[20]

Although the extension of air power to the sea made scant impact on the course of the war, naval capability was affected by it. Britain took the lead, employing airships and aircraft for reconnaissance, attacks against shipping, and for patrols against submarines. In July 1918, Britain conducted the first raid by planes flown off an improvised aircraft carrier. In the following month, British seaplanes eliminated an entire naval force: six coastal motorboats. In September, HMS *Argus*, an aircraft carrier capable of carrying 20 planes with a flush deck unobstructed by superstructure and funnels – the first clear-deck aircraft carrier – was commissioned by the British, although she did not undergo sea trials until October 1918. At the end of the war, the Royal Naval Air Service had 2949 aircraft and was planning an attack on the German High Seas Fleet in harbour.

Although the war was not settled (or apparently settled) by a major naval battle, as navalists claimed the Spanish-American (1898) and Russo-Japanese conflicts (1904–5) had been, it was one in which the overwhelming naval power of the Allies had played a crucial role. Without this power, the alliance could not have operated: it would have lacked both operational reach and the ability to move and use resources across the Channel and the Atlantic.[21] Moreover, the traditional means of surface blockade applied by the British against Germany offered them more than it had done against France in the Napoleonic Wars. In part, this difference was a product of long-term developments in naval effectiveness, specifically the replacement of sail by steam, but it was also due to the nature of the international system. Germany was unable to dominate continental Europe, as Napoleon had done, while the USA was willing to accept the consequences of British naval power, unlike the American anger displayed during the earlier period, which had culminated in the Anglo-American War of 1812.

Inter-war developments

The Armistice at the close of the First World War was followed by the surrender of the German fleet to the British. At Harwich 176 U-boats surrendered, and 9 battleships and the other ships of the High Seas Fleet at Scapa Flow. The Germans ceased to be a significant naval power. They scuttled their ships at Scapa Flow in 1919, while the Peace of Versailles denied Germany permission to build a new fleet. Moreover, as part of the 1919 peace settlement, the merchant ships seized from Germany were allocated to the victors in proportion to their wartime maritime losses. The Austrian fleet ended with the collapse of the

Habsburg monarchy. Although not so seriously affected, Russia was also hard-hit, with its navy badly affected by the civil war of 1917–22.

The war led to a transformation in naval power politics. The naval challenge to Britain now came from her wartime allies, the USA and Japan. Competition from these two was to be played out after the war in the diplomacy of naval limitation that led to the Washington Naval Treaty of 1922. However, wartime alliance followed by the success of these negotiations ensured that naval competition ceased to be the key theme that it had been prior to the outbreak of the First World War. Under pressure from fiscal circumstances and demands for social welfare, the British accepted naval parity with the Americans, the leading industrial and financial power in the world, and both states acknowledged the fact of Japanese naval power in the Pacific. A 5:5:3 ratio in capital ship tonnage for Britain, the USA and Japan was agreed in the Washington Naval Treaty,[22] while the quotas for France and Italy were 35 per cent of the capital ship tonnage of Britain. More generally, the treaty comprised an agreement to scrap many battleships and to stop new construction for ten years. The latter provision was extended by the London Naval Treaty of 1930.

The Washington Naval Treaty appeared to end the prospect of naval races. The treaty also limited warships other than capital ships to 10,000 tons and 8-inch guns (reduced to 6-inch in 1930). In the inter-war period, there was a building of heavy cruisers that met these limits, rather than of the battleships built prior to 1914. Britain, indeed, did not lay down any battleships between January 1923 and December 1936. The treaty also included a clause stopping the military development of American colonies in the Western Pacific and also of many of Japan's island possessions. However, despite British efforts in 1922 and 1930, there were no limitations on submarines, although the Peace of Versailles in 1919 had banned Germany from using them. The French were keen to prevent limits on submarine warfare and built the most in the 1920s.[23]

The combined impact of submarines and air power in the First World War, and their likely future impact, suggested to many a fundamental change both in naval capability and in the tactical, operational and strategic aspects of naval power.

As a consequence, naval goals had to be rapidly rethought. Thus, submarines altered the nature of commerce-raiding and made blockade more difficult. Submarine warfare also emphasised a major difference between naval and land capability: the former was restricted to a few powers, and thus the options to be considered in terms of goals and doctrine were limited. Jellicoe argued that submarines destroyed the feasibility of close blockades, forcing a reliance for trade protection on convoys protected by cruisers. He was worried that Britain had insufficient cruisers both to do this and to work with the battle fleet in a future war. Admiralty concern about naval limitations on the size and number of ships was also expressed by Admiral Sir Charles Madden in a meeting of the Cabinet Committee preparing for the 1930 London Naval Conference. He

> explained that it was not possible to build a battleship of less than 25,000 tons with the necessary quantities of armament, speed and protection, which would include an armoured deck of 5" and 6", to keep out bombs and plunging shell, and have sufficient protection under water against mines, torpedoes and bombs … The Admiralty required a sufficient number of cruisers to give security to the overseas trade of the Empire against raiding forces of the enemy and a battlefleet to give cover to the trade-protecting cruisers.[24]

The problem with negotiating parity agreements was that every naval power had different force requirements to meet its strategic needs; for example the Americans needed far fewer cruisers than the British, and this led to a serious Anglo-American dispute over cruiser numbers at and after the Geneva Naval Conference of 1927.

As had been the case before the First World War, there was a drive to develop naval strength and weaponry, but there was also acute controversy over the potential of different weapons systems in any future naval war. The respective merits of air power, both from aircraft carriers and shore-based, of surface gunnery, and of submarines, were all extensively discussed, as well as their likely tactical and strategic combinations.

Although some theorists argued that battleships were now obsolete in the face of air power and submarines, big surface warships had a continued appeal and not simply for the European powers. Indeed, there was opposition to a stress on carriers becoming the key capital ship; in the 1930s, both the Americans and the British put a major emphasis on battle-fleet tactics based on battleships. This emphasis was not simply a sign of conservatism; for the British displayed adaptability in their tactics.[25] The Germans were also fascinated by battleships.

The role of such ships was enhanced by the absence of a major change in battleship design comparable to those in the late nineteenth century and the 1900s. Indeed, with the arrival of the dreadnoughts, battleship architecture had reached a new period of relative stability. For example, the USS *New York* (BB-34) and *Texas* (BB-35) of 1914 and *Nevada* (BB-36) of 1916 participated in the D-Day bombardment in 1944. The *Texas*'s ten 14-inch guns could fire 1½ rounds per minute; each armour-piercing shell weighing 1500 lb. There was still great interest in such weaponry, both for ship destruction and for shore bombardment. Moreover, there were considerable efforts to strengthen battleships in order to increase their resistance to air attack. Armour was enhanced, outer hulls added to protect against torpedo attack, and anti-aircraft guns and tactics developed. This improvement is a reminder of the danger of assuming that a weapons system is necessarily static.

In the Second World War, surface ships were crucial for conflict with other surface ships, not least because, although there were spectacular losses, many battleships took considerable punishment before being sunk by air attack. Until reliable all-weather day and night reconnaissance and strike aircraft were available (which was really in the 1950s), surface ships provided the means of fighting at night and battleships were still necessary while other powers maintained the type. For the British, such an air capability was further unlikely until 1937, while the Royal Air Force (RAF) controlled the delivery of maritime air power and had to choose between maritime air power and its preferred strategic bombing force.

Naval air power

There was no experience with conflict between aircraft carriers, but there was considerable confidence in their potential. In 1919, Jellicoe pressed for a British Far East Fleet, to include four carriers as well as battleships, in order to deter Japan, while, in 1920, Rear Admiral Sir Reginald Hall MP argued in *The Times* that, thanks to aircraft and submarines, the days of the battleship were over. This argument, however, was of scant interest to the British Admiralty, which remained wedded to the battleship. Carriers were used when Britain intervened against the Communists in the Russian Civil War, while HMS *Argus* was stationed near the Dardanelles during the Chanak crisis between Britain and Turkey in 1922. There was also a carrier on the China Station in the late 1920s (first *Hermes* and then *Argus*) and another, *Furious*, took place in the major naval exercises in the late 1920s.[26]

At sea, air power was restricted in the 1910s and 1920s by the difficulty of operating aeroplanes in bad weather and the dark, by their limited load capacity and range, and by mechanical unreliability, but improvements were made, especially in the 1930s. New arrester gears were fitted which helped slow planes down while landing, and, in addition, they could be reset automatically. The Americans and Japanese made major advances with naval aviation and aircraft carriers, in part because they would be the key powers in any struggle for control of the Pacific.[27] Germany, Italy and the Soviet Union, however, did not build aircraft carriers in the inter-war period, and France only had one, a converted dreadnought-type battleship. Britain's carrier construction therefore gave an important added dimension to her naval superiority over other European powers: four 23,000-ton carriers, the *Illustrious* class, each able to make over 30 knots and having a 3-inch armoured flight deck, were laid down in 1937, following the 22,000-ton *Ark Royal* laid down in 1935.

Naval air power in Britain lacked a separate institutional framework, because the Fleet Air Arm was placed under the RAF between 1918 and 1937, when it was returned to the navy by the Inskip Award, and the RAF was primarily concerned with land-based aeroplanes, and had little time for their naval counterparts.[28] In the USA, there was a very different situation thanks to the Bureau of Aeronautics of the American navy, which stimulated the development of effective air–sea doctrine, operational policies, and tactics. The *Langley*, a converted collier, was, in 1922, the first American aircraft carrier to be commissioned, followed, in 1927, by two converted battle cruisers, the

Lexington and the *Saratoga*. Aside from developments in aircraft carriers, there were also marked improvements in aircraft. Thus, the Americans benefited from the development of dive-bombing tactics in the 1920s and, subsequently, of dive-bombers. These proved more effective than torpedo-bombers: aircraft launching torpedoes, which were vulnerable to defensive fire.[29] More generally, air spotting for naval gunfire also developed in the 1930s.

Tasks and roles

The likely geostrategic character of any future major conflict ensured that there would be different requirements to those on the eve of the First World War. In particular, the focus was less on the confined waters off north-west Europe, the centre of attention in that conflict, and, instead, on the vast expanses of the Pacific. Even before the close of the First World War, there had been an awareness that new technology was likely to lead to a very different naval situation in any future conflict. Balfour argued in May 1918 that a peace settlement that left the Germans with colonies would pose a great problem: 'a piratical power, prepared to use the submarine as Germany had used it in this war, and possessed of well placed bases in every ocean, could hold up the sea-borne commerce of neutral and belligerent alike, no matter what were the naval forces arrayed against it'.[30] The following year, an Admiralty memorandum warned that the British navy was likely to be weaker than that of Japan in the Far East. It suggested that using Hong Kong as a base would expose the fleet, and, instead, that Singapore should be developed, as it was sufficiently far from Japan to permit reinforcement without peril.[31]

The Americans were increasingly concerned about Japanese intentions and naval strength. Furthermore, there were specific American interests in the western Pacific, including the territories of the Philippines, Guam and Samoa, trade, and a strong commitment to the independence of China. This concern led to planning for war with Japan, planning that was a bridge from the naval thought of the Mahanian period to the strategy pursued in the Second World War. Plan Orange of 1924 called for the 'through ticket': a rapid advance directly from Hawaii to Manila, a decisive battle, and then starving Japan by blockade. This plan was superseded by greater interest in a slower process of seizing the Japanese islands in the Pacific – the Marshalls, Carolines and Marianas, which they had gained from Germany in the First World War treaty settlement. Their capture would provide the Americans with forward bases, and deny them to the Japanese. Without control of this area, it was argued, a naval advance to the Philippines would be unsuccessful.

The likely character of a major future war led to a new geography of commitment and concern that was reflected in the development of naval bases, for example those of Britain at Singapore, which in 1932 the Cabinet decided to complete, and of the USA at Pearl Harbor on the Hawaiian island of Oahu. In addition, it was assumed that there would be a far greater role for aircraft carriers in the Pacific than in the North Sea and the Mediterranean. As tensions mounted in the Far East in the 1920s and, even more, 1930s, with Japanese expansionism at the expense of China from 1931 and full-scale war from 1937, and an increase in the size of the Japanese navy, so it was necessary to plan for conflict across very large bodies of water.

This need accentuated the problems for Britain and the USA, powers with commitments in both Atlantic and Pacific, for they had to think about how best to distribute naval forces, and how vulnerabilities would affect policy. There was a *de facto* division of spheres of activity, with the USA dominant in the Pacific, but having no naval role in the Indian Ocean, while the British were more prominent in the South Atlantic and in East Asian waters. The British planned to send much of their fleet to Singapore in the event of war with Japan. Indeed, in 1941, Churchill decided to send a modern battleship to Singapore in order to deter the Japanese and impress the Americans.[32]

In 1935, in the Second London Naval Conference, Japan demanded higher naval ratios. The American rejection of Japanese naval superiority in the Pacific led to the collapse of the conference, the unilateral Japanese disavowal of existing limits, and the launching of the Marusan Programme of shipbuilding designed to achieve superiority over British and American fleets.[33] The militaristic nature of Japanese naval policy and culture calls into question claims that navies have generally been associated with liberal, commercial values.[34]

Despite Japanese efforts, their fleet, by 1940, was only 7:10 in strength relative to the American. The Vinson–Trammel Act of March 1934, followed by the 'Second Vinson Act' of May 1938, had set out to rearm the American navy, and remedy an earlier situation in which there had been a failure to construct what was allowed by the Naval Conferences. In July 1940, when Britain appeared defeated by Germany, Congress passed the Two Ocean Naval Expansion Act, which was designed to produce a fleet larger than that of the second- and third-ranking naval powers combined. This fleet would enable the Americans to wage naval war against both Germany and Japan.

The development of the German and Italian navies indicated that both powers would contest European waters. Under the Anglo-German Naval Treaty of 1935, an attempt to provide an acceptable response to German demands for rearmament, the Germans were to have a quota equivalent to that of France or Italy under the 1922 treaty, with a surface fleet up to 35 per cent the size of that of Britain, although the submarine fleet could be the same size. Hitler, however, ignored these restrictions in his naval build-up. Like Stalin, who planned a 46,000-ton battleship, but was thwarted in his plans to order the world's largest battleship from an American yard,[35] Hitler was fascinated by battleships, and to the detriment of smaller, frequently more effective, warships. Indeed, Germany only had 57 submarines at the outset of the Second World War.[36] The Japanese also built up their navy, which included the largest capital ships in the world, the 'super-battleships' *Yamato* and *Musashi*, each displacing 72,000 tons. They were to be sunk by the Americans in 1944 and 1945, respectively.[37]

Benito Mussolini, the Italian dictator from 1922, greatly developed the Italian navy in order to challenge the British position in the Mediterranean, the crucial axis of the British empire and one that was dependent on naval power and related bases at Gibraltar, Malta and Alexandria.[38] Indeed, the two powers came close to conflict as a result of the Italian invasion of Abyssinia (Ethiopia) in 1935–6, a step condemned by the League of Nations. Despite weaknesses, including a lack of sailors, reserves and anti-aircraft ammunition, the Royal Navy was confident of success. The British government considered oil sanctions as well as closing the Suez Canal, but did not wish to provoke war with

Italy, not least as it hoped to keep Mussolini and Hitler apart, and did not intend to antagonise the Americans by stopping their tankers. The British failure to intimidate Italy was more a consequence of an absence of political will than of a lack of naval capability.[39] Lesser powers also developed their navies, Chile seeking to order two 8-inch gun cruisers from British yards, but being thwarted by the British government.

As a consequence in part of the social policy and disarmament priorities of the Labour government of 1929–31, British naval expenditure had been cut seriously in 1929–34, leading by 1936 to a degree of obsolescence. However, the threatening international situation then led to naval rearmament.[40] The February 1934 report of the Defence Requirements Sub-Committee of the Committee of Imperial Defence noted of the navy: 'The greatest potential threat lies in the acquisition of submarines and aircraft by Germany.'[41] They were therefore prepared for a far more varied conflict than what might result from a German battle-fleet offensive alone. From 1936, the Admiralty was free to pursue ambitious policies. A large number of carriers, battleships, cruisers and destroyers were laid down, and the Fleet Air Arm was greatly expanded. Radar sets were installed in warships from 1938.

Amphibious operations were not to the fore in inter-war naval thinking, which, in part, was a consequence of the lack of joint (i.e. joint service) structures and planning. Nevertheless, there was more interest in specialised landing-craft, especially by the USA, than there had been during the First World War. The Japanese, who used amphibious attacks in their war with China from 1937, made the most progress, both in developing types of landing-craft and in building a reasonable number of ships. Their *Dai-Hatsu* had a ramp in its bows, and this was to become the key type of landing-craft.

The Second World War, 1939–45

In the run-up to the Second World War, and during the conflict itself, naval staffs and lobbies played key roles in the discussion of maritime plans and operations, but less so in the question of overall strategy. The situation, however, varied greatly by country, while individual navies were also divided in their views. In Japan, the navy played a major role in Pacific policy, and, in 1941, naval pressure for an attack on the American Pacific naval base at Pearl Harbor, as a prelude for covering amphibious invasions against Malaya, the Philippines and the Dutch East Indies, was successful.[42] The navy lacked a comparable sphere in German policymaking, partly because the Atlantic did not weigh as heavily in overall policymaking, but mainly because the navy was less important to the politics and symbolism of the German war effort and the Nazi regime; although that did not mean that Hitler was unprepared to support strategies of naval attack. Thus, the conquest of Norway in 1940 was seen as a way to outflank Britain by sea, both to limit British blockade and to provide access to the Atlantic.[43] Similarly, the French navy was able to advocate distinctive policies, pushing plans directed against Italy in 1937–9,[44] but had only modest impact on overall policy, whereas the Royal Navy benefited in Britain from the central role it played in ideas of (and plans for) imperial defence.

Naval conflict played a greater role in this war than in the First World War, because the Pacific, for the first time, became a major war theatre, while the conflict in the Mediterranean was more important than in the previous world war because of the North African and Italian campaigns, and the Germans made a more serious and sustained effort to cut routes across the Atlantic. In addition, the German success in overrunning France in 1940 ensured that the subsequent defeat of Germany would entail a major Allied amphibious invasion of occupied Western Europe, a task that had not been envisaged prior to the war, which helps explain the limited nature of British amphibious preparations.

In the meanwhile, the strength of the Royal Navy was crucial to preventing Germany from launching an invasion of southern England in 1940. Although the Royal Air Force gained lasting fame for repelling the *Luftwaffe* (German air force) in the Battle of Britain, sea power was the key element in stopping the Germans from launching Operation Sea Lion. The losses suffered by the German navy during the Norway campaign meant that its supporting an invasion was unlikely, while the *Luftwaffe* could only try to prevent British naval interference in daylight, allowing the German invasion fleet, which could not cross the Channel and return in daylight, to be attacked at night.

Nevertheless, there was great pressure on British naval resources, especially prior to America's entry into the war against Japan and Germany in response to the Japanese attack on Pearl Harbor in December 1941. In September 1941, the British First Sea Lord complained of a shortage of cruisers, adding 'the destroyer situation is even worse', when explaining why he could send none to the Far East.[45]

British prominence on the Allied side prior to American entry was further secured by the fate of the French navy after the fall of France to the Germans in June 1940. The fleet was left under the Vichy French regime, and British uncertainty about the ability of the Vichy government to keep it out of German control led to a destructive attack on the North African squadron at Mers-el-Kébir near Oran on 3 July 1940. One French battleship was sunk and two were damaged. In contrast, an attack proved unnecessary in order to ensure an acceptable oversight of the French warships in Alexandria, Plymouth and Portsmouth. In some respects, the attack at Mers-el-Kébir was a blunder, as it seriously weakened support within France for Charles de Gaulle and the cause of continued resistance to Germany and made it easier for Vichy. When the Germans occupied Vichy France in November 1942, the remainder of the French fleet at Toulon was scuttled, although the battleship *Richelieu* sailed from Dakar to join the British.

Air power was very important to the naval war in the Mediterranean which followed Italian entry on the German side in June 1940. Sea lanes there were crucial to both the British and the Axis war effort, not least to the Italian hope of turning the Mediterranean into a *Mare Nostrum*. Early in the war, successful British attacks on the Italian fleet, involving both surface ships and aeroplanes, especially by 21 torpedo-bombers against battleships moored in Taranto (11 November 1940), combined with the failure of the large Italian submarine force to make a major impact, ensured that the British became the leading naval power in the Mediterranean. On 28 March 1941, off Cape Matapan, in Britain's last major high-seas fleet battle, the navy sank three Italian cruisers and damaged a battleship, thanks to the use of torpedo aircraft, battleship firepower and ships' radar.[46] The Taranto operation, in which three battleships and two cruisers were severely damaged, by torpedoes operating in less than half the depth of water previously thought necessary, possibly inspired the Japanese attack on Pearl Harbor a year later, although the idea had been discussed in the inter-war period, and the Americans were aware of it as a possibility.

The British position in the Mediterranean, in turn, was challenged by German air and submarine forces, from January and October 1941, respectively. Thus, the carrier *Illustrious*, which had launched the Taranto raid, was severely damaged by German dive-bombers the following January. The last German submarine base in the Mediterranean – at Salamis – was not evacuated until October 1944, and German submarines put pressure on the British in the Mediterranean, although, as a reminder of the need to adopt a wider context, submarine operations there weakened the more significant German effort in the Atlantic.[47]

Equally, British surface ship, air and submarine forces in the Mediterranean sought to limit the operational possibilities and re-supply capability of Axis land forces. The British failed to prevent the German conquest of Crete in May 1941, losing three cruisers and six destroyers in the process as their vulnerability to air power was cruelly exposed. However, thanks in large part to bitterly fought convoy battles against German air attacks, the British hung on to their base of Malta, thus repeating the differing success of Christendom against attacks by the Ottoman Turks in 1565 (Malta survives) and 1669 (Crete falls). In 1943, moreover, the British succeeded in crippling the supply routes to Rommel's army in Tunisia, building on earlier efforts in 1940–2 to cut Axis supply routes to Libya.[48]

The problems of German-Italian co-operation were less important to the equations of naval power at the global scale than the lack of concerted operations between Germany and Japan, a lack that was both product and cause of the Allied dominance of the oceans. Indeed, although the world war was one between two alliances each of which controlled large naval forces, the Axis alliance (Germany, Italy and Japan) suffered because it was able to devote less of its attention to naval activity. Instead, for Germany, the core struggle from 1941 was the land war with the Soviet Union, while, although the Pacific war with the USA was crucial to the Japanese navy, much of the Japanese military effort was committed to a land war with China.

In one respect, this difference in emphasis between Allies and Axis appears to vindicate views on the centrality of naval activity, as the Allies won and were able to employ their naval superiority in order to guarantee maritime routes, and thus provide the mutual support that enabled them not only to remain in the war but also to mount attacks from a variety of directions. Thus, the oceanic alliance won the battle for the oceans, and then the war. This approach, however, is overly comforting, as greater Axis success on land against the Soviet Union in 1941 would have made it difficult to Britain and the USA to mount a successful assault on occupied Western Europe in 1944. Moreover, although very important, American naval power and amphibious capability did not ensure the defeats of Japanese forces on land, especially in Burma and Manchuria in 1945 by the British and Soviets, respectively, while the knock-out blow of the American atomic bombs that August came from the air.

There was German interest in acquiring Atlantic bases such as the Canary Islands from where it would be possible to threaten British convoy routes, to increase German influence in South America, and to challenge American power. This interest reflected the goal of the naval staff in Germany becoming a power with a global reach provided by a strong surface navy. However, although Hitler wanted Germany to regain the overseas colonies it had lost in the First World War, this goal was tangential to his central concern with creating a new Europe, a concern which involved him in having to consider the trade-off between beginning war with the Soviet Union and, on the other hand, continued confrontation with Britain and the prospect that it might win American support. The goal of a new Europe won out in 1941, although, in part, that reflected the conviction that Soviet defeat would make Britain more accommodating.[49] British naval power, it was anticipated, would therefore be trumped by German success on land.

The high point of German–Japanese coordination was in December 1941, with Germany's decision to declare war on the USA after Pearl Harbor, an attack Hitler had sought to encourage by pressing forward operations against Moscow; but this declaration did not lead to any concerted attempt at Axis grand strategy. The only sphere in which such concerted action might have been possible was the Indian Ocean, with German pressure on the Middle East interacting with Japanese advances on India and in the Indian Ocean. As Churchill told the Secret Session of the House of Commons on 23 April 1942: 'while we are at war with Germany and Italy we do not possess the naval resources necessary to maintain the command of the Indian Ocean against any heavy detachment from the main Japanese fleet'.[50] William Joyce, 'Lord Haw Haw', a Nazi propagandist broadcasting from Germany, declared on 28 December 1941 that 'the demands on the Royal Navy were such that every single warship had to do the work of at least half a dozen'.

The Japanese were well placed to advance, but their devastating naval raid by six carriers into the Indian Ocean in April 1942 was not the prelude to further operations, even though they lost no warships in the operation but, rather, sank two British heavy cruisers and a carrier, all inadequately protected against dive-bombers. Instead, the Japanese navy launched the Pacific operation that led to disaster at Midway. Also in the Indian Ocean, British fears that the Vichy-governed island of Madagascar might become a Japanese submarine base were ended by the British conquest of the island in 1942, although German and Italian submarines did link up in that ocean with the Japanese.[51]

Prior to America's entry into the war, the strengthening of Anglo-American relations was expressed through a series of steps for sharing power and responsibility in the North Atlantic. In July 1940, American occupation forces replaced the British in Iceland as part of their attempt to protect the Western Hemisphere, a policy outlined at the Havana Conference of that month. Two months later, as an important gesture, the USA provided 50 surplus destroyers (7 of them to the Canadian navy), in return for 99-year leases on British bases in Antigua, the Bahamas, Bermuda, British Guiana, Jamaica, Newfoundland, St Lucia and Trinidad. In practice, the deal was of limited immediate use as the ships took time to prepare, but the psychological value captured the sense of strength through joint naval capability. In March 1941, the passage by Congress of the Lend-Lease Act opened the way for the shipping of American military supplies to Britain, while, during the Placentia Bay Conference of August 1941, Churchill and Roosevelt agreed to allocate spheres of strategic responsibility, with the Americans becoming responsible, alongside the Canadians, for escorting convoys in the western Atlantic. By 1942, 500 Canadian warships were in commission and, by the end of the war, Canada had the world's third largest navy.

Unlike in the First World War, there was no major clash between warship fleets in the Western Hemisphere, in part because the Germans divided their powerful fleet and relied on squadron moves and individual raids, rather than on fleet actions where they feared the greater strength of the Royal Navy. Unlike in the earlier war, the Germans had the geostrategic position for waging an Atlantic war with surface warships, but the German Supreme Naval Command felt that it lacked the necessary battle fleet. The most well known of the German operations was that of May 1941, by the *Bismarck*, which was sent out to attack British convoys. Probably the most powerful battleship in the Atlantic, and named significantly after the Chancellor who had united Germany, the *Bismarck* sank the largest inter-war British warship, the *Hood*, commissioned in 1920; but the *Bismarck*, damaged by shellfire, was eventually crippled by airborne torpedo attack and was then sunk.[52]

More generally, the war showed the vulnerability of surface ships to air power. In responding inadequately in April 1940 to the German invasion of Norway, British warships proved unable to cope effectively with German air power, leading Admiral Sir Dudley Pound, the First Sea Lord, to note: 'The lesson we have learnt here is that it is essential to have fighter protection over the Fleet whenever they are within reach of the enemy bombers.'[53]

The torpedoing of the heavy cruiser *Lützow* off Norway by British air attack in June 1941 ended the surface raiding of Atlantic sea routes. This vulnerability led the Germans to withdraw their major warships from Brest in February 1942. Norway was an important base for operations against British convoys taking supplies to the Soviet Union, but the inroads of German aeroplanes and submarines were not matched by surface ships. Instead, the German warships fell victim, the *Scharnhorst* to a British fleet escorting a convoy on 26 December 1943 in the Battle of the North Cape; and the *Tirpitz*, which had sailed to Trondheim in January 1942 to take refuge in the Norwegian fjords, being sunk by heavy bombers based in Britain on 12 November 1944.

The vulnerability of surface ships to air power was also shown in the attacks by British Coastal Command on German convoys operating off continental Europe. Initially, the British were outgunned by the effective flak defences of the convoys, but the Beaufighter, introduced in 1942, carried cannon, machine-guns, torpedoes, or eight 25-lb rockets which had the force of a destroyer's salvo. From 1943, the fire of German flak-ships was suppressed and a considerable tonnage of merchantmen was sunk.

The U-boat war

The German submarine (U-boat) assault on the North Atlantic was very serious for the British, and scarcely a peripheral struggle as this conflict was central to the eventual ability to apply American power against Germany. Moreover, the German submarine and air assault on British trade was unrestricted from the outset. The German conquests of Norway and France in 1940 exposed more of British trade to submarine attack than in the First World War; while submarines were more sophisticated than in the First World War, and became yet more so during the war. Moreover, a battle of technological innovation ensued. For example, in 1943, the Germans recalled their submarines in order to fit *schnorkel* devices which allowed them to recharge their batteries while submerged, thus reducing their vulnerability to Allied air power, while the Allies introduced qualitative and quantitative improvements in both sensors and weapons, including more powerful depth-charges, ship-borne radar, and better Asdic detection equipment. In 1943, the Germans also introduced the T5 acoustic homing torpedo.

In 1942, 1664 merchantmen, amounting to nearly eight million tons, were sunk by U-boats, seeking to meet their tonnage objectives, while the U-boat losses were less than new launchings as a result of the increase in the monthly launches: 58 U-boats were lost in July–December 1942, a period in which 121 were completed. For the first time, there were enough U-boats to organise comprehensive patrol lines across North Atlantic convoy routes. Yet, a range of factors helped the Allies win, including greater resources; effective anti-submarine tactics, by both convoy escorts and aircraft; enhanced anti-submarine weaponry, such as improved Asdics, better depth charges and Leigh Lights for aircraft; and signals intelligence. As a consequence, the number of submarines sunk per year was much greater than in the First World War, while the percentage of

Allied shipping lost was less. Moreover, a large number of convoys was not attacked, which in some respect was more important than individual victories and defeats.

A change in tactics also played a major role in defeating the German assault. British policymakers had initially failed to understand the lessons of the First World War and to appreciate the need to focus aircraft and surface escorts on convoy protection. Instead, they preferred to emphasise the value of attacking the Germans, by air attacks on submarine bases and yards, and by hunting groups at sea. Once returned to office as First Lord of the Admiralty in 1939, Winston Churchill maintained this flawed approach.[54] Success in the Atlantic, in part, depended on its abandonment and on a return to convoy protection.

The size of the American contribution in warships and merchantmen, and of their shipbuilding industry, posed a strategic problem for the Germans. American shipbuilding, with its more effective prefabrication and flow production methods, played the crucial role. In contrast, whereas, thanks to shipbuilding, the British had replaced most of their merchantmen sunk during the First World War, they were unable to do so in the Second World War. Instead, the British merchant fleet in 1945 was 70 per cent the size it had been in 1939. Thanks to the Americans, the Allies built more ships than the U-boats sank in the first quarter of 1943. By the end of the third quarter, the Allies had built more than had been sunk since the start of the war.

Allied success simply spurred Karl Dönitz, Commander-in-Chief of the German navy from 1943, to become steadily more radical in his pursuit of victory, demanding fanaticism from his men and accepting increasingly more hazardous operating conditions, which led to a very high rate of fatalities in the German submarine service: 754 out of the 863 submarines in commission were lost and 27,491 crew were killed.

The strategic issue posed for the Germans by Allied shipbuilding interacted with the tactical and operational challenges offered by improved Allied proficiency in anti-submarine warfare, not least in the use of air support. Shore-based long-range B-24 Liberator aircraft were the key to closing the mid-Atlantic air-gap in the spring of 1943.[55] The Allies really won the Battle of the Atlantic in 1943, especially in clashes from March to May that led the Germans to decide to halt continuous U-boat operations in the North Atlantic, although the key decisions were those of late 1942 when the British finally decided to allocate adequate resources to maritime airpower, notably the provision of very long-range aircraft. The number of these aircraft began to rise from February 1943 onwards. The Allied conquest of France in late 1944 was another fundamental blow to U-boat operations.

Strategy, tactics and resources were all important to Allied victory, and helped to explain the greater success which the Allies enjoyed in preserving sea links across the Atlantic when compared to the Japanese failure in the same period to protect their routes.

During the Second World War, carrier-based planes became crucial in naval actions, as in the British pursuit of German warships in the Atlantic and nearby waters. The clear British need for carrier support led to the laying down of 10 light fleet carriers between June 1942 and January 1943, as it was correctly anticipated that they would be finished more quickly than large carriers. More generally, aircraft played a central role in opposing German submarine operations.

War in the Pacific

Air power was also vital to the Pacific war, both in conflict between fleets and in support of amphibious attacks. This began when Japanese aircraft from six carriers sank five American battleships at Pearl Harbor on 7 December 1941.[56] Japan rapidly created an extensive empire in South-East Asia and the Western Pacific in the winter of 1941–2, in large part as a result of successful amphibious operations, with air power providing a powerful aid against Allied navies.

Concerned about the war with Germany, the British had mistakenly hoped that the defence of Malaya and Singapore would benefit from the strength of the American fleet in the western Pacific, and they also seriously mishandled their own naval units in the face of Japanese air power. A powerful squadron from Singapore was sent to contest the Japanese landings in Malaya, but, on 10 December 1941, Japanese land-based naval bombers sank the battleship *Prince of Wales* and the battle-cruiser *Repulse*. These were the first ships of these types sunk in open sea solely by air attack, and their loss demonstrated the vulnerability of capital ships without air cover to enemy air attack. The poorly-conceived and executed plan of the force commander, Admiral Sir Tom Phillips, reflected wider issues, including of British air-sea coordination.[57]

Two months later, in the Battle of the Java Sea, Allied naval forces unsuccessfully attacked a Japanese fleet en route for Java. The Japanese fleet was well coordinated, enjoyed superior air support, and benefited from better torpedoes, whereas the American, Australian, British and Dutch warships lacked an able commander and experience of fighting together.

The Japanese sought to strengthen their empire in the South-West and Central Pacific, but were checked by the American navy in the Battle of the Coral Sea on 7–8 May. This was a new kind of naval battle, one of carrier air-power from fleets beyond the reach of gun-power. Coral Sea indicated the failure of the Pearl Harbor attack to wreck American naval power. In an early instance of their superiority in intelligence operations, the Americans had intercepted and decoded Japanese messages and were waiting for the Japanese fleet. Both sides suffered losses, including the American carrier *Lexington*, but the Japanese had not handled the operation of the battle as well as their earlier successes in the war might suggest. They failed to achieve the necessary concentration of force, a characteristic they were also to show in other naval battles. Coral Sea also demonstrated a serious problem with naval warfare in the period: the difficulty of accurate surveillance. All too often during the war there were to be mistaken estimates of opposing strength, location and direction. Coupled with this, the capability of naval air power in this period should not be exaggerated. The battle led the Japanese to abandon an attempt to mount an amphibious attack on Port Moresby in New Guinea.

Rather than focusing on Australia and the South-West Pacific, Admiral Yamamoto preferred a decisive naval battle aimed at destroying American carriers. To that end, he proposed to seize Midway Island and to lure the American carriers to destruction under the guns of his battleships. The Battle of Midway, on 4 June 1942, however, led to the loss of four Japanese aircraft carriers to American carrier-based air attack. This was a battle in which the ability to locate opposing ships was crucial. In addition, as with combined arms operations on land, the combination of fighter support with carriers in defence and with bombers in attack was important. Initial American attacks by torpedo-bombers failed, due to a lack of fighter support, but, as a result of these attacks, the Japanese fighters were unable to respond, not least because they were at a low altitude, to the arrival of the American dive-bombers. In only a few minutes, three carriers were wrecked. A fourth, the *Hiryu*, successfully took evasive action, and later launched a wave of planes that inflicted heavy damage on the *Yorktown*, but was then caught and crippled by American dive-bombers.

The American carriers then retired to avoid the approach of the Japanese battleships. The Japanese defeat owed much to American command quality,[58] to the American ability to seize advantage of unexpected opportunities, and to the more general resilience of American naval capability. Japanese failure reflected factors particular to the battle, as well as more general issues, including the use of their submarines.[59]

Midway demonstrated that battles at sea would now be dominated by air power rather than the exchanges between battleships seen at Tsushima (1905) and Jutland (1916). Indeed, although the Japanese built the *Yamato* class of battleships with an 18-inch main armament that surpassed those mounted by other navies' battleships, these battleships, the *Yamato* and *Musashi*, were to fall victim to American carrier-based air power, while the third in the class was converted during construction into an aircraft carrier. The *Musashi* was sunk in 1944, while the 71,659-ton *Yamato*, sunk on 7 April 1945, fell victim, with most of its accompanying warships, to attack by over 375 planes when it unsuccessfully attempted to disrupt the American invasion of the island of Okinawa. In turn, the Americans cancelled the large battleships of the projected *Montana* class, as well as scrapping two unfinished ships of the *Iowa* class.

Midway also changed the arithmetic of Pacific air power because the Americans proved far more able to replace trained pilots; although the extent to which this battle was a turning point can be taken only so far.[60] More generally, alongside the availability of superior resources, the effective use of American air power, and the development not only of carrier tactics but of successful air–naval co-operation, was instrumental in the defeat of Japanese forces. Multiple tasking included fighter combat to gain control of the skies, dive-bombing and torpedo attack to destroy ships, and ground attack to help amphibious operations. For example, on 3–4 March 1943, a convoy carrying troops to reinforce New Guinea was attacked by American and Australian planes with the loss of over 3600 Japanese troops and four destroyers.

Yet, after Midway, the Japanese still had a large navy that was particularly strong in battleships, cruisers and destroyers, and was adept at night actions where American air superiority was of limited value. Off the island of Guadalcanal in the South-West Pacific, from August 1942 to February 1943, there was a struggle for the naval dominance correctly seen as crucial to the struggle there onshore. In the Battle of the Santa Cruz Islands on 26 October 1942, a strong Japanese fleet including four carriers attacked an American fleet containing only two carriers, and the Americans lost one of their carriers. However, the heavier loss of Japanese aircraft and, even more, aircrew, was a major blow. From mid-November, however, the Americans were successful in defeating the Japanese off Guadalcanal.

The strength and nature of the American industrial base played a key role. After being practically matched by Japan in naval construction in 1937–41, the Americans outbuilt the Japanese by a wide margin in 1942–5 in all ship types, and most dramatically in carriers. The Japanese built 10, while the Americans had 88 carriers of all types and sizes in commission in March 1945, with another 25 under construction. Although the majority of the carriers were relatively small 'escort' carriers, 26 fast carriers were in service in March 1945, with another 16 in construction. An additional 31 carriers were on order. American shipbuilding was linked to the commissioning of more modern ships, such that those commissioned in the late 1930s, were in some respects obsolete by the close of the war.

Owing to their losses in 1942, the Japanese had lost their lead in carrier strength and, by the spring of 1943, only one fleet carrier was prepared for conflict. The others listed were damaged or were light carriers. Three more fleet carriers were due for completion that year, but the Americans were planning or building far more. There was also a major disparity as far as cruisers, destroyers and submarines were concerned. The marked difference in the industrial capability and effective war mobilisation of the two powers was readily apparent, and this difference was to be accentuated by naval action. Whereas the Japanese navy could not strike at the American economy, the inroads of American submarines affected the movement of raw materials to Japan and, therefore, its industrial capability. The contrast between the two economies was also seen in the construction of merchant shipping, in which the Americans opened up a massive lead.

The British were able to deploy only limited naval strength against Japan until the closing year of the war. The Japanese concentration on the Pacific from May 1942 ensured that there were no raids into the Indian Ocean, and no British warship was lost there in 1943. The British fleet focused on the Mediterranean and Atlantic and, whereas the British had had two carriers to cover the attack on Madagascar in May 1942, from January 1943 there were none until October, when an escort carrier arrived.

In the Pacific, the use to which resources were put was crucial. Thus, logistics interacted with operational considerations, as it was very important to manage fuel resources in order to meet the repeated need to refuel ships.[61] The Japanese were less effective than the Americans at convoy protection and anti-submarine warfare and devoted fewer resources to them, not least through not providing adequate air cover. In addition, they achieved little with submarine warfare, partly because they insisted on hoarding torpedoes for use against warships. Despite initial problems with their torpedoes, which, for example, affected operations off the Philippines in the winter of 1941–2, effective long-range American submarines sunk 1114 Japanese merchantmen, and forced the Japanese to abandon many of their convoy routes in 1944. The Japanese failed to build sufficient ships to match their losses, their trade was dramatically cut, and the Japanese imperial economy was shattered. The USA thus became the most successful practitioner of submarine warfare in history. The submarine assault was also supported by mining by naval aircraft.[62]

From late 1943, as new carriers reached Pearl Harbor, the American Pacific navy benefited from a clear superiority in naval resources. The Americans created self-sufficient carrier task-groups supported by at-sea-logistics groups which did not depend on a string of bases.[63] This capability permitted the rapid advance across an unprecedented distance, with a great deal of island-hopping that destroyed any hope that the Japanese might retain a defensive perimeter in the Pacific.

Superiority in battle was also crucial. Thus, in the Battle of the Philippine Sea in June 1944, an American fleet with 15 carriers and 902 aircraft devastated its Japanese opponent, which had 9 carriers and 450 aircraft, and this victory enabled the Americans to overrun the Marianas, a decisive advance of Allied power into the Western Pacific. In the battle, the Japanese air attacks on 19 June, located by American radar, were shot down by American fighters and by anti-aircraft fire from supporting warships, with no damage to the American carriers, while the Japanese lost two carriers to American submarines. The following day, the Americans sunk or severely damaged three Japanese carriers with a long-range air attack in the failing light. The Japanese carriers were protected by a screen of Zero fighters but, as a clear sign of growing Japanese weakness in the air, this screen was too feeble to resist the fighter aircraft that supported the American bombers. The Japanese navy lacked the capacity to resist the effective American assault, and also suffered from poor doctrine and an inadequate understanding of respective strategic options. The Americans also benefited from more experienced pilots.[64]

Although carriers were the key, battleships, cruisers and destroyers also played a major role, not least in the shore bombardments that assisted the sequencing of American landings that put pressure on the Japanese. There were also significant clashes between surface ships. Thus, on 14 November 1942, off the contested island of Guadalcanal, the radar-controlled fire of the battleship *Washington* pulverised the Japanese battleship *Kirishima*. Covering the landing on Bougainville in the Solomon Islands on 1 November 1943, a force of American cruisers and destroyers beat off an attack that night by a similar Japanese squadron, with losses to the latter in the first battle fought entirely by radar. In October 1944, in the Battle of the Surigao Strait, the last battle between battleships, the long-range radar-controlled fire of the American battleships was again decisive. Destroyer torpedo attacks could also be very effective, as when used by the Japanese off Guadalcanal on 13 and 30 November 1942.[65]

The Battle of the Surigao Strait was part of the larger Battle of Leyte Gulf (23–26 October), a struggle waged by the Japanese in order to thwart the American invasion of the Philippines, just as the Battle of the Philippine Sea was a response to the invasion of the island of Saipan. In contrast, the German fleet lacked an ability to respond in a comparable fashion to Anglo-American invasions in the European theatre. Leyte Gulf was the result of Operation Sho in which the Japanese sought to intervene by luring the American carrier fleet away, and then using two striking forces to attack the American landing fleet. This characteristically complex scheme, which posed serious problem for the ability of American admirals to read the battle (and for their Japanese counterparts in following the plan), nearly succeeded as one of the strike forces was able to approach the landing area. In the event, the net effect of the battle was heavy destruction of the Japanese fleet, with the loss of four carriers, three battleships and ten cruisers.[66]

In response to American naval strength, the Japanese, from October 1944, employed kamikaze attacks in which aircraft would be flown into ships, making the aircraft themselves bombs or, rather, manned missiles. These attacks led to the sinking of 49 ships, with another 300 damaged, and were designed to sap American will. Initially, the percentage of hits and near-misses were over a quarter, but the success rate fell the following spring as the Japanese increasingly relied on inexperienced pilots, while American air defences improved with more anti-aircraft guns and fighter patrols. The Japanese lost about 4000 men in these attacks.

Amphibious warfare

Both in the Pacific and in Europe, the Americans acquired great experience in ship-to-shore operations. The war saw amphibious operations of an hitherto unprecedented scale and complexity, with close coordination by air, land and sea forces. All major powers practised such operations, but the scale varied greatly. The Germans focused on short-range amphibious invasions, most obviously of Norway in 1940, but their strength on land, combined with their weakness at sea relative to the British navy, ensured that most German invasions were primarily land attacks. The Soviets subordinated naval units to land operations, and their amphibious advances, for example against the Japanese in the Kurile Islands and southern Sakhalin in August and early September 1945, were small-scale. In contrast, the Americans and the British used amphibious operations as the building blocks of strategy, most obviously in the invasions of Italy in 1943 and France in 1944. Specialised landing vessels were developed, not only seagoing ships, but also smaller landing-craft, and truly amphibious vehicles. This development enhanced the tempo of amphibious assaults.

The military writer J.F.C. Fuller pointed out that Operation Overlord, the Allied landing in Normandy on D-Day, 6 June 1944, registered a key transformation in amphibious operations as there was now no need to capture a port in order to land, reinforce and support the invasion force. Fuller wrote in the *Sunday Pictorial* of 1 October 1944:

> had our sea power remained what it had been, solely a weapon to command the sea, the garrison Germany established in France almost certainly would have proved sufficient. It was a change in the conception of naval power which sealed the doom of that great fortress. Hitherto in all overseas invasions the invading forces had been fitted to ships. Now ships were fitted to the invading forces ... how to land the invading forces in battle order ... this difficulty has been overcome by building various types of special landing boats and pre-fabricated landing stages.

To Fuller, this development matched the tank in putting the defence at a disadvantage. The preliminary attack on the German-held French port of Dieppe on 19 August 1942, in effect a small-scale practice for the Allied landing on D-Day, had shown that attacking a port destroyed it. This assault on a well-fortified position led to heavy Allied, mainly Canadian, casualties, to accurate machine-gun, artillery and mortar fire. The failure at Dieppe underlined the problems of amphibious attacks on a port, and also those posed by a landing in the face of unsuppressed defensive fire. In 1944, instead, the Allies decided to bring two prefabricated harbours composed of floating piers with the invasion, although to sustain subsequent operations, it was necessary to gain control of ports, particularly Antwerp, in order to deal with logistical problems. The same was true of the Allied invasion of the South of France, Operation Dragoon, and the need to gain control of Marseilles.

By 1944, the Allies had totally taken the lead in the development and production of landing-craft. Aside from the general landing-craft with bows that became ramps, new specialised landing-craft were produced that could land vehicles. In 1940, the British launched their first Landing-craft Tank (LCT). There was also a marked improvement in landing-craft for troops. For example, the American Marines first used Higgins boats, also known as Eurekas, which were wooden infantry landing-craft. Constructed at first for civilian use, they could be easily withdrawn from a beach, but their wooden hulls proved vulnerable, and they were replaced in 1943. Faced by the coral reefs of the Pacific in the Tarawa landing that November, the Americans employed tracked landing vehicles, as well as tank landing ships, and the dock landing ships that could flood their decks so that landing boats could be dispatched through the stern gates.

The Mediterranean provided the Allies with important experience with amphibious landings. Operation Torch – the largely American invasion of Vichy-ruled Morocco (Atlantic beaches) and Algeria (Mediterranean) in 1942 – was followed by Anglo-American invasions of Sicily and mainland Italy in 1943. The success of the Torch landings was only a limited indicator of capability, as opposition to them had been weak. The landings of 1943, in contrast, like that at Anzio in Italy in January 1944, provided ample warnings about the difficulty of invading France, notably in progressing from landings to breakout in the face of strong German resistance. Breakout was not a matter of naval operations and, unless it could be readily achieved, the value of the naval capability that permitted an invasion was limited. Nevertheless, the ability to mount amphibious attacks and then to sustain the troops that had been landed was such that Anglo-American land operations were in large part an expression of maritime power.

The Americans also acquired considerable experience of amphibious operations against the Japanese in the Pacific. Powered landing-craft ensured that it was possible to attack defended coastlines along a wide front and simultaneously, which greatly limited options for the defenders. The British and Americans thus gained important cumulative experience in successful amphibious operations, including the use of landing-craft, and in their coordination with naval and air support. Thus, the American landing on the Pacific island of Saipan in June 1944 benefited from the lessons learned when attacking the island of Tarawa the previous November. The Allies' development of effective specialised craft and weapons, including tracked landing vehicles, amphibious tanks, and tanks developed by the British to attack coastal defences, for example Crab flail tanks for use against minefields, contributed to their improved capability.

The position of Japan in the summer of 1945 was an indication of the great value of naval power and a product of the American success in destroying the Imperial Japanese Navy. Although the Japanese still ruled large areas in East and South-East Asia, these forces were isolated. American submarines operated with few difficulties in the Yellow and East China Seas and the Sea of Japan. Carrier-borne planes attacked Japan, while warships bombarded coastal positions, including by daylight. As in Germany toward the close of the war, naval construction ended under Allied attack. The Americans could plan where they wanted to mount an invasion of Japan. The atomic attacks on Hiroshima and Nagasaki in August 1945 were launched from islands captured by amphibious attack, and the bombs were transported by sea. Just as the Battle of the Atlantic had ended in Allied triumph, so the naval war in the Pacific had been decisively won.

7 1945–2010

The changing nature of naval power

In the post-war world, the potential of warships as a delivery system for hitherto unprecedented power developed. Part of the importance of air and later, sea, more specifically submarine, power lay in their role as delivery platforms for nuclear bombs and later, missiles. The American *George Washington* was the first fleet ballistic missile submarine, commissioned in late 1959 and firing the first Polaris missile from under water in July 1960. *George Washington* and its four sister submarines were the prototypes of the first generation of American, British and French fleet ballistic missile submarines, with sixteen missiles in two rows in the central part of the hull. The Soviet Union, in contrast, originally built several smaller ballistic missile submarines with only a few missiles each in the turret, but they soon changed to the 16-missile configuration, ensuring a remarkable standardisation in type. The first British Polaris test missile was fired from a submarine in 1968, and the French commissioned their first ballistic missile submarine in 1969.

Nuclear-powered propulsion meant that the submarines did not have to come to the surface, and could thus benefit, in hiding from attack, from the vastness of the oceans, while the availability of submarine-based nuclear weapons ensured that submarines acquired a strategic capability for both attack and deterrence. As a consequence, anti-submarine warfare also took on a strategic dimension. The American navy deployed a large number of attack submarines to counter the Soviet ballistic missile submarines.

As with earlier periods, however, it would be misleading to assess only the high-spectrum end of naval power and to focus on such a narrow definition of capability, not least because the ballistic missiles were never employed. Instead, it is necessary to consider the wide range of functions that were discharged by navies. Their competitor, air power, in some respects, complemented or even superseded its naval counterpoint, as in the rapid dispatch of troops to distant trouble-spots. Nevertheless, naval power also had an increasing attraction to major powers as colonial positions were challenged and, later, as these states sought to project their strength and to influence newly-independent 'Third World' countries. The sea was a safer, and less contentious, dimension than land for a number of reasons, both political and military. Power deployed over the horizon was less conspicuous and less vulnerable. In part, navies also benefited in avoiding attack from the degree to which irregular forces operated far less at sea than on land. In addition, at sea, it was easier for warships to distinguish and assess other vessels, and thus to avoid the situation on land in which guerrillas could be indistinguishable from the civilian population. The sea, in short, could be known.

Naval power therefore offered reach, mobility and logistical independence, and provided a dynamic quality that was lacking from fixed overseas garrisons. Navies could also seem to provide a way for states to demonstrate resolve without running the risks attendant on such commitment on land. The display character of such naval power was seen in both peace and war, for example with the deployment of the British Pacific Fleet in 1945, which was in part an effort, notably by Churchill, to ensure that Britain retained imperial power in Asia.[1] The potential such power offered for enabling states to 'punch above their weight' encouraged investment in major capital ships, which meant aircraft carriers as it had earlier meant battleships. This display character, however, was dominated by the USA, as the American position at sea matched that of Britain after 1815, albeit with a greater capability. As with Britain in the earlier period, this was not a position that was matched on land.

The USA as the naval superpower

From 1945, the Americans oversaw the oceans to a degree unmatched in history. The war ended as the *Midway*, the first of a new generation of three 45,000-ton American aircraft carriers, was completed. It was considerably larger than earlier carriers, and had both increased aircraft capacity (144 planes) and an armoured flight deck.[2] The complement, including the air group, was 4100 men, and the *Midway* carried 18 5-inch guns as well as 84 Bofor and 28 Oerlikon anti-aircraft guns. The *Midway*'s sister ship, the *Roosevelt*, was sent to the eastern Mediterranean in 1946 to bolster Western interests in the face of Soviet pressure on Greece and Turkey, and from late 1947 there was at least one American carrier in the Mediterranean.[3]

The American navy, however, was in competition with the other services, and, in 1949, its programme was rejected and its major construction project cancelled, in favour of the Air Force's plans for strategic bombing.[4] Ground-based air power appeared more potent than hitherto as a result of the development of aerial refuelling. It is ironic that the President at the time, Truman, wielding the axe and cancelling what would have been the first American super-carrier, the *United States*, now has a *Nimitz*-class carrier named in his honour.

Nevertheless, technology combined with economic resources to give the US fleets a strength and capability that the British navy had lacked even at the height of its power. The American navy also had a role. In the 1950s and early 1960s, their carriers were assigned strategic bombing duties, not least the use of a nuclear strike capability. The three ships of the *Midway* class had their flight decks strengthened and in 1950 the first launch of a nuclear-armed plane from a carrier took place from the *Coral Sea*.[5]

Moreover, the USA was able to deploy and apply a formidable amount of naval strength in the Korean and Vietnam Wars, and carrier-based aviation played a crucial part in both conflicts, notably for ground support and for bombing. The Korean War saw the Americans use the turbojet aircraft that had entered service in 1949; the first successful carrier landing of a jet aircraft had taken place on the British carrier *Ocean* in December 1945. This deployment led to the first all-jet air battles, as American jets fought Soviet MiG-15s. In addition to air combat, naval jets attacked ground targets, such as bridges across the River Yalu. The scale of American naval airpower was indicated by the number of F9F-2 to F9F-5 jets manufactured for the navy and the Marine Corps up to January 1953, 1385 in total. By late 1954, the navy had 16 carrier air groups.

Aside from the firepower of naval ordnance and aircraft, the American navy provided amphibious capability, shown, most significantly during the Korean War, by the Inchon landing in September 1950 and the Hungnam evacuation three months later, and also offered logistical strength. Most of the American troops and supplies that crossed the Pacific to Korea and Vietnam came by sea. The North Koreans, North Vietnamese and their Soviet and Chinese supporters were in no position to attack American supply lines and did not try to do so.[6]

In the Vietnam War, there was an additional commitment and capability, that of riverine warfare by a large brown-water navy, which was part of the interdiction process designed to prevent the movement of supplies from North Vietnam to the Viet Cong. Offshore, American warships including submarines also contributed to the interdiction, as did the South Vietnamese navy. Earlier, and in controversial circumstances, a clash at sea, with North Vietnamese torpedo boats attacking American warships in the Gulf of Tonkin, had played a key role in the escalation of American involvement in the conflict.[7] In both the Korean and the Vietnam Wars, the warships of America's allies, such as Australia in both and Britain in the Korean War, also played a role.

However, as the Vietnam War demonstrated, naval and/or air power, in both of which the USA was unmatched, can rarely win wars: the killer punch on the ground has to be administered by an army, but, more generally, there is the problem of relating military effort to a viable political strategy for victory. Output is not the same as outcome.

The building of new ships[8] and the upgrading of weaponry and communications kept the Americans in the leading position. During the period of the so-called 'balanced navy', from 1949 to 1968, the navy emphasised force projection, specifically an amphibious capability able to seize and hold forward bases and to intervene throughout the world, as well as an ability to hold sea lanes to critical theatres, especially Europe, a task that led to anti-submarine requirements, and a role in aerial and later ballistic attack on the Soviet Union. A key capacity for American naval intervention was that in Western Europe in the event of Soviet invasion. In 1946, the American navy asked the British to provide a detailed survey of their beaches in order to aid invasion after a Soviet conquest. In Operation Sandstone, British Naval

Intelligence had surveyed half the coastline by 1965, including the likely invasion area of South Wales twice.

The emphasis was on force projection and not on a Mahanian focus on fleet engagements at sea with a Soviet navy.[9] Indeed, in 1962, the American navy successfully isolated the Soviet client state of Cuba during a crisis created by the deployment of Soviet missiles. The American navy enforced the blockade and employed a total of 183 warships.[10] Soviet ships seeking to reach Cuba were intercepted and turned back, an American capability that encouraged the Soviet Union to build up its navy.

The USA also dominated the naval influence offered by the disposal of surplus vessels. The 1944 Surplus Property Act permitted the sale of minor vessels at low prices. A transfer of major warships to Latin America took place in 1951 under the auspices of the Mutual Defense Assistance Plan, with Argentina, Brazil and Chile each receiving two heavy cruisers. By 1956, every state on the continent which had an American naval mission had signed a bilateral defence agreement under which they received financial help in return for specialising in anti-submarine warfare. British influence declined markedly, with, for example, the US establishing a naval mission in Chile after Britain in 1944 decided that to do so would anger the Americans.

The Cold War

American naval strength, however, was challenged in the Cold War between the Western and Communist blocs by the growth of rival navies, notably a Soviet navy threatening transatlantic routes and a submarine-launched missile attack on the USA, which became a major concern from 1953.[11] The American navy was also threatened by the development of anti-ship weaponry, specifically the missiles that took forward the threat posed in the Second World War by German radio-guided glide-bombs. The potential of missiles was demonstrated in October 1967, during the Egyptian–Israeli conflict, when the destroyer *Eliat*, the Israeli flagship (a Second World War ship purchased in 1955), was sunk by Soviet-supplied Styx missiles (employing radar homing) used by the Egyptians. This sinking, the first strike against an enemy ship by surface-to-surface missiles, and the first wartime use of a cruise missile,[12] was a major challenge to the USA as it was no longer trying to develop this type of weapon, an early version of which, the ASM-N-2 or Bat, had been developed in 1945–8. In response to the sinking of the *Eliat*, the USA pushed ahead with a cruise missile programme, as did the French.

The Soviet Union also responded to the enhanced American submarine capability. The American nuclear-propelled *Nautilus*, capable of sailing submerged around the world at 25 knots as it did not need to surface in order to replenish batteries, had represented a revolution in such capability, one demonstrated in 1958 when the *Nautilus* sailed under the Arctic polar ice cap, a voyage encouraged as a way of restoring American prestige after the launch of the Soviet *Sputnik* satellite. The Soviets responded with the *Moskva* class of helicopter carriers equipped with dipping sonars and nuclear-tipped anti-submarine missiles. Anti-submarine capability also improved, with Magnetic Anomaly Detection equipment and new homing torpedoes.

The build-up of the Soviet fleet that began in the 1950s under Admiral Sergei Gorshkov quickly made the Soviet Union the world's number two naval power,[13] supplanting Britain by 1971, although the geographical range of the Soviet fleet was less than that of Britian had been. Soviet warships, for example, rarely visited the Indian Ocean, the Caribbean, the South Atlantic or the South Pacific, although a global network of bases was established in client states such as Somalia, Syria and Vietnam. Soviet success in attaining the position of number two was facilitated by the earlier American wartime destruction of the Japanese navy and by the post-war decline of the British navy.

The British navy in the early 1950s still saw itself as committed to protect the worldwide interests of greater Britain,[14] but this mission was to come under lethal pressure. Britain's failure in the Suez Crisis of 1956 was followed by a retreat from empire. The Anglo-French attack on Egypt was politically misconceived and also poorly planned, in part a reflection of the lack of operational capability that arose from the failure to create a strong doctrine, an institutional focus for amphibious forces, and adequate forces and shipping.[15] Nevertheless, the invasion saw a large-scale display of military power, including three British and two French carriers, before American opposition led to its abandonment.[16] Although there was no immediate relationship with the crisis, 1956 saw Britain cede its position as the leading ship-building country to Japan.

Lord Mountbatten, then First Sea Lord, wrote in 1956: 'The [British] Navy has begun to assume its new streamline form for the atomic age',[17] but streamlining was followed by repeated adjustments downwards due to financial stringency. The British navy was also challenged by the protagonists of land-based air power. The 1957 Defence White Paper declared that 'the role of naval forces in total war is uncertain'. The Reserve fleet, including four of the surviving five battleships, was scrapped, and the number of naval personnel cut, although Mountbatten successfully lobbied to save the carriers in the face of a Minister of Defence who regarded them as expensive and outmoded. The Chiefs of Staff had reported that it was crucial to retain the Fleet Air Arm as it offered a way to deploy air power in regions where ground-based planes could not be used.[18] The abolition of the Board of Admiralty in 1964 symbolised the abandonment of past structures.

British naval retrenchment led other powers to adopt roles previously played by the Royal Navy. From 1949, in response to British overstretch, the Australian navy became largely responsible for the defence of sea communications in the ANZAM (Australia, New Zealand and Malaya) region, and in 1951 the Radford–Collins agreement underlined co-operation between the American and Australian navies.

Looked at differently, the British navy was able to achieve its goals, especially anti-submarine capability in the North Atlantic, and force projection in support of land operations, most prominently in Kuwait (1961), Brunei (1962) and in north Borneo during the confrontation with Indonesia in 1963–6. The navy then played a defensive role by blocking Indonesian incursions, and offensive roles with its helicopters and aircraft, and in terms of force projection and logistics.[19] As a more minor action, the navy, in 1953, landed Royal Marines in Deception Island in the contested South Shetland Islands off Antarctica, removing Argentinian and Chilean bases that were seen as a threat to the British position in the Falkland Islands. In 1964, mutinies by military units in newly independent Kenya, Tanganyika and Uganda led to a successful British response, which included the transport of troops by sea at Aden and their helicopter landing at Dar-es-Salaam. Alliance with the USA, notably through the North Atlantic Treaty Organisation (NATO), lessened the threat to British maritime security posed by the rise of Soviet naval power, and, in combination with the Americans, the British navy was able to act as a major force.

No other Western European navy rose to a position comparable to Britain in the 1950s, nor to that of the Soviet Union. Wrecked in the war, the French navy and its infrastructure were revived in the early 1950s, in part with American help, but this revival was compromised by Franco-American differences, and French naval construction and deployment were reduced in the late 1950s.[20] The navy did not have an important role in France's major military commitment in the late 1950s and early 1960s, that of combating insurrection in Algeria, while France's military commitment to NATO was largely that of defending a share of the frontier along the Iron Curtain.

The Canadian navy, which had been the world's third largest in 1945, continued thereafter to develop the anti-submarine capability it had rapidly expanded to provide during the Second World War, although now the goal was Soviet threats to Canadian sea-routes. In the 1970s, however, Canadian naval expenditure fell rapidly.[21] The surviving German navy was dismantled by the Allies in 1945, but a West German navy was established from 1955, largely financed by the USA, which provided equipment, including destroyers. The provision of assistance reflected the American concern to establish NATO's anti-submarine capability, especially by bottling up Soviet submarines in the Baltic. In the 1960s, the American-provided ships were supplemented by German-built destroyers and frigates as well as American destroyers armed with guided missiles. By the 1980s, the West German navy was, in conjunction with NATO allies, operating as a true blue-water navy.[22]

Aside from changes in the respective position of the naval powers, naval force-structures and doctrines changed greatly after 1945. The age of the battleship passed, as those built in the inter-war period were scrapped to be followed by others launched during the Second World War. The 44,500-ton *Vanguard*, the largest battleship built for a European navy, laid down in 1941 and commissioned in 1946, was the only European battleship commissioned after the war, and it was scrapped in 1960. When

NATO, and particularly the Royal Navy, became concerned about the development of the *Sverdlov*-class cruisers by the Soviet Union in the late 1940s and early 1950s, *Vanguard* was recommissioned, as her 15-inch guns and the 6-inch guns of the cruiser force were considered better *Sverdlov* killers than the current daylight-only strike aircraft. However, in the mid-1950s, having also disposed of the Axis powers' battleships in the Second World War, the American and British navies reduced their reliance on battleships as all-weather strike aircraft were becoming a possibility, for example with the British De Havilland Sea Venom FAW21, followed by the Supermarine Scimitar. The manpower demands and cost of maintaining battleships were also factors. The French *Jean Bart* was the last European battleship to be completed, although it had fought as a coastal battery at Casablanca in 1942, in spite of being far from complete. In the Suez Crisis of 1956, the *Jean Bart* became the last European battleship to fire a shot in anger.

In 1949, the American navy only had one battleship (the *Missouri*) and thirteen cruisers in active service, although American battleships subsequently returned to use. The *New Jersey* was recommissioned in 1968 in order to serve off Vietnam, providing gunfire support for American units under attack in South Vietnam. The *New Jersey* was decommissioned in 1968, but American battleships were subsequently in service, including off Lebanon in the 1980s and, the *Missouri* and *Wisconsin*, firing shells and cruise missiles, in the Gulf War of 1991.

The decline of the battleship focused attention on aircraft carriers. Three French carriers operated off Vietnam against the Viet Minh in the unsuccessful French attempt to retain control in 1946–54, while one British carrier was deployed during the Korean War, and three British and two French carriers in the Suez crisis of 1956. The British increased the capability of their carriers with the angled flight deck, the steam catapult, and, in 1960, the first V/STOL, vertical/short takeoff and landing aircraft, based on carriers. These aircraft did not require fleet carriers, and, in 1966, after a major controversy, the British cancelled a planned one, the 50,000-ton CVA-01 (intended as the first of a class of three large strike aircraft carriers), preferring, instead, to rely on land-based air power and, at sea, on smaller carriers.[23] The alleged consequences of this cancellation play a role today in the debate about British needs for carriers.[24]

The cancellation of the CVA-01 marked a major shift from British naval plans earlier in the 1960s, as well as a dramatic reordering of procurement in light of domestic political priorities. In 1960, the carrier *Victorious* had joined the Far East station with several nuclear bombs, and planes able to drop them, aboard. Subsequent war planning called for the use of a carrier able to mount nuclear strikes on southern China, and for a second carrier to be deployed in 1964. The British presence in the India Ocean was anchored with bases in Aden and Singapore. Planning for the new submarines armed with Polaris missiles with nuclear warheads included firing stations in the Indian Ocean designed both to block Himalayan passes (through which the Chinese could advance on India) and to reach targets in southern Russia.[25] However, the mismatch between commitments and resources under pressure from severe fiscal difficulties led the government to announce in January 1968 that it was abandoning Britain's position east of Suez.[26] The previous year, the South Africa and South Atlantic Naval Station was abolished.

Thereafter, British naval priorities were largely defined by NATO roles until the 1990s. The British withdrawal from east of Suez had implications for other powers. Until the 1960s, the Indian navy was equipped with surplus British warships, and links between the two navies were close. Subsequently, the Indians increasingly looked elsewhere. The American role in the Indian Ocean in the early 1960s was minor, with only a small squadron showing the flag in the Persian Gulf, but this changed from the 1970s. The British encouraged the American naval build-up in the Indian Ocean, making the island colony Diego Garcia available to the USA as a naval base. In late 1974, an American carrier entered the Persian Gulf, the first such deployment since 1948.[27]

The USA dominated carrier capability and enhanced the effectiveness of the carriers, swiftly emulating the British innovations of the steam catapults (1951), angled decks (1952) and mirror landing systems (1953). The Americans also integrated carrier strength into other military purposes. Thus, in the 1950s and early 1960s, American carriers were assigned strategic bombing duties in the event of war with the Soviet Union, and the Americans developed carrier-based strategic nuclear bombers; followed by the British with the nuclear strike-capable Blackburn Buccaneer.

The most extensive use of carriers was during the Vietnam War. Then, the absence of hostile submarine attacks offered a mistaken impression of the invulnerability of carriers, which were able to provide a nearby safe base for American operations over both North and South Vietnam. Improvements in supply methods since the Second World War, for example re-supply from other ships, ensured that the American carriers were able to stay at sea for longer than hitherto. During most of 1972, no fewer than six carriers were on station, and, that summer, an average of 4000 sorties were flown monthly.[28] Although the carrier-based planes lacked the payload of the large land-based planes, especially the B-52s, they provided significant firepower both in support of grand operations in South Vietnam and in attacking ground targets in North Vietnam.

Naval conflict

Although the Chinese and Japanese were to become major naval powers in the last quarter of the twentieth century, the limited number of states with any significant naval effectiveness, prior to that, helped ensure that the sea was essentially used for sea-to-land operations, rather than contested between marine powers. There were no major naval conflicts in the three decades after the Second World War. The wars of decolonisation were waged on land, although the imperial powers, Britain, France, the Netherlands and Portugal, used the sea to ensure troop movements and supply, to mount amphibious attacks, and to interdict the movement of insurgents.[29] The vulnerability of warships was demonstrated in the Corfu Channel in 1946, when a force of British warships passing through international waters was shelled by Albanian shore batteries, and, when a demonstration passage was subsequently organised to uphold the law of the sea and Britain's naval prowess, two destroyers were badly damaged by mines laid by the Albanians.

There were hostilities at sea in the Arab–Israeli Wars of 1967 and 1973, and the Indo-Pakistan conflicts of 1965 and 1971, with the Indians successfully using Soviet-supplied Styx missiles in attacks on the port of Karachi; but these hostilities were limited as the wars were waged between contiguous states and most of the fighting took place on land. The same was true of the Iran–Iraq war of 1980–8, in which both sides used Silkworms, the Chinese-manufactured copy of the Styx, more properly known as the HY-2 Hai Ying (Sea Eagle), but attacks then on commercial shipping or oil platforms, while important as economic warfare and as efforts to affect other powers, were subsidiary to the bitter conflict on land.

In contrast, naval operations were crucial to the Falklands War of 1982 between Britain and Argentina. The Falkland archipelago in the South Atlantic had been under British control from 1833 and had a British settler population, but was claimed, as the Malvinas, by the Argentinians. Their navy had long sought to regain the Falklands in order to demonstrate its role in protecting the patrimony, and a desire to propriate naval opinion led the junta who headed the military dictatorship to decide to act. In 1977, threatening Argentinian manoeuvres were countered by the British with a task force of two frigates and a submarine. However, in 1982, a new junta, under pressure from its naval member and convinced that the British government would not respond forcefully, successfully invaded the virtually undefended islands. Their tiny garrison lacked air and naval support.

In the event, assured that the navy could fulfil the task, the British government sent an expeditionary force. A total of 51 ships were to take part in the operation, while, as another sign of British maritime strength and of the continuing need to rely on a broad-based maritime system, 68 ships were 'taken up from trade' – contracted and requisitioned – including the cruise ships *Queen Elizabeth II* and *Canberra*, which were used to transport troops, and the container ship *Atlantic Conveyor*, which, in the event, was to be sunk by an Exocet missile, taking a large amount of stores to the bottom. Indeed, air-launched bombs and Exocets led to the loss of six British ships. Another 11 were damaged, while 13 badly-fused bombs hit ships but failed to explode, a key instance of the role of chance factors. British losses showed that modern anti-aircraft missile systems were not necessarily a match for manned aircraft, and also revealed a lack of adequate preparedness on the part of the navy, which had to rely on missile systems not hitherto tested in war.

Naval support was essential for the mounting of the amphibious assault by which Britain sought to regain the Falklands.

Britain, however, lacked a large aircraft carrier, and therefore airborne early warning (AEW) of attack on its fleet by Argentinian planes, although this lack of AEW was due primarily to strategic policy assumptions about the navy operating only in the East Atlantic, where it was to be covered by the NATO air umbrella, and, specifically, within the range of RAF early-warning aircraft. For the Falklands campaign, there were, nevertheless, two anti-submarine carriers equipped with Sea Harrier short take-off fighter-bombers armed with Sidewinder AIM-L missiles. These contested Argentinian air assaults on the task force, and thanks to the carriers, which the Argentinians were unable to sink, Britain had vital air support (but not superiority) for both sea and land operations.

The sinking, by a British submarine, of the Argentinian cruiser *General Belgrano*, which had been an American cruiser at Pearl Harbor in 1941, suggested (and still suggests) that, while the navies of Latin America and other regional maritime states have continued to purchase and deploy ships decommissioned by the American and European navies, it was clearly foolish to maintain in commission a ship of the size of the *Belgrano* that was over forty years old and clearly obsolete. The sinking of the *Belgrano* was crucial to the struggle for command of the sea as it led the Argentinian navy to desist from threatening attack and to withdraw to Argentinian territorial waters.[30] Thus, the sinking showed that submarines could be a platform for command of the sea rather than simple sea denial.

Once ashore, the British forces outfought the Argentinians, who surrendered. The protection of the Falklands remained thereafter a task for the British military with air power playing a role as well as the navy in supporting the garrison.

American–Soviet competition

The Falklands War, however, was exceptional in this period. As a consequence, the Cold War saw a naval race between the Soviet Union and the NATO powers that was unmediated by conflict. It was a high-cost exercise and one that, as a result of submarines and air power, was more complex than the Anglo-German naval race at the start of the twentieth century. In this naval race, it became necessary both to devise counter-measures and to ensure that the various forces that could operate on, over and under the sea co-operated effectively.

America's naval position was affected by the development of a Soviet fleet designed to support Soviet interests across the world, as well as to challenge the deployment of American and allied forces. The traditional doctrine of Soviet naval power, looking back to the reign of Peter the Great (r. 1689–1725), had emphasised support of land forces in the Baltic and Black Seas and the quest for naval superiority in these areas. However, Soviet forces based in these seas could only gain access to the oceans through straits (such as the Bosporus, Dardanelles and Kattegat) and shallow waters where they were vulnerable. A similar problem affected the Russian naval challenge to Japan from the late nineteenth century and, specifically, the Russian naval base of Vladivostok on the Sea of Japan. Indeed, Japan's contribution to American naval strategy was that of providing submarine support against Soviet ships trying to reach the Pacific.

As a result of this problem of access, the Soviet navy developed their Northern Fleet based at Murmansk. Indeed, the rise of Soviet capability was intricately linked with the foundation of submarine bases that gave the Soviets access to the Atlantic. By 1980, the Kola Peninsula contained the greatest concentration of naval power in the world. This concentration owed much to the Gulf Stream which ensured that the water off the Peninsula remained warm and did not freeze. The Northern Fleet became the largest Soviet fleet, with a particularly important submarine component. This threat obliged NATO powers to develop nearby patrol areas for submarines and underwater listening devices, and also to develop a similar capability in the Denmark Strait between Iceland and Greenland and in the waters between Iceland and Britain through which Soviet submarines would have to travel en route to the Atlantic.

The Soviet navy also built an important surface fleet, especially, from the 1960s, a fleet which included missile cruisers firing sea-to-sea missiles. In 1967 and 1973, the Soviet navy was able to make substantial deployments in the eastern Mediterranean in order to advance Soviet views during Middle Eastern crises and to threaten Israel, thus putting pressure on the USA.[31]

Soviet naval development led the Americans from 1969 to focus on planning for naval conflict with the Soviets, rather than on amphibious operations. Naval Force Atlantic was established as a standing NATO force in 1967. The emphasis was on being able to destroy Soviet naval power in battle and in its home waters before Soviet warships, and notably submarines, could depart for the oceans.[32] NATO's CONMAROPS (Concept of Maritime Operations) proposed the attack on Soviet submarines in depth in order to secure the North Atlantic sea-lines of communication for the supply and re-supply of NATO forces in Europe. This stress led to a focus on big aircraft carriers and large submarines, both intended to attack the Soviet fleet, whether surface or submarine. For example, the American blue-water reorientation in 1986 saw calls for a Maritime Strategy, and a 600-ship navy with 15 carrier groups. There was also a focus on anti-submarine warships, such that the British Type 22 *Broadsword*-class frigates of the 1980s lacked a main gun armament, as this was seen as irrelevant for their anti-submarine duties.

In contrast, the Soviet Union relied on land-based long-range bombers and reconnaissance planes and had only one aircraft carrier, the *Admiral Kuznetsov*, launched in 1985. Nevertheless, the Soviets did compete in large submarines, their *Typhoon*-class against the American *Ohio*-class. Thus, the submarine evolved into an underwater capital ship as large as the First World War dreadnought-class battleship, and with a destructive capacity never seen before (or since) in any other type of warship. The USS *Ohio* and its sister submarines were 170.7 metres long with 18,700 tons submerged displacement. The Soviet *Typhoon*-class was 171.5 metres long with 25,000 tons submerged displacement. In each case, the submerged displacement was somewhat greater than the surface displacement. By comparison, the *Dreadnought* of 1906 was 161 metres long and displaced 18,420 tons. These submarines were in a different league to the German U-boats of the Second World War.

After the Cold War

The last decade of the twentieth century was to witness the rapid decline of the Russian navy after the collapse of the Soviet Union in 1991, and to leave the USA as an even more prominent foremost naval power. Indeed, in 2008, the USA had 11 operational carriers, a number that could surge to 15 or 16 as a result of drawing on the reserve fleet. Each carrier strike force is a key element of power projection. The USA also has ten carrier wings. There has been talk of reducing the numbers to ten carriers and eight wings, but the American carrier capability remains robust and a reminder of the continuing close relationship between American power and naval strength. The launch, in January 2009, of the *Bush*, the last of the nuclear-powered *Nimitz*-class carriers (which displaced 78,000 tons), was a testimony to the American defence economy. The ship, built at Newport News, is to be followed in about three years by the first of four of the new *Ford* class that has been ordered at an estimated cost of $11.2 billion each. This nuclear-powered class is designed to have a more effective form of propulsion, while the planes are to be launched by electro-magnetic power.

At the start of 2009, the total tonnage of the American navy equalled that of the next 17 navies. The relative strength of the USA today mirrors that of the USA after 1945 prior to the Soviet build-up, and indeed of Britain after 1815. In each case, there were questions as to whether such dominance was a normal characteristic of naval power, and of how far traditional naval strategies remained appropriate, both for the leading navy and for others.

This outcome of unmatched American naval power had been less clear in the early 1970s, but, even then, the Americans were helped in comparison with the Soviet navy, not only by greater naval resources and superior infrastructure, but also by more operational experience. This experience was a matter not only of the combat experience of the Korean and Vietnam Wars, but also of peacetime training. American operational experience was maintained by a range of commitments, which included amphibious interventions, as at Beirut in 1982 and Grenada in 1983.[33]

Although the Soviet navy had become the second largest naval power, it became increasingly obsolescent in the 1980s and 1990s as it proved impossible for the Soviet Union to sustain the cost of new units. Under Mikhail Gorbachev, the General Secretary of the Communist Party from 1985 to 1991, military expenditure was reduced, while Boris Yeltsin, the Russian President from 1990 to 2000, cut budgets even more sharply. Moreover, the war he launched in 1994 in inland Chechnya understandably focused on the army. In addition, in the 1990s, the navy not only failed to sustain the operational effectiveness of both warships and bases, but was also gravely affected by the break-up of the Soviet Union. This break-up was especially important in the case of the Black Sea naval base of Sevastopol, which came under the authority of Ukraine, although it was leased to Russia in return for an annual write-off of debt by $97 million. The Baltic fleet base of Liepaja came under Latvia, and many of the ethnic Russians who had settled there returned to Russia.

Naval capability in the new millennium is very different to that on land because fewer states wield naval than land power, while the power of non-state organisations is very limited at sea. As a consequence, it is easier to think in terms of a hierarchy of strength at sea than on land, although, as in earlier periods, issues of force structure, operational effectiveness and political combination ensure that this hierarchy is more than a matter of counting warships.

More generally, American naval policy, like that of other naval powers, reflects not simply an 'objective' assessment of interests and threats, but also 'culturally-situated images of world politics ... and of the military objectives of war'.[34] The 'cultural situation' is a matter of a number of spheres. Aside from the more general views of society as a whole, there are the overlapping suppositions of government and political élites, and the specific views of naval staffs and their supporters. The domestic basis of modern American naval power does not match that of British naval power in the imperial heyday because the navy was then far more central to British concerns and self-image. Moreover, a later alternative, air power, was not a factor in the nineteenth century, and was only a relatively minor one in the early twentieth century.

The USA succeeded Britain as the strongest naval power after the Second World War, but it was also the leading air power, while both army and marines had important roles in American public culture and thus in perceptions of military identity. Thus, the navy did not come first in terms of the number of veterans and related social indices of political commitment. As an instance of the possible significance of political culture, the defeat in the Presidential election of 2008 of John McCain, a former naval pilot, by Barack Obama, a member of a community and political nexus with neither positive views about, nor commitment to naval power, may well be significant as far as the issues and nuances of military power politics are concerned.

Nor did the navy come first with reference to the combat delivery of American power. The lack of naval conflict played a role in this relative lack of centrality, as America's opponents essentially fought on land. Troops and supplies were delivered in large part by sea, as with interventions between 1982 and 2003 in Beirut, Grenada, Panama, Iraq, Somalia, Haiti and the Balkans. The same was true of the commitment to Afghanistan: most of the supplies for Allied forces were shipped to Karachi and then trucked on. However, the dependence of these military operations on naval power did not engage public attention. Indeed, the navy appeared to lose its function as a fighting service. This impression was reinforced by the fact that the strategic role of the submarine force as an invulnerable second-strike nuclear option, for the USA and Britain, was downplayed in public estimation because it was not used and indeed appeared of questionable value after the end of the Cold War.

This apparent redundancy, certainly in comparison with the 'shock and awe' of air power, whether the B-52s of the Vietnam War, or the American (and allied) air assaults on Iraq and Serbia in 1991–2003, led to an attempt by navies to assert a role that would command public attention. The expeditionary mode of American foreign policy in the 1990s and 2000s appeared to offer the navy such a role, in the shape of littoral action, but it also was challenged by air power. Indeed, airborne assault forces had earlier played key parts in Grenada and Panama. The ability to insert forces by air both provided possibilities for the American navy, as its aircraft carriers were an obvious means for launching such attacks, and yet also challenged the navy as air operations could also be based on land. Indeed, the stress, in the 1990s and 2000s, on coalition warfare ensured that such bases were available. Thus, Saudi Arabia provided the key base for the 1991 Gulf War, although most of the Allied equipment and supplies came by sea, which underlined the importance of secure sea routes.

To return to prudential considerations and rational analysis, however, is not all that helpful as impressions of capability and effectiveness rested on more diffuse factors and on irrational assumptions. In particular, the extent to which the sea was seen primarily as another basis for air operations affected the public traction of the American navy.

An economic historian might also suggest that the declining role of heavy industry in the American economy and, in particular, of steel and shipbuilding, hit the naval interest domestically, with the same process also occurring in Britain, each development reversing the change at the close of the nineteenth century. This explanation can also be related to the rise of different regional constituencies. In particular, although there was shipbuilding on the Gulf of Mexico, in Mississippi, as well as the large naval air station at Pensacola, the South, which became far more important not only to American politics but also to its public culture from the late 1960s and, even more, 1970s, had scant commitment to the navy. Instead, the army was the major focus in the South, a legacy that owed much to roots during the Confederacy and to Southern notions of masculinity.

Indeed, the move of America's centre of gravity and power from the North-East can be seen as a move away from the navy, not least because Philadelphia and Norfolk/Newport News, Virginia were established naval centres with significant shipbuilding capacity, while New London in Connecticut had become the major submarine base. The geography of naval (and air) power had already been changed during the Second World War with the rise of manufacturing activity and bases on the West Coast such as San Diego. These interests remained influential thereafter, but, from the overall perspective, the West Coast was more significant in providing a key regional component to the prominence of air power. The role of regional interests can also be probed in Russia, where the navy's headquarters were moved from Moscow to St Petersburg in 2008.

Economic changes and regional interests and images combined to affect the public view of the American navy, which, in turn, contributed greatly to the more general situation of naval power because the USA had the strongest navy. As this navy could not dominate the public's military imagination in the USA, so it was not surprising that there was not the knock-on effect elsewhere. Moreover, American influence in other countries, for example in training, was more a matter of the army than the navy, as in South America. In addition, in many states, for example China, Russia, India and Germany, the national navy's role had for long been secondary and it had scant public impact.

Newly independent colonies that acquired the naval bases of empire frequently made only limited use of the facilities. Thus, Aden was not to be the basis of South Yemeni naval power, although there were interesting changes in function, with a church built for the British military in 1863 requisitioned in 1970 as a naval store and gymnasium.

Writing about the recent, current and likely future situation is difficult because the views of naval staffs and their supporters tend to dominate discussion. Indeed advocacy plays an important role in analysis. There are major differences among such commentators over force structure, strategy and doctrine, but it is rare to find a writer on naval matters arguing that navies are anything other than fundamental to military capability and vital for national, indeed international, interests and security. These arguments became more pronounced from the 1990s.[35] In part, this rise in advocacy reflected the end of the Cold War, because, although that confrontation was a dynamic situation with changing strategic landscapes, interacting with the competing interests of particular services, the Cold War was more fixed than what was to follow.

First, the end of the Cold War led to pressure for a 'peace dividend' in the shape of lower military expenditure, and this pressure sharpened service competition, including in the USA and Britain. Secondly, and as a related factor, the strategic landscape appeared unclear in the 1990s. Thirdly, the 'War on Terror' that took centre stage from 2001 gave point and focus to this service competition. Fourthly, the relationship between this 'War on Terror' and the revival of great-power confrontation from the mid-2000s became a matter of contention that was directly linked to competing priorities in procurement, strategy and deployment.

Naval staffs played a central role in each of these developments, and the sense of opportunity and concern for the service was readily communicated both by them and by other commentators on the navy. The latter included historians. It would be reckless to imagine that value-free historical (and current) analysis is possible, but, attending conferences and reading publications, it is noteworthy that naval historians do not generally query the value of naval power nor of building more warships; a remark that will guarantee critical reviews for this book.

Power projection

In the case of the 1990s and 2000s, admirals and commentators responded to the challenges facing naval power by emphasising the inherent value of naval power,[36] by arguing the importance of littoral power projection,[37] and by seeing this projection as a key role that also provided the intellectual case for maintaining naval strength. In *From the Sea*, an 'institutional vision' statement from the American Department of the Navy issued in 1992, there was a call for a transformation towards joint operations conducted from the sea. Indeed, joint structures, operations and plans owed much to naval advocates, for example in the American Department of the Navy's *Sea Power 21* and the British Navy Board's strategic vision *Future Navy*.[38] The 1998 British Strategic Defence Review focused on an expeditionary, and thus by definition, maritime, capability.

Enhanced capability played a valuable role. Cruise missiles and helicopter-borne assault forces provided the opportunities to deliver ordnance into the interior, as well as troops from the sea without the need to fight their way across a defended beach. In 1998, for example, the USA fired 79 sea-launched cruise missiles at terrorist targets in Afghanistan and Sudan. This bombardment, however, was an impressive but futile display of force which did not stop the terrorists. Indeed, Osama bin Laden was able to raise funds by selling missiles that did not detonate to the Chinese, who were interested in cutting-edge American military technology.

Cruise missiles were also employed against Serbia in 1999 as part of a combined NATO air and missile assault designed to ensure that Serb forces withdraw from Kosovo. In 1998, the submarine *Splendid* achieved Britain's first firing of a cruise missile, which had been bought from the USA. The following year, *Splendid* fired these missiles at Serb targets in Kosovo as part of NATO operations there. During the attack in 2001 on the Taliban regime in Afghanistan – like Serbia, an inland state – cruise missiles were fired from American warships in the Arabian Sea.

Power projection was not simply a matter of delivering ordnance. There was also a greater emphasis, seen most obviously with the American and British navies, on the provision of capacity to move and land troops and supplies. Thus, the American fleet acquired 19 aircraft carrier-sized Large Medium-Speed Roll-On/Roll-Off ships,[39] while the Japanese built the *Kunisaki*, a landing platform ship.

Power projection, littoral action, the end of the Cold War and the War on Terror combined to encourage changes in force structure, doctrine and organisation, including the rise in joint command and training structures, and indeed an interest by historians in amphibious operations.[40] In 1999, *British Maritime Doctrine*, the second edition of what had been published in 1995 as *The Fundamentals of British Maritime Doctrine*, declared:

> The maritime environment is inherently *joint* ... Naval forces themselves exist to influence events ashore; they have never operated strategically in an exclusively naval environment ... the sea is a pre-eminent medium because, above all, it provides access at a time and place of political choice ... Ultimately maritime forces can only realise their considerable potential when integrated fully into a joint force.[41]

The British *Naval Strategic Plan* of 2006 stated: 'The development of new maritime Equipment Capability will provide the Future Navy with the expeditionary and versatile capabilities essential for success in the future Joint environment.'[42]

By 2009, among the NATO powers, Denmark had created a projection navy reliant on uniform-model ships that could be adapted to different tasks, Italy was building an aircraft carrier, Britain had ordered two 65,000-tonne carriers (although, in December 2008, the first, the *Queen Elizabeth*, was postponed to 2015), Spain was building a strategic projection vessel, and the Americans were developing littoral combatant ships. Japan is to acquire helicopter-equipped destroyers in order to support power projection, while Sweden has 140 Combat Boat 90 fast-attack craft capable of moving troops to the shore, as well as 3 hovercrafts. The USA is deploying twelve landing platform docks, Britain has three and the Dutch, who are putting a focus on All-Water Operations (i.e. including littoral, rivers and lakes), have two. The extent to which the recession that began in 2008 will lead to the shelving of such plans is unclear, but there were already serious and varied problems with resources. In 2008, Australia only had sufficient manpower for three of its six submarines.

Power projection against the land takes a variety of forms. In 2008, there were suggestions that if Israel attacked Iranian nuclear facilities, they might use missiles fired from recently acquired German-built submarines, rather than air attack. Africa's largest navy, that of South Africa, centred on new ships, including the largest, a support ship for amphibious operations, as well as German-built frigates and submarines. This investment, which is due to be continued with landing craft, is more impressive in the context of the cuts in overall South African military expenditure.

Trade protection

The fundamentals of maritime power and concern, however, were not those of attacks on rogue states nor other aspects of amphibious intervention, but, rather, the extent to which trade continued to be dominated by ships. Indeed, in the mid-2000s, it was estimated that there were about 40,000 merchant ships and that more than 90 per cent of global trade was carried by sea. This approach, however, underrated the importance of land transport to freight movements within states, notably the USA, China and Russia, each of which is very large, while most trade within the European Union was carried by land. Moreover, land routes are being developed to link regions, for example German Railways seeking to create routes into the Balkans.

The construction of long-distance oil and gas pipelines can be an aspect of this process, as with the movement of Russian gas to European markets, but some pipelines go under water, while others move supplies to ports for subsequent shipping, as with pipelines planned, constructed or begun for the movement of central Asian oil to Pakistan, Georgia or Turkey.

Alongside the qualifications above, maritime trade is also important for domestic as well as international trade, and overall maritime trade rose considerably in the 1990s and 2000s, increasing at a faster rate than the growth in world GDP. In 2005, two-thirds of the world's hydrocarbon energy flows moved by sea, with 20 per cent of the oil supply moving through the Straits of Hormuz. These trade flows across the global commons of the high seas, however, were vulnerable to military action, and notably so for seas and oceans to which access was gained through choke points, such as the Indian Ocean and Mediterranean, Baltic and Black Seas; whereas such choke points were absent in the Atlantic and Pacific. Other key economic elements include the undersea fibre-optic cables, which carry most international telecommunications, and offshore energy platforms producing and pumping for both oil and gas. A more traditional resource, fish, also proved the source of confrontation and indeed conflict, notably with the Turbot War between Canada and Spain in 1995, and with Japan and Korea staging a stand-off over rocks that would provide fishing rights in the Sea of Japan the following year.

The protection of trade routes was an important aspect of the Japanese view of sea power as a key constituent of national strategy. The navy was also seen as a visual statement of political purpose, with Japan sending minesweepers to the Persian Gulf in 1991 and destroyers to the Indian Ocean from 2001 on. Moreover, in December 2008, Taro Aso, the Prime Minister, instructed the Defence Ministry to find a way to deploy warships against pirates off Somalia.

Trade is a fundamental indication of the globalisation that became a more important theme in political discussion from the early 1990s, and this discussion affected strategic thought, not least when terrorism was seen in terms of a challenge to this globalisation. The two together led to pressure for distinctive, if not new, ideas in thinking about navies, notably a challenge to the basic concept of discussing procurement, doctrine and strategy in terms of the traditional practices and uses of competing navies. In particular, in consultation with many other navies, the American navy developed the concept of a maritime strategy based around a coalition navy, indeed a 1000-ship coalition navy, an idea advocated by Admiral Michael Mullen, Chief of Naval Operations from 2005 to 2007, and the basis of the Global Maritime Partnership Initiative. The American navy in late 2008 contained 275 combat and support ships.[43] The American experience of working with allied navies from the 1940s on had demonstrated its value in the two Gulf Wars and in other activities.

While piracy, terrorism and other anti-normative behaviour offered prospects for such co-operation, the revival of great-power competition from the late 2000s challenged the viability of the 1000-ship navy or suggested that any coalition might or would be another version of such competition, or could be regarded as such. In September 2008, President Sarkozy of France highlighted the challenge from piracy, especially that based in Somalia, but, by then, the possibility of co-operation spanning the USA, Britain, France and also Russia, China and Iran had greatly receded. Indeed, in the winter of 2008–9, Iran sent two destroyers to the Gulf of Aden on the pretext of fighting piracy, destroyers that were suspected of taking part in the movement of arms from Iran to the Hamas government in Gaza. At the same time, the American naval task force deployed against the pirates was instructed to track such shipments.

International co-operation would ease action against pirate bases in Somalia, which is necessary if effective steps are to be taken against pirates; a lesson clearly shown by British operations against pirates and slavers in the nineteenth and early twentieth centuries, including in Somalia in 1904.

Debating procurement

Differing prospects for naval activity accentuated debates over force structures; and the age-old interaction of proposed capabilities with projected tasks recurred. In the absence of networks of imperial bases and of what would have been a partial replacement, adequate overflying rights for airborne forces, the concept of carrier and amphibious battle groups seemed sensible as a means of ensuring or threatening intervention. At the same time, surface ships are vulnerable to modern submarines carrying modern spearfish torpedoes. This threat appears countered by the concept of a balanced fleet, with hunter-killer submarines designed to keep the threat from hostile submarines suppressed and out of range; but the equations of adequate balance will only be discovered as a result of conflict, and that will be too late. On the other hand, the same point can be made about all modern military systems.

The issue of adequate balance in fighting terms interacts with that of procurement. Thus, investment in two large carriers for the British navy, an investment in ships, planes, crew and bases, threatens the number (both existing and to be commissioned) of frigates and destroyers. However, looked at differently, Admiralty requirements for each of the latter are excessive, and thus ensure high costs, which helps ensure that the number of ships in the navy cannot be maintained. HMS *Daring*, the first of six Type 45 warships, berthed in Portsmouth, her home port, for the first time in January 2009. Designed to replace the Type 42, the Type 45, described as the world's most advanced destroyer, has a greater range and is armed with a new air-defence missile system called Sea Viper, which can track hundreds of targets up to 250 miles away, but the cost of the 7350-tonne ship is £650 million.

Similar problems exist elsewhere, and the high cost of new warships, not least of their complex electronics and of the weapons (aircraft, intercontinental and cruise missiles) they carry and launch, will ensure a pronounced level of volatility in procurement as economies expand or hit difficulties. Thus, the trajectory of growth, decline and revival seen with Soviet/Russian naval power from the 1970s to the present may well be repeated for other navies, not least, but not only, in response to the recession of the late 2000s. It is unclear, for example, whether British naval plans are sustainable, and this will doubtless be debated in the Defence Review that, in 2009, was widely anticipated as a likely consequence of the next election. Already the Ministry of Defence's Planning Round 09 saw major struggles over expenditure on new warships.

Conclusions

Such trajectories reflect not only economic and fiscal strength but also the competing constituencies of interest within the overlapping worlds of military, government and society. The high costs of a large-scale, cutting-edge naval capability are underlined by the fact that, unlike a millennium or even half a millennium ago, there is no overlap between this cutting-edge capability and direct benefit in the shape of selling naval protection, taking part in privateering or engaging in trade; although discussion of the threat from piracy will emphasise the relationship. At any rate, navies risk following air forces, at least at the cutting edge, in pricing themselves out of the business for most powers. This situation may accentuate the asymmetry in capability that is such a readily apparent feature of modern warfare.[44] Conversely, cutting-edge capability may well be the best way to deal with asymmetrical threats.

The relationship between this asymmetry at sea and asymmetry in air power is worthy of consideration, and notably if exposure to sea and air power are included in the asymmetrical relationships. The problems of suppressing violent opposition and insurrections in Iraq and Afghanistan in the mid-2000s led to greater emphasis on the difficulties that major states faced in asymmetrical warfare. These difficulties ensure that the value of investment in weapons systems such as cruise missiles and carrier-borne aircraft that project power, but often can only produce limited results on the ground, will be debated alongside the issue of the tension between output and outcome, although the two questions are not coterminous. Navies will argue for the particular value of the sea as a sphere in which power has to be maintained and also as a basis for power projection. Each argument is of great value but, in order for capability to be understood in terms of effectiveness, these arguments will need to be considered alongside the limitations and qualifications of this power.[45]

8 The future

Looking to the future, in the short term of the next few decades, the basic assumption tends to be that weapons systems similar to those of the present will continue to dominate the military situation and the equations of force and capability. This view, a key aspect of what is termed 'future proofing', may be a mistake, but it is argued that aircraft carriers, submarines, destroyers, frigates and assault vessels will be the essential warships, and that they will serve as the basis for delivering firepower (via aircraft, cruise missiles and shells) and troops. These suppositions assume that there will be scant equivalent at sea to the movement towards remotely controlled aircraft (drones) for air warfare, or that the existing platforms can be used as the basis for such weaponry. Thus, the two large British carriers ordered in 2008 are intended to remain in service until 2070 and are designed to have the space to carry new systems. The latter goal is also seen in the design of the British Type 45 destroyers.

Although there is some discussion of the consequences of electromagnetic pulses, the general assumption of identical or similar platforms to the present is matched by that about the participants in the naval power system, essentially still the major powers of today. Again, that may be mistaken, and this view also implies no equivalent at sea to the possibility of changes on land with a rise there of irregular warfare mounted by those rejecting the power and authority of existing states. Recent advances in missile, mine, submarine and aircraft technology, for example air-independent propulsion systems for diesel-electric submarines, challenge large surface ships, such as carriers, but the ability of modern navies to confront such challenges is impressive.[1]

China: The next naval great power?

If the same cast of powers is to be assumed, then the major questions at present revolve around the likely development of

America's relations with both China and Russia. China is seen as the more unpredictable and the state best able to develop naval power, a view, however, that may underplay the capacity of Russia under both heads. In 2008, China overtook Germany to become the world's third largest economy (after the USA and Japan), and did so five years earlier than the Americans had predicted as recently as five years before.

At the same time, there are very different views of Chinese naval proficiency, and of the significance of its future development. These differences extend to the helpful advice offered by the two academic readers for the synopsis of this book, one of whom remarked: 'An additional chapter is needed beyond Chapter 8 dealing with China', while the other wrote that 'the focus on China ... would be unwise. The Chinese Navy is no threat to anyone.'

The likely trajectory of Chinese naval power is clearly of importance to the global situation. Although its navy is part of the structure of the People's Liberation Army, and is indeed subordinated to the army, China is determined to develop the navy. This stronger navy is designed to be able to protect China's capacity to act against Taiwan, for example by ensuring a blockade or an invasion or, more seriously, a defence against an American attack on China mounted from the Pacific, most obviously an attack similar to that by NATO against Serbia during the Kosovo crisis of 1999. In 1996, a Chinese threat to Taiwan led to the dispatch of two American carrier battle-groups. The concern among Chinese policymakers about protecting China's ability to act against Taiwan is linked to the long-term maritime strategy outlined by Admiral Liu-Huaqing in 1987, a strategy that has been adjusted from one of peacetime build-up to one of war preparation. Chinese plans include not only amphibious operations and missile strikes, but also submarine ambushes to restrict American access to crucial areas. The launching of major surface warships by China in the 2000s has been at more than twice the rate of the 1990s, and this build-up is intended to give substance to the access-denial operations that are seen by Chinese planners as crucial, for conflict over Taiwan, for any war with the USA, and for a role for the Chinese navy.

The doctrine of sea denial provides the weaker (Chinese) navy with an opportunity to thwart the stronger (American) navy, and plans to do so entail asymmetric capabilities such as saturation missile strikes against American carrier battle-groups. China intends to have an ability for sea denial up to the First Island Chain (which includes Taiwan and Okinawa) by 2020, and a global capability by 2050.[2] The latter goal entails escort-carrier fleets able to protect trade from the Indian Ocean, notably oil through the Straits of Malacca, the source of most Chinese energy imports; and, in the meantime, submarine warfare offers a deterrent designed to protect this trade by being able to pose a threat to the trade of other powers. In December 2008, China dispatched two modern destroyers and a supply ship from Hainan to the Gulf of Aden as part of the international opposition to piracy. Wu Shengli, the head of the navy, declared when the ships set sail on 26 December: 'It is the first time we go abroad to protect our strategic interests armed with military force.' In part these deployments reflected the extent to which Chinese ships and trade had been exposed to piratical attacks in 2008 and in part to a desire to match India's role in combating piracy.

Yet the development of Chinese capability, while primarily intended to prevent the USA from pre-empting China over Taiwan, in turn leads to responses by other powers, especially Japan, the strength of whose navy has to be included when assessing Chinese capabilities. Taiwan, moreover, has sought to develop a submarine force to help protect it against invasion. Australia, Malaysia, Singapore and South Korea are among the other powers building up their naval strength in response to China's growing navy. Chinese territorial interests involve claims on a range of islands and waters including the Spratleys and much of the Yellow Sea. These claims entail disputes with Russia, Japan, North and South Korea, Vietnam and the Philippines, and help fuel regional interest in naval procurement.[3] The naval bases at Yulin and Sanya on the southern coast of the island of Hainan provide China with a convenient entry into the South China Sea.

Chinese military plans include the acquisition of a carrier capability. From the 1980s, the development of such a capability has been rumoured and, in December 2008, senior Defence Ministry figures stated that it was under serious consideration. Indeed, Colonel Huang Xueping declared: 'An aircraft carrier is a symbol of the country's overall national strength as well as the competitiveness of the country's force.'[4] As yet, however, there are no

Chinese carriers. Anyway, they will probably be unable to counter superior American carrier strength which, instead, is threatened by the cost of new carriers and by the improvement in Chinese submarine capability. In 2006, a Chinese submarine was able to surface five miles from the American carrier USS *Kitty Hawk* and its battle group without apparently being detected prior to that.

A different type of threat from China is indicated by the Jin-class nuclear ballistic missile submarines, each equipped with twelve Chinese 8,000-kilometre-range nuclear ballistic missiles. These missiles, which are certainly not intended for coastal defence,[5] will give the Chinese a potent second-strike ability in any nuclear conflict, although such operations depend on supporting facilities that include a sophisticated satellite-based targeting system. It is a great challenge for China to deploy such a system. For example, after letting its satellite-based targeting system deteriorate from 1991, the Russian navy still has not recovered this capability. Nevertheless, Chinese developments mean that the USA needs to revitalise its anti-submarine warfare capability, which has been downgraded with the end of the Cold War and has deteriorated markedly since 1991.

Strengthening relations between China and Russia complicate the situation for the West. A key forum for co-operation between the two powers is the Shanghai Co-operation Organization, which in 2005 held joint military manoeuvres, Peace Mission 2005. These manoeuvres appeared to be a practice for an amphibious attack on Taiwan. Arms sales are another important aspect of co-operation. They have increased since the 1996 Sino-Russian Summit, with Russia selling guided-missile destroyers and submarines to China, not least eight Kilo-class submarines in 2002.

The Chinese naval challenge is also apparent as an aspect of an increasingly far-flung Chinese defence system. For example, China's alliance with Iran threatens Western interests in the Middle East and South Asia, especially trade routes in and from the Persian Gulf. The provision of Chinese weaponry is part of the problem, and serves as a reminder that naval power is increasingly an aspect of an equation in which land-based strength plays a major role. Thus, advanced C-series Chinese-supplied missiles make the Strait of Hormuz a choke point vulnerable to Iranian power, and this vulnerability is exacerbated by Iran's mine-laying capability and its ownership of Russian Kilo-class submarines. China has developed a naval base at Gwadar on the Baluchi coast for Pakistan, from which China could overlook the approaches to the Persian Gulf, as well as an offshore listening station on the Burmese coast to keep an eye on Indian naval moves, and is building a deep-water port at Hambatota on Sri Lanka.

With over half of the world's proven oil reserves in countries that adjoin the Persian Gulf, and with these states more able to sustain oil production at current rates than others elsewhere, the security of maritime routes in and from the Persian Gulf is clearly foremost. Indian support for the USA is relevant as it strengthens the American position in the Indian Ocean, which is the ocean from which action can be taken in the Persian Gulf. Moreover, India may be able to block Chinese naval moves beyond the Strait of Malacca, an area in which the Chinese have acquired naval facilities in Burma, Pakistan and Sri Lanka. India, which purchased the carrier *Hermes* from Britain in 1986 and leased a nuclear-powered submarine from the Soviet Union between 1988 and 1991, was also due to lease, from 2009, in a deal allegedly worth £415 million over ten years, the *Nerpa*, a Russian nuclear-powered submarine that had an accident in 2008. India has also ordered three carriers and six nuclear submarines, and has negotiated a strategic understanding with Japan.

In addition, the Indian navy has a role in providing a second-strike deterrent against a nuclear-armed Pakistan. There would be a much more level playing-field between the two powers were it not for India's sea-based strike capacity. At the same time, China is India's largest trading partner. India is looking for growth in co-operation and not competition, and China's priority is Taiwan, not the Indian Ocean. Indeed, the Chinese navy will act there only if there is war over Taiwan and the USA intervenes. In order to get on with India, China has separated its Indian policy from its Pakistan policy. Similarly, Australia, which is investing in submarines armed with cruise missiles, is a key strategic partner of the USA and yet also a major economic partner of China.

Russian naval moves

Russia has greater naval strength than China at present, and the dramatic decline in Russian naval power has in part been lessened by an increase in military expenditure from 2007. Russia also has a more powerful technological base than China. Moreover, the impression of serious deficiencies was unduly magnified by the accidental sinking of the nuclear (i.e. nuclear-powered) submarine *Kursk* in 2000, although the frequent repairs that the *Admiral Kuznetsov*, the sole Russian aircraft carrier, has required indicate more general problems. These were longstanding. Between 1969 and 2002, four Soviet submarines sank, leading to an estimated 43 lost nuclear warheads.[6] Moreover, in 2003, a decommissioned nuclear submarine sank, in 2004 a holding tank on another exploded, in 2006 a fire broke out on another, and in 2008, the *Nerpa*, a new nuclear submarine undergoing tests, had an accident with its fire-extinguishing system, leading to 20 deaths. Much of the Russian navy consists of Cold War vessels rather than newer warships equipped with more recent electronic systems. The Russian navy certainly lacks a capability akin to that of the USA, and the announcement by Vladimir Putin in July 2008 that Russia would build five aircraft carriers, each to be the basis of a carrier group, lacked credibility, not least due to a lack of shipyards. *The Military Balance*, a report by the International Institute for Strategic Studies published on 27 January 2009, claimed that Russia had only 12 nuclear-powered submarines, 20 major surface warships and one carrier still in service, and that most of the fleet had to rest anchored in port as there was insufficient money to keep it at sea.

Yet Russia is ambitious to be a superpower anew and the Russian navy is a challenge, especially if combined with Russia's air and missile power. Continued Russian investment in their submarine force after the fall of the Soviet bloc, especially with the Akula I (in service from 1982) and II (in service from 1986 or 1991; opinion is divided)[7] classes, provides an insight into the importance of the submarine within the Russian perception of naval power. By 2008, the Russians had deployed a new long-range cruise missile with a range of up to 3,000 kilometres (1,900 miles) and were experimenting with a very fast torpedo, the *Shkval*. The *Nerpa*, an Akula II class submarine, has a speed of up to 35 knots. As a result of Russian strength, the deployment of American warships to the Black Sea in 2008, in order not only to provide humanitarian aid to Georgia after its disastrous war with Russia, but also to offer both symbolic support and a presence that would deter further Russian attacks, represented a commitment that would have been difficult to support had hostilities with Russia ensued, certainly in so far as safeguarding American warships there was concerned.

There is also concern about Russian activities and capability in the Arctic Ocean and linked seas, such as the Norwegian Sea. Russian claims to territory affect underwater minerals, oil and gas, while melting ice ensures that the Arctic may become a strategic route between the Atlantic and the Pacific, both to the north of Asia and to the north of North America. The extent to which this prospect represents both challenge and opportunity to the major powers, as well as to regional powers such as Canada, is still unclear, but the resulting equations of interest will affect naval planning and procurement. Canada, in particular, is now keen to bolster its naval position as a support to its territorial claims in Arctic waters.

More generally, the dynamics of alliance politics suggest all sorts of combinations in the future. If Russia and China cooperate against the USA, the latter may well be supported by the other NATO powers as well as Japan and India. That none provided support to the USA during the Vietnam War offers no indication for the future. Naval confrontation or conflict among the great powers would anyway probably be subsumed into a missile, and therefore nuclear, confrontation or conflict which would displace the equations of naval power. The same might be the case in the event of confrontation or conflict with second-rank powers, such as Iran, as the latter might receive support from Russia and/or China. To that extent the equations of the Cold War have in part been restored, with the added complication that China now has maritime aspirations and naval strength. Indeed the Chinese navy has moved from a coastal force to one capable of true blue-water policies. Co-operation with Russia gives this development added edge.

The geopolitics of the Cold War have been altered as well as maintained. Thus, in the autumn of 2008, Russian warships set sail for an exercise with the Venezuelan navy in the Caribbean, a new project, and also prepared to call at Tripoli in Libya and the port of Tartus in Syria, where Soviet warships called during the Cold War. Russian assistance has also played a role in the development of a new facility at the Syrian port of Latakia, while there has been discussion about re-establishing a naval base in Cuba. One of the far major ships sent to the Caribbean, in an exercise proclaimed by a Russian newspaper as delivering 'a Russian fist into America's belly', was the nuclear-powered guided missile cruiser, *Peter the Great*, although it had been out of commission in 2004. In 2007, the carrier *Admiral Kuznetzov* was sent into the Atlantic and then the Mediterranean, the first deployment of major warships since 1995, but it was escorted by two tugs in case of need. Having carried out manoeuvres with the Venezuelan navy, the destroyer *Admiral Chabanenko* sailed through the Panama Canal in December 2008, the first Russian warship to do so since the Second World War, before sailing to Cuba. Moreover, a Russian warship joined the anti-piracy patrols in the Gulf of Aden. Such moves aided the lobbying of Congress by American admirals. By 2008, Russian defence expenditure, in real terms, had returned to the figures for 1991, and for 2009 a 27 per cent increase is planned, although the marked fall in the price of oil in late 2008 called such plans into question.

Counter-insurgency at sea

There are of course other tasks for naval power, some of them drawing on concepts of policing and constabulary tasks[8] and extending to roles that are reminiscent of discussion of army functions in terms of counter-insurgency (COIN). Piracy is a key problem, not least because it threatens vital, not peripheral, economic targets, both trade routes and offshore oil facilities, the latter particularly off Nigeria. Attacks are far out to sea, including over 500 miles off Somalia. The apex of the piracy problem has changed. For long, it centred on the Straits of Malacca, the key economic lifeline between China and the Indian Ocean. A total of 63,000 ships passed through the Straits in 2006. Piracy in the Straits profited from the opportunities provided by the withdrawal of British naval power and from a lack of regional co-operation. Pirates also benefited from the rebellion in Atceh province in Sumatra and also from the difficulty of policing the Straits' many inlets. Co-operation between the navies of Singapore, Malaysia and Indonesia, however, has reduced that threat, moving the regional focus of piracy to the southern Philippines, where the authority of the state is limited.

More serious problems have developed in the Indian Ocean off Somalia, a failed state with Africa's longest coastline, where authority is weak and weaponry widely available, as well as off Nigeria. Rocket-propelled grenades provide pirates with potent weapons and are now supplemented by shoulder-held missiles. Major maritime routes are threatened. Somali pirates threaten the 10 per cent of the world's shipping that passes through the Gulf of Aden and by 2007 raised a considerable sum, maybe over $30 million a year, from ransoms. By November 2008, a total of $150 million had been paid. That month, a fully laden supertanker en route to the USA with a cargo of oil worth an estimated $100 million was seized 450 miles off Kenya by Somali pirates, and, the following month, another ship was seized the same distance off Tanzania.

Tackling the threat of piracy is now a major commitment, both for local naval forces and for those of major powers, not least those with a vested interest in the security of trade routes. The latter operated through the Gulf of Aden Combined Task Force 150. A United Nations Security Council resolution of 2008 allowed naval forces to move into Somali waters. However, although pirates can be deterred from existing platforms, it is very difficult to deal with a pirated ship. A complex military operation is required in order to retake such ships without causing damage. Moreover, the legal basis for trying pirates is weak.

Alongside a recourse to naval strength, which reassures legitimate users of the seas, has come a reliance on non-governmental means that offers echoes of the past variety of force at sea. Off Somalia there is now a reliance on private security companies to provide armed protection on board ships as well as advice on pirate movements. This reliance suggests the way in which the sea can become again a sphere for competing forces that are not constrained by the exigencies and claims of the navies of sovereign powers.

Some of the issues involved in piracy play a role in the drug trade, where there is a particularly strong maritime dimension in the Caribbean and off Africa. Drug money is a threat to the stability of West Indian states, which, however, have tiny navies, largely of patrol craft. Instead, it is the navies of major powers that have a Caribbean presence, the USA, Britain and France, each of which also have colonies there, that play a key role, one that is greatly facilitated by aerial surveillance and interception capabilities. Naval action against pirates, drug smugglers and people traffickers, the last a major task for the navies of Spain, Italy and Greece, is reminiscent of the moral agenda of nineteenth-century naval power, more particularly action against pirates and slavers. Humanitarian action also played a role in the response to the Indian Ocean tsunami (tidal wave) of 26 December 2004.

The diversity of naval powers

Most states do not have navies with the capability of China, Russia, Britain and France, let alone the USA. Yet there are likely to be national goals that encourage weaker states to exert naval power. The most significant will probably arise from competition over resources, particularly offshore oil and gas, and the related pursuit of territorial claims. Thus, in 2009 Iraq took delivery of the first of four Italian-built patrol ships designed to help protect offshore oil installations. The impact of competition over resources varies greatly, and is generally not militarised, but, where that is not the case, then it is likely that naval strength will be maintained, at least to the extent that it can remain a factor. Warships will provide a key means for action, but will probably be joined by air power, including aerial surveillance.

Institutional continuity will also be a factor. Navies will assert their value, and this assertion will be particularly important in states where they have traditionally had political weight and been centrally related to attempts at national assertion, for example Chile, Argentina and, to a lesser extent, Brazil. In most states, however, navies have far less political clout than armies and play a smaller role in national self-image. This latter situation is true, for example, of Turkey, Iran, India and Pakistan.

Yet issues of military need and power politics complicate such situations. For example, the quest for a regional political role judged commensurate to its population size, economic development, resource concerns and political pretensions will continue to ensure that India seeks naval strength. Turkey may develop naval strength to support its desire to act as a Black Sea power, although the prime drive, for domestic political as well as strategic reasons, will be that of an enhanced army. Iran is concerned about power politics and resources in the Persian Gulf. Iran seeks to exert pressure on maritime routes there, as well as on the states on the southern shore, such as Dubai, and is also concerned about the American naval presence in the Persian Gulf, a presence that protects these states. These power equations, however, are not simply naval. Indeed, Iran's military position in the Persian Gulf owes much to its missiles.

Military need plays a direct role in the Israeli situation and will continue to do so. Warships provide an ability to act at a distance from Israel's borders, not least in putting pressure on Lebanon, as in 2006, their missiles extend the range of Israeli's rocket capability, and they offer an ability to support blockades, particularly those aimed against arms shipments, for example to Hamas in the Gaza Strip. In 2002, Israeli naval commandos stormed an Iranian cargo ship in the Red Sea, seizing arms en route for the Palestinian Authority. In 2009, Israeli warships took part in the bombardment of Hamas positions, with Hamas responding to the warships with missiles.

Israeli warships and ports are vulnerable to missiles, as the 2006 war with Hizbollah showed: the corvette *Hamit* was hit by a radar-guided C-802 missile fired from southern Lebanon, while Hizbollah rockets also hit the port of Haifa. By 2008, Ashkelon, the southernmost Israeli port on the Mediterranean, was within range of these rockets. Moreover, investment in the Israeli navy will go on being far less than that in army or air force. Each of the latter will continue to provide a greater capability, for both attack and defence, and each will continue to be more powerful, both politically and institutionally.

The sensitivity of arms supplies to Hamas and Hizbollah both exposed the limitations of naval power, with Hizbollah resupplied by air from Iran via Damascus, and also its potential. The sea was an obvious route to resupply Gaza, and in January 2009 the Egyptian Foreign Minister warned Britain, France and Germany against sending warships to block this route.

The role of naval power in opposing terrorist activity was also seen with Sri Lanka, with the Sri Lankan navy seeking to cut the supply routes from India of the rebel Tamil Tigers as well as to prevent their attacks and, instead, to be able to support operations against Tamil strongholds. In turn, the Tamils used the sea both to ensure the movement of supplies and as a sphere for attack. Thus, in October 2008, three 'Black Sea Tiger' suicide boats tried to ram two Sri Lankan freighters carrying supplies to the northern coast. The Sri Lankan navy fired on the boats, two of which exploded, and the third of which capsized. The navy admitted slight damage to one of the freighters, while the Tamil Tigers acknowledged the loss of two of their boats but claimed that they had sunk one of the freighters and severely damaged another. This episode indicated the role of naval clashes in providing an impression of success. The following January, the Sri Lankan navy destroyed at least four Tamil Tiger boats tying to escape from their last enclave.

Most maritime states lack the naval resources of Israel. Indeed, there is an important contrast between the extension of national jurisdiction over the seas, a jurisdiction that covered more than a third of their extent in 2008, and the fact that many states cannot ensure their own maritime security. This point is true for example of Oceania, of the Caribbean, and of Indian Ocean states such as Mauritius, the Maldives and the Seychelles. These weaknesses encourage the major powers to maintain naval strength and intervene but also led to initiatives for regional solutions, such as that supported by India since 2007.[9]

Conclusions

Reminders of the variety of political contexts within which naval goals will persist in being formulated serve as a limitation to any capability-driven account of the future development of navies largely in terms of the capabilities of warships, important as they are. As a separate point, the sea, described in the British *Future Navy Vision* (2006) 'as the indispensable medium for trade and access to areas of strategic interest',[10] will continue to enjoy advantages over the air as a medium for force projection, not least the advantages presented by the greater ease of transporting and supporting numbers of troops. As a base for the delivery of firepower, however, differences between sea and air will possibly erode further. The two have been linked in operational and resource terms since the mid-twentieth century. Thus, in July 1942, the Australian War Cabinet cabled Churchill: 'superior sea power and airpower are vital to wrest the initiative from Japan and are essential to assure the defensive position in the Southwest Pacific Area'.[11]

Looked at in another light, the sea will remain a key basis for this delivery of aerial firepower because navies lack the vulnerabilities and sensitivities of land bases. The role of navies will therefore remain crucial whether for fighting other navies, controlling trade routes, or projecting power into land masses. Yet, none of these roles can be discharged only by navies, and they will have to demonstrate particular values in each, values that will be expressed in terms of the strategic cultures and institutional practices of individual states. Thus, while naval functions will continue to be important, justifying much of the rhetoric and self-interest of naval power, the reality will be that it is not only navies that can seek to delivery these functions.

Similarly, the American navy plays a role in the programme for a Ground-based Missile Defense System that was launched in 2002, with the Aegis BMD defence system intended to engage missiles in the eco-atmospheric phase of flight. In 2008, 10 warships had this capability, a number that by 2009 is to be expanded to 3 Aegis cruisers and 15 destroyers. This System is aimed against threats posed by Iran and North Korea, and entails ships deployed in the Sea of Japan and the Mediterranean. Yet, the System is not restricted to the sea, nor necessarily dependent on the navy.

Alongside the far from automatic relationship between navies (ship-based organisations) and the deployment of force on, over and from the oceans, there is also the need to stress the centrality of war on land, and the related extent to which conflict and disorder at sea are generally related to causes and sources ashore.[12] As such, naval power becomes a key instrument for the pursuit of interests, but one that has to be understood in terms of its ability to fulfil its functions and serve its constituencies, rather than as, in some fashion, a force of timeless value.

9　Conclusions

Naval power has to be understood not as a free-floating variable but as a phenomenon shaped in and by particular contexts. This shaping involves a dynamic interaction of capabilities and tasks. The tasks are more important as far as individual powers are concerned, although the capabilities tend to set general parameters, as is captured in phrases such as 'the Age of Steam'. The dynamic interaction between capabilities and tasks owes much to the coalitions of social, political and economic interests which provide the basis for naval organisation and doctrine. Thus, reinterpretations of state interests were linked to investment in navies and to tasks for naval activity.[1]

The shaping of differing capabilities and tasks helps explain varied emphases not only in the practice of naval power but also in the definition of it. As this book has indicated, notions of control, protection or denial of maritime routes, bodies of water and areas for amphibious attack have all played a role in the definition of naval power, but these roles have been far from fixed. Variations have been not only chronological but also by individual power in any particular period. No single definition of sea power works even for one navy, in part because of the tension between any general theory of sea power and the historically specific conditions of the sea power of individual states. Thus, in the 2000s navies such as those of Australia, Italy and Spain took prominent action to restrict or control immigration, a role that was of limited importance over the previous century.

There have also been significant variations in the constraints affecting naval operations, not least the unpredictability of naval operations and their contribution to the imponderability of war. Thus, storms were not only a problem for the Age of Sail. In the two world wars, German U-boats found it difficult to put to sea in storms and could not get near enough to the surface safely to torpedo merchant ships, while, in turn, Allied convoys were scattered by storms. At the same time, the operational and tactical consequences of such constraints were different to those in the Age of Sail.

Naval capability has been less central to history than its land equivalent for a number of reasons, but primarily because man lives on the land. Some states lack coasts, or extensive or economically fruitful ones, but more important has been the ability of armies to act not only to support interests abroad, but also to maintain internal control. Navies have played a role in the latter process, but nowhere near to the same extent. This factor helps explain their relative marginality in political terms in many states, whatever the rhetoric about maritime destiny. However, trying to make a division between armies and navies only works in some cases. It is also important to note the function of navies in expeditionary warfare in keeping armies where they are, and, indeed, in putting them there in the first place. Armies and navies must, of necessity, coexist if water is anyway involved, and often when it is not.

Yet, if naval power has not been as universal as land power, nor as prominent in the history of such major states as China, France, Germany, India, Russia and Spain, naval power has, nevertheless, played a role in the history of these states. In part, this is a matter of their inability to wield naval power for any sustained period at a decent level of operational effectiveness, at least as assessed in terms of victory at sea. It is also pertinent to ask such counterfactual questions as, 'What if early modern Spain had focused more effort on naval activity?', or 'What if Louis XIV had not shifted naval policy after France's naval defeat at Barfleur?', or 'What if Napoleon had devoted more attention to his navy?', or 'What if China, both between 1500 and 1850 and since 1950, had developed a navy commensurate with its economic resources?' On the other hand, such questions also suggest the secondary role of naval power in the strategic culture of these states.

From another perspective, however, naval power has been crucial during the last half-millennium in permitting the development of far-flung economic and political systems. Some, but not all, of these systems took the character of empires or were partly represented in that form, but all were dependent on an ability to pursue trans-oceanic interests and to benefit from maritime links. This ability, which was expressed in naval and mercantile capability, was crucial to world history. These systems have all been Western, although other regions of the world provided portions of the collectivities and constituencies of interests that comprised them. Thus, for example, Indian economic, labour and military resources were very important to the British Empire from the 1750s to the 1940s, especially, but not only, in Asia and East Africa.

Without any comparable structure of imperial rule, East Asian and Middle Eastern capital inflows are highly significant to American power at present, and, indeed, provide further reason for the defence of maritime trade routes and the capability to project naval strength. In the modern world, moreover, the movement of oil is in large part by sea, and can be deliberately threatened by powers seeking to exert pressure on the international system, as in the Iran–Iraq War of 1980–8, when attacks on shipping in the Persian Gulf led to convoying by Western navies.[2] Naval power, therefore, should not be treated as a separate subject; rather, naval power is integral to global history over the last half-millennium, which makes the subject at once important and challenging.

Notes

Chapter 1

1   A. Spilhaus, 'Maps of the Whole World Ocean', *Geographical Review*, 32 (1942), pp. 431–5, 'To See the Oceans Slice Up the Land', *Smithsonian*, 10/8 (Nov. 1979), p. 116, and 'World Ocean Maps: The Proper Places to Interrupt', *Proceedings of the American Philosophical Society*, 127/1 (Jan. 1983), pp. 50–60, Spilhaus and J.P. Snyder, 'World Maps with Natural Boundaries', *Cartography and Geographic Information Systems*, 18 (1991), pp. 246–54.

2   M.W. Lewis and K.E. Wigen, *The Myth of Continents: A Critique of Metageography* (Berkeley, California, 1997).

3   For a useful corrective, B. Cunliffe, *Facing the Ocean: The Atlantic and its Peoples, 8000 BC–AD 1500* (Oxford, 2001), and for the current situation, J. Lindley-French and W. van Straten, 'Exploiting the Value of Small Navies: The Experience of the Royal Netherlands Navy', *Royal United Services Institute Journal*, 153 (Dec. 2008), p. 66.

4   J. Thomson, *Pirates, Mercenaries and Sovereigns: State-Building and Extraterritorial Violence in Early Modern Europe* (Princeton, New Jersey, 1994).

5   J.S. Morrison and J.F. Coates, *The Athenian Trireme: History and Reconstruction of an Ancient Greek Warship* (Cambridge, 1986); B. Jordan, *The Athenian Navy in the Classical Period* (Berkeley, California, 1972).

6   L. Carson, *Ships and Seamanship in the Ancient World* (Princeton, New Jersey, 1971) and *Ships and Seafaring in Ancient Times* (Austin, Texas, 1994).

7   J.H. Pryor, *Geography, Technology and War: Studies in the Maritime History of the Mediterranean, 649–1571* (Cambridge, 1988).

8   B. Strauss, *The Battle of Salamis: The Naval Encounter That Saved Greece – and Western Civilisation* (New York, 2004).

9   J.F. Lazenby, *The First Punic War* (Stanford, California, 1996); F. Meijer, *A History of Seafaring in the Ancient World* (New York, 1986).

10 C. Martin, 'Water Transport and the Roman Occupations of North Britain', in T.C. Smout (ed.), *Scotland and the Sea* (Edinburgh, 1992), pp. 6–8.

11 J. Haywood, *Dark Age Naval Power* (London, 1991); S. Rose, *Medieval Naval Warfare, 1000–1500* (London, 2001).

12 S. Rose, *Southampton and the Navy in the Age of Henry V* (Winchester, 1998).

13 L. Levathes, *When China Ruled the Seas: The Treasure Fleet of the Dragon Throne, 1405–1433* (Oxford, 1994).
14 K. Hall and J.K. Whitmore (eds), *Explorations in Early Southeast Asian History* (Ann Arbor, Michigan, 1976); G.W. Spencer, *The Politics of Expansion: The Chola Conquest of Sri Lanka and Srivijaya* (Madras, 1983); K. Hall, *Maritime Trade and State Development in Early Asia* (Honolulu, Hawaii, 1985); P. Shanmugam, *The Revenue System of the Cholas, 850–1279* (Madras, 1987); J. Abu-Lughod, *Before European Hegemony* (Oxford, 1989); G. Hourani, *Arab Seafaring* (Princeton, New Jersey, 1995).

Chapter 2

1 The best introduction to the subject, particularly good on shifts in the maritime power structure, is J. Glete, *Warfare at Sea, 1500–1650: Maritime Conflicts and the Transformation of Europe* (London, 2000). For the statistical background, Glete, *Navies and Nations: Warships, Navies and State Building in Europe and America, 1500–1860* (Stockholm, 1993). For an earlier account, J. Black, *European Warfare, 1494–1660* (London, 2002), pp. 167–95.
2 G. Parker, *The Grand Strategy of Philip II* (New Haven, Connecticut, 1998).
3 B. Lavery, *The Arming and Fitting of English Ships of War, 1600–1815* (Annapolis, 1987).
4 R. Romano, 'Economic Aspects of the Construction of Warships in Venice in the Sixteenth Century', in B. Pullan (ed.), *Crisis and Change in the Venetian Economy in the Sixteenth and Seventeenth Centuries* (London, 1968), pp. 59–87.
5 J.D. Tracy (ed.), *The Rise of Merchant Empires: Long-Distance Trade in the Early Modern World, 1350–1750* (Cambridge, 1990) and (ed.), *The Political Economy of Merchant Empires* (Cambridge, 1991).
6 A. Lewis and T. Runyon, *European Naval and Maritime History, 300–1500* (Bloomington, 1985).
7 R. Gardiner and J. Morrison (eds.), *The Age of the Galley: Mediterranean Oared Vessels since Pre-classical Times* (London, 1995).
8 R. Gardiner and R.W. Unger (eds.), *Cogs, Caravals and Galleons: The Sailing Ship, 1000–1650* (London, 1994); J. Glete (ed.), *Naval History 1500–1680* (Aldershot, 2005), p. xvi.
9 R.W. Unger, *The Ship in the Medieval Economy, 600–1600* (London, 1980).
10 C.R. Boxer, *The Portuguese Seaborne Empire, 1415–1825* (Harmondsworth, 1973).
11 C. Cipolla, *Guns, Sails and Empires: Technological Innovation and the Early Phases of European Expansion 1400–1700* (London, 1965).

12 N.A.M. Rodger, *The Safeguard of the Sea: A Naval History of Britain, Vol. I, 660–1649* (Harmondsworth, 1997).

13 A. de Silva Saturnino Monteiro, 'The Decline and Fall of Portuguese Seapower, 1583–1663', *Journal of Military History*, 65 (2001), pp. 19–20.

14 D. Ayalon, 'The Mamluks and Naval Power: A Phase of the Struggle between Islam and Christian Europe', *Proceedings of the Israel Academy of Sciences and Humanities*, 1 (1965), p. 1; A. Fuess, 'Rotting Ships and Razed Harbors: The Naval Policy of the Mamluks', *Mamlūk Studies Review*, 5 (2001), pp. 67–70; A.C. Roy, *Mughal Navy and Naval Warfare* (Calcutta, 1972).

15 Y. Park, *Admiral Yi Sun-shin and his Turtleboat Armada: A Comprehensive Account of the Resistance of Korea to the 11th Century Japanese Invasion* (Seoul, 1973).

16 Parker, 'The *Dreadnought* Revolution of Tudor England', *Mariner's Mirror*, 82 (1996), pp. 269–300.

17 K. DeVries, 'The Effectiveness of Fifteenth-Century Shipboard Artillery', *Mariner's Mirror*, 84 (1998), pp. 389–99, esp. p. 396.

18 N.A.M. Rodger, 'The Development of Broadside Gunnery, 1450–1650', *Mariner's Mirror*, 82 (1996), pp. 301–24.

19 R.W. Unger, *The Art of Medieval Technology: Images of Noah the Shipbuilder* (New Brunswick, New Jersey, 1991); I. Fried, *The Good Ship: Ships, Shipbuilding and Technology in England, 1200–1520* (Baltimore, 1995).

20 A.B. Caruana, *The History of English Sea Ordnance, 1523–1875. I: The Age of Evolution, 1523–1715* (Rotherfield, 1994). For the list, see Parker's review of D. Loades's *Tudor Navy*, *Sixteenth Century Journal*, 24 (1993), p. 1022.

21 S. Rose, 'Islam Versus Christendom: The Naval Dimension, 1000–1600', *Journal of Military History*, 63 (1999), p. 577.

22 F.C. Lane, 'Naval Actions and Fleet Organisation, 1499–1502', in J.R. Hale (ed.), *Renaissance Venice* (London, 1973), pp. 146–73.

23 J.F. Guilmartin, *Gunpowder and Galleys: Changing Technology and Mediterranean Warfare at Sea in the Sixteenth Century* (Cambridge, 1974).

24 J.H. Pryor, *Geography, Technology and War: Studies in the Maritime History of the Mediterranean, 649–1571* (Cambridge, 1988).

25 A.C. Hess, 'The Evolution of the Ottoman Seaborne Empire in the Age of the Oceanic Discoveries, 1453–1525', *American Historian Review*, 74 (1970), pp. 1892–1919.

26 Guilmartin, *Gunpowder*, pp. 42–56.

27 E. Bradford, *The Great Siege* (1961); Guilmartin, *Gunpowder*, pp. 176–93.

28 Guilmartin, *Gunpowder*, pp. 221–52 and 'The Tactics of the Battle of Lepanto clarified: The Impact of Social, Economic, and Political Factors on Sixteenth-Century Galley Warfare', in C.L. Symonds (ed.), *New Aspects of Naval History* (Annapolis, 1981), pp. 41–65;

N. Capponi, *Victory of the West: The Story of the Battle of Lepanto* (London, 2006). For recent Turkish work see I. Bostan, 'Inebahti Deniz Savasi', in *Türkiye Dinayet Vakfi Islam Ansiklopedisi*, vol. 22 (Istanbul, 2000), pp. 287–9. I owe this reference to Gabor Ágoston.

29 C. Imber, 'The Reconstruction of the Ottoman Fleet after the Battle of Lepanto', in Imber, *Studies in Ottoman History and Law* (Istanbul, 1996), pp. 85–101.

30 Guilmartin, *Gunpowder*, pp. 253–73.

31 C. Imber, *The Ottoman Empire, 1300–1650: The Structure of Power* (2002); E. Zachariaou (ed.), *The Kapudan Pasha: His Office and his Domain* (Rethymnon, 2002).

32 J. Glete, 'Bridge and Bulwark: The Swedish Navy and the Baltic, 1500–1809', in G. Rystad, K-R. Bohme and W.M. Carlgren (eds), *The Baltic and Power Politics, 1500–1990* (Lund, 2 vols, 1994), I, pp. 10–58.

33 M. Bellamy, *Christian IV and His Navy: A Political and Administrative History of the Danish Navy, 1596–1648* (Leiden, 2006).

34 J.D. Tracy, 'Herring Wars: The Habsburg Netherlands and the Struggle for Control of the North Sea, *c.* 1520–1560', *Sixteenth Century Journal*, 24 (1993), pp. 267–71.

35 C. Martin and Parker, *The Spanish Armada* (1988); M.J. Rodríguez-Salgado, *Armada, 1588–1988* (London, 1988); F. Fernandez-Armesto, *The Spanish Armada: The Experience of War in 1588* (Oxford, 1988); J. McDermott, *England and the Spanish Armada: The Necessary Quarrel* (New Haven, Connecticut, 2005).

36 D. Loades, *The Tudor Navy: An Administrative, Political and Military History* (Aldershot, 1992); K.R. Andrews, *Elizabethan Privateering: English Privateering during the Spanish War, 1585–1603* (Cambridge, 1964); R.T. Spence, *The Privateering Earl: George Clifford, 3rd Earl of Cumberland, 1558–1605* (Stroud, 1995).

37 J.R. Bruijn, *The Dutch Navy of the Seventeenth and Eighteenth Centuries* (Columbia, South Carolina, 1993).

38 C.R. Phillips, *Six Galleons for the King of Spain: Imperial Defence in the Early Seventeenth Century* (Baltimore, 1992); D. Goodman, *Spanish Naval Power, 1589–1665: Reconstruction and Defeat* (Cambridge, 1996).

39 J.I. Israel, *Dutch Primacy in World Trade* (Oxford, 1989).

40 R.A. Stradling, *The Armada of Flanders. Spanish Maritime Policy and European War, 1568–1668* (Cambridge, 1992).

41 J.I. Israel, *The Dutch Republic and the Hispanic World, 1606–1661* (Oxford, 1982).

42 M. Vergé-Franceschi, 'Les Politiques et le développement de la puissance maritime sous l'Ancien Régime', in C. Buchet, J. Meyer and J.-P. Poussou (eds), *La Puissance maritime* (Paris, 2004), p. 557.

43 A. James, *The Ship of State: Naval Affairs in Early Modern France, 1572–1661* (Woodbridge, 2002).

44 Andrews, *Ships, Money and Politics: Seafaring and Naval Enterprise in the Reign of Charles I* (Cambridge, 1991).

45 B. Capp, *Cromwell's Navy: The Fleet and the English Revolution* (Oxford, 1989).

46 S.C.A. Pincus, *Protestantism and Patriotism: Ideologies and the Making of English Foreign Policy, 1650–1685* (Cambridge, 1996).

47 J.R. Jones, *The Anglo-Dutch Wars of the Seventeenth Century* (Harlow, 1996).

48 R. Harding, *Seapower and Naval Warfare 1650–1830* (London, 1999), pp. 73–5; W. Maltby, 'Politics, Professionalism and the Evolution of Sailing Ships Tactics', in J.A. Lynn (ed.), *Tools of War: Instruments, Ideas and Institutions of Warfare, 1445–1871* (Chicago, 1990), pp. 53–73; M.A.J. Palmer, 'The Military Revolution Afloat: the era of the Anglo-Dutch Wars', *War in History*, 4 (1997), pp. 123–49.

49 D.F. Allen, 'Charles II, Louis XIV and the Order of Malta', *European History Quarterly*, 20 (1990), pp. 323–40; P. Bamford, *Fighting Ships and Prisons: The Mediterranean Galleys of France in the Age of Louis XIV* (Minneapolis, 1973), p. 23.

50 J.M. Wismayer, *The Fleet of the Order of St John, 1530–1798* (Valletta, 1997), p. 232.

51 J.E. Dotson, 'Foundations of Venetian Naval Strategy from Pietro II Orseolo to the Battle of Zonchio, 1000–1500', *Viator*, 32 (2001), p. 125.

52 C. Imber, 'The Navy of Süleyman the Magnificent', *Archivum Ottomanicum*, 6 (1980), pp. 211–82.

53 T. Kirk, *Genoa and the Sea: Policy and Power in an Early Modern Maritime Republic, 1589–1684* (Baltimore, 2005).

54 N.A.M. Rodger, 'Drowning in a Sea of Paper: British Archives of Naval Warfare', *Archives*, 32 (2007), p. 111.

55 Glete, *Warfare at Sea, 1500–1650*, eg. pp. 186–7; C.R. Phillips, review of Glete, *Warfare at Sea, 1500–1650*, in *Journal of Military History*, 64 (2000), p. 1144.

56 Bruijn, 'States and Their Navies from the Late Sixteenth to the End of the Eighteenth Centuries', in P. Contamine (ed.), *War and Competition between States* (Oxford, 2000), pp. 78–9.

57 James, *Ship of State*, conclusion.

58 J. Black, *European Warfare 1660–1815* (London, 1994).

59 A. Pérontin-Dumon, 'The Pirate and the Emperor: Power and the Law on the Seas, 1450–1850', in Tracy (ed.), *Political Economy*, pp. 196–227.

60 P. Earl, *Corsairs of Malta and Barbary* (1970); W. Bracewell, *The Uskoks of Senj: Piracy, Banditry and Holy War in the Sixteenth Century Adriatic* (Ithaca, New York, 1992); A. Tenenti, *Piracy and the Decline of Venice, 1580–1615* (Berkeley, 1967).

61 V. Ostapchuck, 'Five documents from the Topkapi Palace Archive on the Ottoman Defence of the Black Sea against the Cossacks', *Journal of Ottoman Studies*, 2 (1987), pp. 49–104; C. Imber, *The Ottoman Empire, 1300–1650: The Structure of Power* (Basingstoke, 2002).

62 K.R. Andrews, *The Spanish Caribbean: Trade and Plunder, 1530–1630* (New Haven, Connecticut, 1978); D.D. Hebb, *Piracy and the English Government, 1616–1642* (Aldershot, 1994); V.W. Lunsford, *Piracy and Privateering in the Golden Age Netherlands* (Basingstoke, 2005).

63 J.H. Ohlmeyer, *Civil War and Restoration in the Three Stuart Kingdoms: The Career of Randal MacDonnell, Marquis of Antrim, 1609–1683* (Cambridge, 1993), p. 230.

64 M.A.J. Palmer, '"The Soul's Right Hand": Command and Control in the Age of Fighting Sail, 1652–1827', *Journal of Military History*, 61 (1997), pp. 679–706.

Chapter 3

1 S. Hornstein, *The Restoration Navy and English Foreign Trade, 1674–1688: Study in the Peacetime Use of Seapower* (Aldershot, 1991); J. Glete, *Navies and Nations: Warships, Navies and State Building in Europe and America, 1500–1860* (Stockholm, 1994), p. 192.

2 J. Glete, 'The Sea Power of Habsburg Spain and the Development of European Navies, 1500–1700', in E.G. Hernán and D. Maffi (eds), *Guerra y Sociedad en La Mondraquía Hispánica* (2 vols, Madrid, 2006), I, 859–60.

3 P. Williams, 'The Strategy of Galley Warfare in the Mediterranean, 1560–1620', in Hernán and Maffi, *Guerra y Sociedad*, I, 892.

4 J.G. Coad, *The Royal Dockyards 1690–1850* (Aldershot, 1989), pp. 7–10, 92–7; M. Duffy, 'The Establishment of the Western Squadron as the Linchpin of British Naval Strategy', in Duffy (ed.) *Parameters of British Naval Power 1650–1850* (Exeter, 1992), pp. 61–2 and 'The Creation of Plymouth Dockyard and its Impact on Naval Strategy', in *Guerres maritimes 1688–1713* (Vincennes, 1990), pp. 245–74.

5 J. Ehrman, *The Navy in the War of William III* (Cambridge, 1953); E.B. Powley, *The Naval Side of King William's War* (Hamden, Connecticut, 1972); P. Aubrey, *The Defeat of James Stuart's Armada 1692* (Leicester, 1979).

6 D. Baugh, 'What Gave the British Navy Superiority?', in L.P. de Esosura (ed.), *Exceptionalism and Industrialisation: Britain and its European Rivals, 1688–1815* (Cambridge, 2004), pp. 235–57; A.V. Coats, 'Efficiency in Dockyard Administration, 1660–1800: A

Reassessment', in N. Tracy (ed.), *The Age of Sail* (London, 2002), pp. 116–32.

7   N. Elias, *The Genesis of the Naval Profession* (Dublin, 2007).

8   J.R. Bruijn, *The Dutch Navy of the Seventeenth and Eighteenth Centuries* (Columbia, South Carolina, 1993), p. 215.

9   D. Pilgrim, 'The Colbert–Seignelay Naval Reforms and the Beginnings of the War of the League of Augsburg', *French Historical Studies*, 9 (1975–6), pp. 235–62. For a more positive view, J. Meyer, 'Louis XIV et les puissances maritimes', *XVIIe Siècle*, 123 (1979), p. 170. For criticism of Louis, G.J. Ames, 'Colbert's Grand Indian Ocean Fleet of 1670', *Mariner's Mirror*, 76 (1990), pp. 236–9.

10   G. Symcox, *The Crisis of French Naval Power, 1688–1697* (The Hague, 1974).

11   S.F. Gradish, 'The Establishment of British Seapower in the Mediterranean, 1689–1713', *Canadian Journal of History* (1975), pp. 1–16.

12   J.M. Stapleton, 'The Blue-Water Dimension of King William's War: Amphibious Operations and Allied Strategy during the Nine Years' War, 1688–1697', in D.J.B. Trim and M.C. Fissel (eds), *Amphibious Warfare 1000–1700: Commerce, State Formation and European Expansion* (Leiden, 2006), p. 348.

13   Marquis of Carmarthen to Duke of Marlborough, 3 Apr. 1705, BL. Add. 61308 f. 36.

14   Colonel John Richards to Marlborough, 10 May 1706, BL. Add. 61309 f. 50.

15   Shovell to Earl of Sunderland, 10 Aug. 1707, BL. Add. 61311 f. 50.

16   J.S. Bromley, 'The French Privateering War, 1702–13', in H.F. Bell and R.L. Ollard (eds.), *Historical Essays, 1600–1750, Presented to David Ogg* (New York, 1963), pp. 203–31 and 'The North Sea in Wartime, 1688–1713', *Bijdragen en Mededelingen Betreffende de Geschiedenis der Nederlanden*, 92 (1977), pp. 270–99.

17   Ellis to Stepney, 17 Oct. 1701, BL. Add. 7074 f. 49.

18   Blathwayt to Stepney, 28 Feb. 1702, New Haven, Connecticut, Beinecke Library, Osborn Shelves.

19   Ibid., 6 Aug. 1703, Beinecke, Osborn, Blathwayt Box 21.

20   H.C. Owen, *War at Sea under Queen Anne* (Cambridge, 1934).

21   J. Hattendorf, 'Admiral Sir George Byng and the Cape Passaro Incident, 1718: A Case Study in the Use of the Royal Navy as a Deterrent', in *Guerres et Paix* (Vincennes, 1987), pp. 19–38; J.D. Harbron, *Trafalgar and the Spanish Navy* (London, 1988), p. 31.

22   Craggs to Duke of Newcastle, 10 Aug. 1719, BL. Add. 32686 f. 137.

23   Hedges to Charles Delafaye, Under-Secretary, 8 Feb. 1727, Tyrawly to Newcastle, 17 Jul. 1729, NA. SP. 92/32 f. 128, 89/35 f. 188.

24 I have benefited from discussing piracy with Guy Chet.
25 Townshend to William Stanhope, 11 Aug. 1726, NA. SP. 94/98.
26 Newcastle to Wager, 12, 18 July, 12 Sept., Townshend to Wager, 6 Aug. 1727, NA. SP. 47/78 f. 95, 98, 104–6, 101–2.
27 Newcastle to Townshend, 13 June 1729, NA. SP. 43/77.
28 *Wye's Letter*, 24, 26, 29 July, 12 Aug. 1729.
29 Newcastle to Horatio Walpole, 23 May 1726, BL. Add. 32746 f. 136.
30 Du Bourgay to Townshend, 17 May 1726, NA. SP. 90/20.
31 Horatio Walpole to Newcastle, 6 July 1728, BL. Add. 32756 f. 419.
32 Charles Caesar to 'James III', 20 Feb. 1726, Windsor Castle, Royal Archives, Stuart Papers 90/133.
33 J. Black and A. Reese, 'Die Panik von 1731', in J. Kunisch (ed.), *Expansion und Gleichgewicht. Studien zur europäischen Mächtepolitik des ancien régime* (Berlin, 1986), pp. 69–95.
34 Anon., *A Letter from a By-Stander to a Member of Parliament: Wherein is Examined What Necessity there is for the Maintenance of a Large Regular Land Force in this Island* (London, 1742).
35 Stone to Edward Weston, 2 Aug., Stephen to Edward Weston, 25 Dec. 1745, Farmington, Weston Papers 16.
36 Newcastle to Cumberland, 12 Dec. 1745, RA. Cumberland Papers (hereafter CP) 8/9.
37 For differing views, H.W. Richmond, *The Navy in the War of 1739–1748* (3 vols., Cambridge, 1920) II, pp. 154–89; F. McLynn, 'Sea Power and the Jacobite Rising of 1745', *Mariner's Mirror*, 67 (1981), pp. 163–72.
38 R. Harding, 'The Ideology and Organisation of Maritime War: An Expedition to Canada in 1746', in R.T. Sánchez (ed.), *War, State and Development. Fiscal-Military States in the Eighteenth Century* (Pamplona, 2007), pp. 159–60.
39 Newcastle to Cumberland, 3 July 1746, BL. Add. 32707 f. 390.
40 J. Pritchard, *Anatomy of a Naval Disaster: The 1746 French Naval Expedition to North America* (Montreal, 1996).
41 S.W.C. Pack, *Admiral Lord Anson* (London, 1960), pp. 153–60.
42 R. Mackay, *Admiral Hawke* (Oxford, 1965), pp. 69–88.
43 Newcastle to Cumberland, 27 Oct. 1747, RA. CP. 29/145; Newcastle to Lieutenant-General Bland, 30 Oct. 1747, NA. SP. 54/37 f. 14.
44 Sandwich to Anson, 14 Nov. 1747, BL. Add. 15957 f. 29.
45 Newcastle to Cumberland, 11 Mar. 1748, RA. CP. 32/245.
46 D.J. Starkey, *British Privateering Enterprise in the Eighteenth Century* (Exeter, 1990).
47 C. Swanson, *Predators and Prizes: American Privateering and Imperial Warfare, 1739–1748* (Columbia, South Carolina, 1991).
48 D. Crewe, *Yellow Jack and the Worm: British Naval Administration in the West Indies, 1739–1748* (Liverpool, 1993).

49 C. Wilkinson, *The British Navy and the State in the Eighteenth Century* (Woodbridge, 2004).

50 N. Rogers, *The Press Gang* (London, 2007).

51 Holdernesse to Rochford, 4 Oct. 1751, NA. SP. 92/59 f. 170.

52 Newcastle to Keith, 22 Oct., Keith to Newcastle, 3 Nov. 1753, NA. SP. 80/192.

53 *Sbornik Imperatorskogo Russkogo Istoricheskogo Obshchestva* (148 vols, St Petersburg, 1867–1916), C111, 259–60, 275; D. Aldridge, 'The Royal Navy in the Baltic 1715–1727', in W. Minchinton (ed.), *Britain and the Northern Seas* (Pontefract, 1988), pp. 75–9.

54 R. Koser (ed.), *Politische Correspondenz Friedrichs des Grossens* (46 vols, Berlin, 1879–1939), IX, 345.

55 C. Baudi di Vesme, *La politica Méditerranea inglese nelle relazioni degli inviati italiani a Londra durante la cosidetta Guerra di successione d'Austria* (Turin, 1952); J. Black, 'The Development of Anglo-Sardinian Relations in the First Half of the Eighteenth Century', *Studi Piemontesi*, 12 (1983), pp. 48–60.

56 Vernon to Dashwood, 29 July 1749, Oxford, Bodleian Library, Ms. D.D. Dashwood B11/12/6.

57 Duke of Bedford, Secretary of State for Southern Department, to Earl of Albemarle, envoy in Paris, 5 Apr. 1750, London, Bedford Estate Office vol. 23; J. Black, 'British Intelligence and the Mid-Eighteenth Century Crisis', *Intelligence and National Security*, 2 (1987), pp. 209–29.

58 Newcastle to Yorke, 26 June 1753, NA. SP. 84/463.

59 Cumberland to Holdernesse, 31 May, 18 June, Holdernesse to Cumberland, 13 May 1757, BL. Eg. Mss 3442 f. 99–100, 122, 74–5.

60 T.C.W. Blanning, *The Culture of Power and the Power of Culture. Old Regime Europe, 1660–1789* (Oxford, 2002).

61 R. Middleton, 'British Naval Strategy, 1755–1762: The Western Squadron', *Mariner's Mirror*, 75 (1989), pp. 349–67; Duffy, 'Western Squadron'.

62 Hardwicke to Newcastle, 4 Aug. 1755, BL. Add. 32857 f. 571.

63 H.W. Richmond (ed.), *Papers Relating to the Loss of Minorca* (London, 1915); B. Tunstall, *Admiral Byng and the Loss of Minorca* (London, 1928).

64 P. Padfield, *Guns at Sea* (London, 1973), pp. 90–2, 100.

65 G.J. Marcus, *Quiberon Bay: The Campaign in Home Waters, 1759* (London, 1960).

66 J.F. Bosher, 'Financing the French Navy in the Seven Years' War: Beaujon, Goosens et Compagnie in 1759', *Business History*, 28 (1986), pp. 115–33; Pritchard, *Louis XV's Navy, 1748–1762: A Study in Organisation and Administration* (Quebec, 1987), pp. 185–202.

67 D. Syrett, 'The Methodology of British Amphibious Operations during the Seven Years' and American Wars', *Mariner's Mirror*, 58 (1972), p. 277.

68 J. Cresswell, *British Admirals of the Eighteenth Century* (London, 1972), p. 254; M.A.J. Palmer, 'The "Military Revolution" Afloat: The Era of the Anglo-Dutch Wars and the Transition to Modern Warfare at Sea', *War in History*, 4 (1997), pp. 147–8. The social dimension of naval service can be approached best through N.A.M. Rodger's *The Wooden World: An Anatomy of the Georgian Navy* (London, 1986).

Chapter 4

1 For European equivalents, D.J.B. Trim, 'Medieval and Early-Modern Inshore, Estuarine, Riverine and Lacustrine Warfare', in Trim and M.C. Fissel (eds), *Amphibious Warfare 1000–1700: Commerce, State Formation and European Expansion* (Leiden, 2006), pp. 357–420.

2 R. Tregaksis, *The Warrior King: Hawaii's Kamehameha the Great* (New York, 1973).

3 H. Moyse-Bartlett, *The Pirates of Trucial Oman* (London, 1966) and L.R. Wright, 'Piracy in the Southeast Asian Archipelago', *Journal of Oriental Studies*, 14 (1976), pp. 23–33; B. Sandin, *The Sea Dayaks of Borneo: Before White Rajah Rule* (London, 1967).

4 N.A.M. Rodger, 'Form and Function in European Navies, 1660–1815', in L. Akveld et al. (eds), *In het Kielzog* (Amsterdam, 2003), pp. 85–97.

5 C.O. Philip, *Robert Fulton* (New York, 1985), p. 302.

6 J. Glete, *Warfare at Sea, 1500–1650* (London, 2000) and *War and the State in Early Modern Europe* (London, 2002).

7 R. Harding, *Seapower and Naval Warfare 1650–1830* (London, 1999), p. 205.

8 S. Chaudhury and M. Morineau (eds), *Merchants, Companies and Trade: Europe and Asia in the Early Modern Era* (Cambridge, 1999).

9 T. Andrade, 'The Company's Chinese Pirates: How the Dutch East India Company Tried to Lead a Coalition of Pirates to War against China, 1621–1662', *Journal of World History*, 15 (2005), pp. 442–4.

10 C. Totman, *Early Modern Japan* (Berkeley, California, 1994).

11 J.A. Millward, *Beyond the Pass: Economy, Ethnicity and Empire in Qing Central Asia, 1759–1864* (Stanford, California, 1998).

12 M. Malgonkar, *Kanhoji Angrey, Maratha Admiral* (Bombay, 1959).

13 L. Lockhart, 'Nadir Shah's Campaigns in Oman, 1734–1744', *Bulletin of the School of Oriental and African Studies*, 8 (1935–7), pp. 157–73.

14 B. Vale, *A War Betwixt Englishmen: Brazil Against Argentina on the River Plate, 1825–1830* (London, 2000).

15 A. DeConde, *The Quasi-War: The Politics and Diplomacy of the Undeclared War with France, 1797–1801* (New York, 1966).

16 S.C. Tucker, *The Jeffersonian Gunboat Navy* (Columbia, South Carolina, 1993); C.L. Symonds, *Navalists and Antinavalists: The Naval Policy Debate in the United States, 1785–1827* (Newark, Delaware, 1980).

17 A. Deshpande, 'Limitations of Military Technology: Naval Warfare on the West Coast [of India], 1650–1800', *Economic and Political Weekly*, 25 (1992), pp. 902–3.

18 J.C. Beaglehole, *The Exploration of the Pacific* (3rd edn, Stanford, California, 1966).

19 J.P. Merino Navarro, *La Armada Española en el Siglo XVIII* (Madrid, 1981), p. 168.

20 J. Glete, *Navies and Nations: Warships, Navies and State Building in Europe and America, 1500–1860* (2 vols, Stockholm, 1993), I, 313.

21 R. Morriss, *The Royal Dockyards during the Revolutionary and Napoleonic Wars* (Leicester, 1983); C. Wilkinson, *The British Navy and the State in the Eighteenth Century* (Woodbridge, 2004).

22 P. Crimmin, '"A Great Object With Us is to Procure This Timber…" The Royal Navy's Search for Ship Timber in the Eastern Mediterranean and Southern Russia, 1803–1815', *International Journal of Maritime History*, 4 (1992), pt. 2, pp. 83–115.

23 J.E. Talbott, *The Pen and Ink Sailor: Charles Middleton and the King's Navy, 1778–1813* (London, 1998); C. Wilkinson, *The British Navy and the State in the Eighteenth Century* (Woodbridge, 2004).

24 J. Dull, *The French Navy and the Seven Years' War* (Lincoln, Nebraska, 2005).

25 Rockingham to Earl of Hardwicke, *c.* Apr. 1781, Sheffield, City Archive, Wentworth Woodhouse Mss. R1-1962; J.E. Talbott, 'Copper, Salt, and the Worm', *Naval History*, 3 (1989), p. 53, and 'The Rise and Fall of the Carronade', *History Today*, 39/8 (1989), pp. 24–30; R.J.W. Knight, 'The Royal Navy's Recovery after the Early Phase of the American Revolutionary War', in G.J. Andreopoulos and H.E. Selesky (eds), *The Aftermath of Defeat: Societies, Armed Forces, and the Challenge of Recovery* (New Haven, Connecticut, 1994), pp. 10–25; R. Cock, '"The Finest Invention in the World": The Royal Navy's Early Trials of Copper Sheathing, 1708–1770', *Mariner's Mirror*, 87 (2001), pp. 446–59.

26 M. Duffy, 'The Gunnery at Trafalgar: Training, Tactics or Temperament?', *Journal for Maritime Research* (August 2005), www.jmr.ac.uk.

27 Glete, *Navies*, pp. 402, 405. Glete employs a different system of measurement from that traditionally used and the tonnages are therefore higher by 500–750 tons than normally given.

28 J. Pritchard, 'From Shipwright to Naval Constructor', *Technology and Culture* (1987), pp. 19–20; L.D. Ferreiro, *Ships and Science: The*

Birth of Naval Architecture in the Scientific Revolution, 1600–1800 (Cambridge, Massachusetts, 2007).

29 N.A.M. Rodger, *The Command of the Ocean: A Naval History of Britain, II, 1649–1815* (London, 2004), p. 422.

30 M. Duffy, '"... All Was Hushed up": The Hidden Trafalgar', *Mariner's Mirror*, 91 (2005), pp. 216–40.

31 J. Gwyn, *Ashore and Afloat: The British Navy and the Halifax Naval Yard before 1820* (Toronto, 2004).

32 R. Buel, Jr., *In Irons: Britain's Naval Supremacy and the American Revolutionary Economy* (New Haven, Connecticut, 1999).

33 P. Krajeski, 'The Foundation of British Amphibious Warfare Methodology during the Napoleonic Era, 1793–1815', *Consortium on Revolutionary Europe: Selected Papers 1996* (Tallahassee, Florida, 1996), pp. 191–8.

34 D. Syrett, *The Royal Navy in American Waters, 1775–1783* (Aldershot, 1989).

35 J.R. Dull, *The French Navy and the Seven Years' War* (Lincoln, Nebraska, 2005).

36 N.A.M. Rodger, *The Insatiable Earl: A Life of John Montagu, 4th Earl of Sandwich* (London, 1993), pp. 365–77.

37 J.R. Dull, *The French Navy and American Independence: A Study of Arms and Diplomacy, 1774–1787* (Princeton, New Jersey, 1975).

38 S. Willis, 'The Capability of Sailing Warships, Part 2: Manoeuvrability', *Le Marin du Nord/The Northern Mariner*, 14 (2004), pp. 57–68.

39 N.A.M. Rodger, 'Image and Reality in Eighteenth Century Naval Tactics', *Mariner's Mirror*, 89 (2003), pp. 281–2.

40 S. Willis, 'Fleet Performance and Capability in the Eighteenth-Century Royal Navy', *War in History*, 11 (2004), pp. 373–92.

41 Blankett to Earl of Shelburne, 29 July 1778, BL., Bowood papers 511 fols 9–11. For the role of the weather gauge, not least the contrast between theory and practice, S. Willis, *Fighting at Sea in the Eighteenth Century: The Art of Sailing Warfare* (Woodbridge, 2008), pp. 113–28.

42 W.S. Cormack, *Revolution and Political Conflict in the French Navy, 1789–1794* (Cambridge, 1995).

43 R. Harding (ed.), *A Great and Glorious Victory: New Perspectives on the Battle of Trafalgar* (Barnsley, 2008).

44 George III to William Pitt the Younger, First Lord of the Treasury, 4 Mar. 1797, NA. 30/8/104 fol. 145.

45 D.D. Howard, 'British Seapower and its Influence on the Peninsular War, 1810–18', *Naval War College Review*, 21 (1978), pp. 54–71; C.D. Hall, 'The Royal Navy and the Peninsular War', *Mariner's Mirror*, 79 (1993), pp. 403–18.

46 D.J. Starkey, 'War and the Market for Seafarers in Britain, 1736–1792', in L.R. Fischer and H.E. Nordvik (eds), *Shipping and Trade, 1750–1950* (Pontefract, 1990), p. 39.

47 P.L.C. Webb, 'The Rebuilding and Repair of the Fleet, 1783–93', *Bulletin of the Institute of Historical Research* 1 (1977), pp. 194–209.

48 T. Jenks, *Naval Engagements: Patriotism, Cultural Politics, and the Royal Navy, 1793–1815* (Oxford, 2006).

49 C. Ware, 'The Glorious First of June. The British Strategic Perspective', in M. Duffy and R. Morriss (eds), *The Glorious First of June 1794: A Naval Battle and its Aftermath* (Exeter, 2001), pp. 38–40.

50 P. Mackesy, *British Victory in Egypt, 1801: The End of Napoleon's Conquest* (London, 1995).

51 F. Crouzet, 'Wars, Blockade and Economic Change in Europe, 1792–1815', *Journal of Economic History*, 24 (1964), p. 585.

52 George III to George, 2nd Earl Spencer, 1st Lord of the Admiralty, 17 Apr. 1795, BL. Add. 75779.

53 R. Morriss (ed.), *The Channel Fleet and the Blockade of Brest, 1792–1801* (Aldershot, 2001); A.N. Ryan, 'The Royal Navy and the Blockade of Brest, 1689–1805: Theory and Practice', in M. Acera, J. Merino and J. Meyer (eds), *Les Marines de Guerre Européenes XVII–XVIIIe Siècles* (Paris, 1985), pp. 175–94.

54 P. Mackesy, *The War in the Mediterranean, 1803–1810* (London, 1957); P.C. Krajeski, *In the Shadow of Nelson: The Naval Leadership of Admiral Sir Charles Cotton, 1753–1812* (Westport, Connecticut, 2000).

55 C. Ware, *The Bomb Vessel: Shore Bombardment Ships of the Age of Sail* (Annapolis, Maryland, 1994).

56 A. Roland, *Underwater Warfare in the Age of Sail* (Bloomington, Indiana, 1978); W.S. Hutcheon, *Robert Fulton, Pioneer of Undersea Warfare* (Annapolis, Maryland, 1981); G.L. Pesce, *La Navigation sous-marine* (Paris, 1906), p. 227.

57 J. Macdonald, *Feeding Nelson's Navy: The True Story of Food at Sea in the Georgian Era* (London, 2004).

58 Fulton to William, Lord Grenville, British Prime Minister, 2 Sept. 1806, BL. Add. 71593 fol. 134.

Chapter 5

1 M.S. Reidy, *Tides of History: Ocean Science and Her Majesty's Navy* (Chicago, 2007), pp. 293–4.

2 T. Jenks, *Naval Engagements: Patriotism, Cultural Politics, and the Royal Navy, 1793–1815* (Oxford, 2006); N. Tracy, *Britannia's Palette: The Arts of Naval Victory* (Montreal, 2007).

3 J.H. Schroeder, *Shaping a Maritime Empire: The Commercial and Diplomatic Role of the American Navy, 1829–1861* (Westport, Connecticut, 1985); F. Leiner, *The End of Barbary Terror: America's 1815 War against the Pirates of North Africa* (New York, 2006).

4   C. Lopez, 'English and American Mariners in Chile's First Squadron, 1817–18', in R.W. Love et al. (eds), *New Interpretations in Naval History* (Annapolis, 2001), pp. 119–32; B. Vale, *Cochrane in the Pacific: Fortune and Freedom in Spanish America* (London, 2007).

5   E.A.M. Laing, 'The Introduction of Paddle Frigates into the Royal Navy', *Mariner's Mirror*, 66 (1980), pp. 221–9.

6   B. Greenhill and A. Gifford, *Steam, Politics and Patronage: The Transformation of the Royal Navy, 1815–54* (London, 1994); A.D. Lambert, 'Responding to the Nineteenth Century: The Royal Navy and the Introduction of the Screw Propeller', *History of Technology*, 21 (1999), pp. 1–28, esp. p. 25.

7   T. Crick, *Ramparts of Empire: The Fortifications of Sir William Jervois, Royal Engineer, 1821–1897* (Exeter, 2009).

8   A.D. Lambert, 'Preparing for the Russian War: British Strategic Planning, March 1853–March 1854', *War and Society*, 7 (1989), pp. 23, 34.

9   N. Tarling, 'The Establishment of the Colonial Régimes', in Tarling (ed.), *The Cambridge History of Southeast Asia* (2nd edn, 4 vols, Cambridge, 1999), III, 41.

10 Stirling to Sir James Graham, First Lord of the Admiralty, 19 Apr., 27 Nov. 1854, BL. Add. 79696 fols 147, 163; A.D. Lambert, *The Crimean War* (Manchester, 1991).

11 W.H. Roberts, *Civil War Ironclads: The U.S. Navy and Industrial Mobilization* (Annapolis, 2002).

12 D.G. Surdam, 'The Union Navy's Blockade Reconsidered', *Naval War College Review*, 51 (1998), p. 104, and 'The Confederate Naval Buildup: Could More Have Been Accomplished?', ibid., 54 (2001), p. 121.

13 R.J. Schneller, 'A Littoral Frustration: The Union Navy and the Siege of Charleston, 1863–1865', *Naval War College Review* (1996), pp. 38–60.

14 G.D. Joiner, *Mr. Lincoln's Brown Water Navy: The Mississippi Squadron* (Lanham, Maryland, 2007).

15 H. Holzer and T. Milligan (eds), *The Battle of Hampton Roads* (New York, 2006).

16 G. Wawro, 'Luxury Fleet: The Austrian Navy and the Battle of Lissa, 1866', in R.W. Love et al. (eds), *New Interpretations in Naval History* (Annapolis, 2001), pp. 176–87.

17 J.W. Kipp, 'The Russian Navy and the Problem of Technological Transfer', in B. Eklof et al. (eds), *Russia's Great Reforms, 1855–1881* (Bloomington, Indiana, 1994), p. 129.

18 H.J. Fuller, '"This Country Now Occupies the Vantage Ground": Understanding John Ericsson's Monitors and the American Union's War against British Naval Superiority', *American Neptune*, 62 (2002), pp. 91–111, and *Clad in Iron: The American Civil War and the Challenge of British Naval Power* (Westport, Connecticut, 2008), p. 282.

19   D. O'Connor, 'Privateers, Cruisers and Colliers: The Limits of International Maritime Law in the Nineteenth Century', *Royal United Services Institute Journal*, 150/1 (Feb. 2005), p. 73.

20   E. Gray, *Nineteenth Century Torpedoes and Their Inventors* (Annapolis, 2004).

21   J. Glete, 'John Ericsson and the Transformation of Swedish Naval Doctrine', *International Journal of Naval History*, 2 (2003), p. 14.

22   N.A.M. Rodger, 'The Idea of Naval Strategy in Britain in the Eighteenth and Nineteenth Centuries', in G. Till (ed.), *The Development of British Naval Thinking* (Abingdon, 2006), pp. 29–30.

23   A. Røksund, *The Jeune École: The Strategy of the Weak* (Leiden, 2007), quote, p. 227.

24   P.J. Kelly, 'Tirpitz and the Origins of the German Torpedo Arm, 1877–1889', in R.W. Love et al. (eds), *New Interpretations in Naval History* (Annapolis, 2001), pp. 219–49.

25   L. Sondhaus, 'Strategy, Tactics, and the Politics of Penury: The Austro-Hungarian Navy and the *Jeune École*', *Journal of Military History*, 56 (1992), p. 602.

26   M. Geyer and C. Bright, 'Global Violence and Nationalizing Wars in Eurasia and America: The Geopolitics of War in the Mid-Nineteenth Century', *Comparative Studies in Society and History*, 38 (1996), p. 651.

27   J.F. Beeler, 'A One Power Standard? Great Britain and the Balance of Naval Power, 1860–1880', *Journal of Strategic Studies*, 15 (1992), p. 570.

28   C. Symonds, *Navalists and Anti-Navalists: The Navy Policy Debate in the United States, 1785–1827* (Newark, New Jersey, 1980).

29   D.H. Olivier, *German Naval Strategy, 1856–1888: Forerunners of Tirpitz* (London, 2005).

30   B.M. Gough, *Gunboat Frontier: British Maritime Authority and Northwest Coast Indians, 1846–1890* (Vancouver, 1984).

31   R. Parkinson, *The Late Victorian Navy: The Pre-Dreadnought Era and the Origins of the First World War* (Woodbridge, 2008).

32   W.H. Thiesen, *Industrializing American Shipbuilding: The Transformation of Ship Design and Construction, 1820–1920* (Gainesville, Florida, 2006).

33   A.D. Lambert, *The Foundations of Naval History: John Knox Laughton, and the Introduction of the Royal Navy and the Historical Profession* (London, 1998).

34   A.T. Mahan, *From Sail to Steam: Recollections of Naval Life* (New York, 1907), p. 277.

35   R.W. Turk, *The Ambiguous Relationship: Theodore Roosevelt and Alfred Thayer Mahan* (Westport, Connecticut, 1987).

36   See the valuable annotated edition by Eric Grove published in 1988.

37   D.M. Schurman, *Julian S. Corbett 1854–1922: Historian of British Maritime Policy from Drake to Jellicoe* (Amherst, New York, 1981); M.R. Shulman, *Navalism and the Emergence of American Sea Power, 1882–1893* (Annapolis, 1995); J.T. Sumida, *Inventing Grand Strategy and Teaching Command: The Classic Works of Alfred Thayer Mahan Reconsidered* (Baltimore, 1997).

38   T.D. Gottschall, *By Order of the Kaiser: Otto von Diederichs and the Rise of the Imperial German Navy, 1865–1902* (Annapolis, 2003).

39   R. Hobson, *Imperialism at Sea, 1875–1914* (Leiden, 2002).

40   S.J. Shaw, 'Selim III and the Ottoman Navy', *Turcica*, 1 (1969), p. 222.

41   N.B. Dukas, *A Military History of Sovereign Hawai'i* (Honolulu, 2004), pp. 147–64; C.V. Reed, 'The British Naval Mission at Constantinople: An Analysis of Naval Assistance to the Ottoman Empire, 1908–1914' (D.Phil. thesis, Oxford, 1995).

42   S. Asada, *From Mahan to Pearl Harbor: The Imperial Japanese Navy and the United States* (Annapolis, 2006).

43   J.T. Sumida, 'The Quest for Reach: The Development of Long-Range Gunnery in the Royal Navy, 1901–1912', in S.D. Chiabotti (ed.), *Military Transformation in the Industrial Age* (Chicago, Illinois, 1996), pp. 49–96.

44   M.S. Seligmann, 'Switching Horses: The Admiralty's Recognition of the Threat from Germany, 1900–1905', *International History Review*, 30 (2008), p. 257.

45   M.S. Seligmann, 'New Weapons for New Targets: Sir John Fisher, the Threat from Germany, and the Building of HMS *Dreadnought* and HMS *Invincible*, 1902–1907', *International History Review*, 30 (2008), p. 325.

46   N.A. Lambert, *Sir John Fisher's Naval Revolution* (Columbia, South Carolina, 1999); J.T. Sumida, 'A Matter of Timing: The Royal Navy and the Tactics of Decisive Battle, 1912–1916', *Journal of Military History*, 67 (2003), pp. 85–136, esp. 131–3.

47   T.G. Otte, '"What we desire is confidence": The Search for an Anglo-German Naval Agreement, 1909–1912', in K. Hamilton and E. Johnson (eds), *Arms and Disarmament in Diplomacy* (Edgware, Middlesex and Portland, Oregon, 2007), p. 47.

48   P.J. Kelly, 'Strategy, Tactics, and Turf Wars: Tirpitz and the Oberkommando der Marine, 1892–1895', *Journal of Military History*, 66 (2002), p. 1059.

49   J.C. Schencking, *Making Waves: Politics, Propaganda, and the Emergence of the Imperial Japanese Navy, 1868–1922* (Palo Alto, California, 2005).

50   Z. Fotakis, *Greek Naval Strategy and Policy, 1910–1919* (London, 2005).

51   J.T. Sumida, *In Defence of Naval Supremacy: Finance, Technology, and British Naval Policy, 1899–1914* (London, 1989).

52 N.A. Lambert, 'Strategic Command and Control for Maneuver Warfare: Creation of the Royal Navy's "War Room" System, 1905–1915', *Journal of Military History*, 69 (2005), pp. 361–413.

53 Re USA: S.K. Stein, *From Torpedoes to Aviation: Washington Irving Chambers and Technological Innovation in the New Navy, 1876–1913* (Tuscaloosa, Alabama, 2007); P.A. Shulman, '"Science Can Never Demobilize": The United States Navy and Petroleum Geology, 1898–1924', *History and Technology*, 19 (2003), pp. 367–71.

Chapter 6

1 G.C. Peden, *Arms, Economics and British Strategy: From Dreadnoughts to Hydrogen Bombs* (Cambridge, 2007).

2 C. P. Vincent, *The Politics of Hunger: The Allied Blockade of Germany, 1915–1919* (Athens, Georgia, 1985).

3 N.J.M. Campbell, *Jutland: An Analysis of the Fighting* (London, 1986).

4 A. Gordon, *The Rules of the Game: Jutland and British Naval Command* (London, 1996), pp. 514–15.

5 Kitchener to Balfour, 6 Nov. 1915, PRO. 30/57/66.

6 C. McKee, *Sober Men and True: Sailor Lives in the Royal Navy, 1900–1945* (Cambridge, Massachusetts, 2002), p. 113.

7 BL. Add. 50294 fol. 6, 49710 fol. 2.

8 M. Wilson, 'Early Submarines', in R. Gardiner (ed.), *Steam, Steel and Shellfire: The Steam Warship 1815–1905* (London, 1992), pp. 147–57.

9 H.H. Herwig, 'Total Rhetoric, Limited War: Germany's U-Boat Campaign, 1917–1918', in R. Chickering and S. Forster (eds), *Great War, Total War: Combat and Mobilization on the Western Front, 1914–1918* (Cambridge, 2000), p. 205.

10 BL. Add. 49714 fol. 29.

11 BL. Add. 49714 fol. 145.

12 BL. Add. 49715 fol. 210.

13 J. Winton, *Convoy: The Defence of Sea Trade, 1890–1990* (London, 1983); J. Terraine, *Business in Great Waters: The U-Boat Wars 1916–45* (London, 1989).

14 G. Penn Fisher, *Churchill and the Dardanelles* (London, 1999).

15 P.G. Halpern, *The Naval War in the Mediterranean 1914–1918* (London, 1987).

16 G. Nekrasov, *North of Gallipoli: The Black Sea Fleet at War, 1914–1917* (Boulder, Colorado, 1992).

17 M.B. Barrett, *Operation Albion: The German Conquest of the Baltic Islands* (Bloomington, Indiana, 2008).

18 W.N. Still, *Crisis at Sea: The United States Navy in European Waters in World War I* (Gainesville, Florida, 2007).

19 D. Horn, *The German Naval Mutinies of World War One* (New Brunswick, New Jersey, 1969); N. Hewitt, '"Weary Waiting is Hard Indeed": The Grand Fleet after Jutland', in I.F.W. Beckett (ed.), *1917: Beyond the Western Front* (Leiden, 2009), p. 69.

20 D.A. Yerxa, *Admirals and Empire: The United States Navy and the Caribbean, 1898*; W.N. Still, *Crisis at Sea 1945* (Columbia, South Carolina, 1991), p. 53.

21 P.G. Halpern, *A Naval History of World War I* (Annapolis, Maryland, 1994).

22 S. Roskill, *Naval Policy between the Wars. I: The Period of Anglo-American Antagonism, 1919–1929* (London, 1968); E.O. Goldman, *Sunken Treaties: Naval Arms Control Between the Wars* (University Park, Pennsylvania, 1994); P.P. O'Brien, *British and American Naval Power: Politics and Policy, 1900–1936* (Westport, Connecticut, 1998); E. Goldstein and J.H. Maurer, *The Washington Naval Conference: Naval Rivalry, East Asian Stability, and the Road to Pearl Harbor* (Ilford, 1994).

23 R.D. Burns, 'Regulating Submarine Warfare, 1921–41: A Case Study in Arms Control and Limited War', *Military Affairs*, 35 (1971), pp. 56–63.

24 NA. CAB. 29/117 fol. 78. R.W. Fanning, *Peace and Disarmament: Naval Rivalry and Arms Control, 1922–1933* (Lexington, Kentucky, 1995); D.C. Evans and M.R. Peattie, *Kaigun: Strategy, Tactics and Technology in the Imperial Japanese Navy, 1887–1941* (Annapolis, 1997).

25 J.T. Sumida, '"The Best Laid Plans": The Development of British Battle-Fleet Tactics, 1919–1942', *International History Review*, 14 (1992), pp. 682–700.

26 I.M. Philpott, *The Royal Air Force … the Inter-war Years. I. The Trenchard Years, 1918 to 1929* (Barnsley, 2005), pp. 194–208.

27 C.G. Reynolds, *The Fast Carriers: The Forging of an Air Navy* (New York, 1968); G. Till, 'Adopting the Aircraft Carrier: The British, American, and Japanese Case Studies', in W. Murray and A.R. Millett (eds), *Military Innovation in the Interwar Period* (Cambridge, 1996), pp. 191–226.

28 G. Till, *Air Power and the Royal Navy, 1914–1945* (London, 1989).

29 T.C. Hone, N. Friedman and M.D. Mandeles, *American and British Aircraft Carrier Development, 1919–1941* (Annapolis, 1999); T. Wildenberg, *Destined for Glory: Dive Bombing, Midway, and the Evolution of Carrier Airpower* (Annapolis, 1998).

30 BL. Add. 49699 fol. 84.

31 BL. Add. 49045 fols 1–2.

32 O.C. Chung, *Operation Matador: Britain's War Plans against the Japanese, 1918–1941* (Singapore, 1997).

33 S.E. Pelz, *Race to Pearl Harbor: The Failure of the Second London Naval Conference and the Onset of World War II* (Cambridge, Massachusetts, 1974); R.G. Kaufman, *Arms Control During the*

Pre-Nuclear Era: The United States and Naval Limitation Between the Two World Wars (New York, 1990).

34 P. Padfield, *Maritime Dominion and the Triumph of the Free World* (London, 2009).

35 T.R. Maddux, 'United States–Soviet Naval Relations in the 1930s: The Soviet Union's Efforts to Purchase Naval Vessels', in D.J. Stoker and J.A. Grant (eds), *Girding for Battle. The Arms Trade in a Global Perspective, 1815–1940* (Westport, Connecticut, 2003), p. 207.

36 H.H. Herwig, 'Innovation Ignored: The Submarine Problem – Germany, Britain, and the United States, 1919–1939', in Murray and Millett (eds), *Military Innovation*, pp. 227–64.

37 T.R. Philbin, *The Lure of Neptune: German–Soviet Naval Collaboration and Ambitions, 1919–1941* (Columbia, South Carolina, 1994), p. xiv.

38 R. Mallett, *The Italian Navy and Fascist Expansionism, 1935–1940* (London, 1998).

39 A. Marder, 'The Royal Navy and the Ethiopian Crisis of 1935–36', *American Historical Review*, 75 (1970), pp. 1327–56.

40 J. Ferris, 'The Last Decade of British Maritime Supremacy, 1919–1929', in K. Neilson and G. Kennedy (eds), *Far Flung Lines* (London, 1997), pp. 155–62.

41 NA. CAB. 16/109, fol. 9.

42 D.M. Goldstein and K.V. Dillon (eds), *The Pearl Harbor Papers: Inside the Japanese Plans* (McLean, Virginia, 1993).

43 A. Claasen, 'Blood and Iron, and *der Geist des Atlantiks*: Assessing Hitler's Decision to Invade Norway', *Journal of Strategic Studies*, 20 (1997), pp. 71–96.

44 R.M. Salerno, 'The French Navy and the Appeasement of Italy, 1937–9', *English Historical Review*, 112 (1997), pp. 102–3.

45 Sir Dudley Pound to Admiral Layton, 15 Sept. 1941, BL. Add. 74796.

46 J.J. Sadkovich, *The Italian Navy in World War II* (Westport, Connecticut, 1994); J. Greene and A. Massignani, *The Naval War in the Mediterranean, 1940–1943* (Rockville Centre, New York, 1999); M. Simpson (ed.), *The Cunningham Papers* I (Aldershot, 1999).

47 L. Paterson, *U-Boats in the Mediterranean* (London, 2007).

48 A.J. Levine, *The War Against Rommel's Supply Lines, 1942–1943* (Westport, Connecticut, 1999).

49 I. Kershaw, 'Did Hitler Miss His Chance in 1940?', in N. Gregor (ed.), *Nazism, War and Genocide* (Exeter, 2005), pp. 110–30.

50 C. Eade (ed.), *Secret Session Speeches* (London, 1946), p. 47.

51 L. Paterson, *Hitler's Grey Wolves: U-boats in the Indian Ocean* (London, 2004).

52 G. Rhys-Jones, *The Loss of the Bismarck: An Avoidable Disaster* (London, 1999).

53 BL. Add. 52560 fol. 120.

54 G. Franklin, *Britain's Anti-Submarine Capability, 1919–1939* (London, 2003).

55 J. Terraine, *Business in Great Waters: The U-Boat Wars, 1916–45* (London, 1989).

56 D.M. Goldstein and K.V. Dillon (eds), *The Pearl Harbor Papers: Inside the Japanese Plans* (Washington, DC, 1993); H.P. Willmott, *Pearl Harbor* (London, 2001).

57 C.M. Bell, 'The "Singapore Strategy" and the Deterrence of Japan: Winston Churchill, the Admiralty and the Dispatch of Force Z', *English Historical Review*, 116 (2001), pp. 604–34.

58 D.V. Smith, *Carrier Battles: Command Decisions in Harm's Way* (Annapolis, 2006), esp. pp. 244–55.

59 C. Boyd and A. Yoshida, *The Japanese Submarine Force and World War II* (Annapolis, 1995).

60 M. Murfett, *Naval Warfare 1919–1945* (Abingdon, 2009), p. 498.

61 J.B. Lundstrom, *Black Shoe Carrier Admiral: Frank Jack Fletcher at Coral Sea, Midway, and Guadalcanal* (Annapolis, 2006).

62 C. Blair, *Silent Victory: The U.S. Submarine War Against Japan* (New York, 1963); M. Parillo, *The Japanese Merchant Marine in World War Two* (Annapolis, 1993).

63 J.H. and W.M. Belote, *Titans of the Seas: The Development and Operations of American Carrier Task Forces During World War II* (New York, 1975); W.R. Carter, *Beans, Bullets and Black Oil: The Story of Fleet Logistics Afloat in the Pacific during World War Two* (Washington, DC, 1952).

64 W.T. Y'Blood, *Red Sun Setting: The Battle of the Philippine Sea* (Annapolis, 1981).

65 T.B. Buell, *The Quiet Warrior: A Biography of Admiral Raymond A. Spruance* (Boston, 1974); E.B. Potter, *Nimitz* (Annapolis, 1976); H.P. Willmott, *The Barrier and the Javelin: Japanese and Allied Pacific Strategies, February to June 1942* (Annapolis, 1983); D.C. James, *The Years of MacArthur, 1941–1945* (New York, 1985); R. Spector, *Eagle Against the Sun: The American War with Japan* (New York, 1985); G. Bischof and R.L. Dupont (eds), *The Pacific War Revisited* (Baton Rouge, Louisiana, 1997); V.P. O'Hara, *The U.S. Navy Against the Axis: Surface Combat 1941–1945* (Annapolis, 2007).

66 H.P. Willmott, *The Battle of Leyte Gulf: The Last Fleet Action* (Bloomington, 2005).

Chapter 7

1 M. Coles, 'Ernest King and the British Pacific Fleet', *Journal of Military History*, 65 (2001), pp. 127–9.

2 P.H. Silverstone, *The Navy of World War II* (New York, 2008), p. 12.

3   N. Polmar, 'Improving the Breed', *Naval History*, 21/5 (Oct. 2007), pp. 22–7.

4   M.A. Palmer, *Origins of the Maritime Strategy: The Development of American Naval Strategy, 1945–1955* (Annapolis, 1990); J.G. Barlow, *Revolt of the Admirals: The Fight for Naval Aviation* (Washington, DC, 1994).

5   J. Miller, *Nuclear Weapons and Aircraft Carriers: How the Bomb Saved Naval Aviation* (Washington, DC, 2001).

6   M.W. Cagle and F.A. Manson, *The Sea War in Korea* (Annapolis, 2000); E.J. Marolda, *The U.S. Navy in the Korean War* (Annapolis, 2007).

7   P. Paterson, 'The Truth About Tonkin', and comment by W. Buehler, *Naval History* (Feb. 2008), pp. 52–9, (Apr. 2008), p. 6.

8   F. Duncan, *Rickover and the Nuclear Navy: The Discipline of Technology* (Annapolis, 1990).

9   E. Grove and G. Till, 'Anglo-American Maritime Strategy in the Era of Massive Retaliation, 1945–60', in J.B. Hattendorf and R.S. Jordan (eds), *Maritime Strategy and Balance of Power: Britain and America in the Twentieth Century* (New York, 1989), pp. 286–99; M.A. Palmer, *Origins of the Maritime Strategy: The Development of American Naval Strategy, 1945–1955* (Annapolis, 1990); S.M. Maloney, *Securing Command of the Sea: NATO Naval Planning, 1948–1954* (Annapolis, 1995).

10   E.J. Marolda, *Cordon of Steel: The United States Navy and the Cuban Missile Crisis* (Washington, DC, 1994).

11   S.M. Maloney, *Securing Command of the Sea: NATO Naval Planning, 1948–1954* (Annapolis, 1995), pp. 197–8.

12   A. Hind, 'The Cruise Missile Comes of Age', *Naval History*, 22/5 (Oct. 2008), p. 55.

13   J. Gorshkov, *The Sea Power of the State* (Annapolis, 1979).

14   G. Kennedy, 'The Royal Navy and Imperial Defence, 1919–1956', in Kennedy (ed.), *Imperial Defence: The Old World Order, 1856–1956* (Abingdon, 2008), pp. 144–5.

15   I. Speller, *The Role of Amphibious Warfare in British Defence Policy, 1945–1956* (Basingstoke, 2001).

16   S. Lucas, *Britain and Suez: The Lion's Last Roar* (Manchester, 1996).

17   Southampton, University Library MB1/I149.

18   S.J. Ball, '"Vested Interests and Vanished Dreams": Duncan Sandys, the Chiefs of Staff and the 1957 White Paper', in P. Smith (ed.), *Government and the Armed Forces in Britain, 1856–1990* (London, 1998), pp. 217–34.

19   J. and D.S. Small, *The Undeclared War: The Story of the Indonesian Confrontation, 1962–1966* (London, 1971).

20   P. Vial, 'National Rearmament and American Assistance: The Case of the French Navy during the 1950s', in W.M. McBride (ed.), *New Interpretations in Naval History* (Annapolis, 1998), pp. 260–88.

21 M. Milner, *Canada's Navy: The First Century* (Toronto, 1999).
22 D.R. Snyder, 'Arming the *Bundesmarine*: The United States and the Build-up of the German Federal Navy, 1950–1960', *Journal of Military History*, 66 (2002), pp. 477–500.
23 A. Gorst, 'CVA-01', in R. Harding (ed.), *The Royal Navy, 1930–2000: Innovation and Defence* (Abingdon, 2005), pp. 172–92.
24 E.g. *Financial Times*, 20 Feb. 2008, p. 13.
25 P. Darby, *British Defence Policy East of Suez, 1947–68* (London, 1973); M. Jones, '"Up the Garden Path": British Nuclear History in the Far East, 1954–1962', *International History Review* 25 (2003), pp. 325–7.
26 J. Pickering, *Britain's Withdrawal from East of Suez* (Basingstoke, 1998).
27 M.A. Palmer, *On Course to Desert Storm: The United States Navy and the Persian Gulf* (Washington, DC, 1992).
28 E.J. Marolda and O.P. Fitzgerald, *The United States Navy and the Vietnam Conflict. II: From Military Assistance to Combat, 1959–1965* (Washington, DC, 1986); J.B. Nichols and B. Tillman, *On Yankee Station: The Naval Air War over Vietnam* (Annapolis, 1987); R.J. Francillon, *Tonkin Gulf Yacht Club: U.S. Carrier Operations off Vietnam* (Annapolis, 1988).
29 N. Stewart, *The Royal Navy and the Palestine Patrol* (London, 2002).
30 D.K. Brown, *The Royal Navy and the Falklands War* (London, 1987); L. Freedman, *The Official History of the Falklands Campaign* (2 vols, London, 2005); S. Badsey, R. Havers and M. Grove (eds), *The Falklands Conflict Twenty Years On: Lessons for the Future* (London, 2005).
31 G.E. Hudson, 'Soviet Naval Doctrine and Soviet Politics, 1953–1975', *World Politics*, 29 (1976), pp. 90–113; B. Ranft and G. Till, *The Sea in Soviet Strategy* (London, 1983).
32 P. Nitze et al., *Securing the Seas: The Soviet Naval Challenge and Western Alliance Options* (Boulder, Colorado, 1979); J.D. Watkins, *The Maritime Strategy* (Annapolis, 1986); E. Rhodes, '"…From the Sea" and Back Again. Naval Power in the Second American Century', *Naval War College Review*, 52/2 (1999), pp. 22–3; D. Winkler, *Cold War at Sea: High Seas Confrontation between the United States and the Soviet Union* (Annapolis, 2000).
33 F.H. Hartmann, *Naval Renaissance: The U.S. Navy in the 1980s* (Annapolis, 1990); J.F. Lehman, *Command of the Seas: Building the 600 Ship Navy* (New York, 1988).
34 E. Rhodes, 'Constructing Peace and War: An Analysis of the Power of Ideas to Shape American Military Power', *Millennium: Journal of International Studies*, 24 (1995), p. 84. For an earlier example, Rhodes, 'Sea Change: Interest-Based vs. Cultural-Cognitive Accounts of Strategic Choice in the 1890s', *Security Studies*, 5/4 (1996), esp. pp. 121–2.

35   N. Friedman, *Seapower as Strategy: Navies and National Interests* (Annapolis, 2001).

36   C.S. Gray, *The Leverage of Seapower: The Strategic Advantage of Navies in War* (New York, 1992), and *The Navy in the Post-Cold War World: The Uses and Value of Strategic Sea Power* (Philadelphia, 2004).

37   W. Hughes, *Fleet Tactics and Coastal Combat* (2nd edn, Annapolis, 2000); E.J. Grove, *The Royal Navy Since 1815* (London, 2005), p. 261.

38   J.B. Hattendorf (ed.), *US Naval Strategy in the 1990s: Selected Documents* (Newport, Rhode Island, 2007); M. Mäder, *In Pursuit of Conceptual Excellence: The Evolution of British Military Strategic Doctrine in the Post-Cold War Era, 1989–2002* (New York, 2004).

39   R.O. Work, 'The Global Era of National Policy and the Pan-Oceanic National Fleet', *Orbis*, 52 (2008), p. 602.

40   A. Dorman et al. (eds), *The Changing Face of Maritime Power* (London, 1999).

41   *British Maritime Doctrine* (2nd edn, London, 1999), pp. 3, 171.

42   *Naval Strategic Plan* (2006), p. 9.

43   K.J. Hagan and M.T. McMaster, 'In Search of a Maritime Strategy: The U.S. Navy, 1981–2008', in Hagan (ed.), *In Peace and War: Interpretations of American Naval History* (2nd edn, Westport, Connecticut, 2008), pp. 291–2.

44   J. Black, *War Since 1990* (London, 2008).

45   For debate over American naval force structure, E. Labs, *Options for the Navy's Future Fleet* (Washington, DC, 2006); R.O. Work, 'Numbers and Capabilities: Building a Navy for the Twenty-First Century', in G.J. Schmitt and T. Donnelly (eds), *Of Men and Materiel: The Crisis in Military Resources* (Washington, DC, 2007), pp. 82–113; F. Hoffman, *From Preponderance to Partnership: American Maritime Power in the 21st Century* (Washington, DC, 2008).

Chapter 8

1   I. Speller, 'Naval Warfare', in D. Jordan et al., *Understanding Modern Warfare* (Cambridge, 2008).

2   D.G. Muller, *China as a Maritime Power* (Boulder, Colorado, 1983); J.W. Lewis and X. Litai, *China's Strategic Seapower: The Politics of Force Modernization in the Nuclear Age* (Stanford, California, 1995); B.D. Cole, *The Great Wall at Sea: China's Navy Enters the Twenty-First Century* (Annapolis, 2001); T.M. Kane, *Chinese Grand Strategy and Maritime Power* (London, 2002); D. Shambaugh, *Modernizing China's Military: Progress, Problems, and Prospects* (Berkeley, California, 2002); J.R. Holmes and T. Yoshihara, *Chinese Naval Strategy in the 21st Century: The Turn*

to Mahan (London, 2008); D. Lei, 'China's New Multi-faceted Maritime Strategy', *Orbis* (winter 2008), pp. 139–57. I have benefited from hearing a paper by You Ji.
3   T. Yoshihara and J.R. Holmes (eds), *Asia Looks Seaward: Power and Maritime Strategy* (Westport, Connecticut, 2008).
4   *The Times*, 27 Dec. 2008, p. 43; A.S. Erickson and A.R. Wilson, 'China's Aircraft Carrier Dilemma', *Naval War College Review* (autumn 2006), pp. 13–45.
5   US Joint Forces Command, *The Joint Operating Environment 2008* (Suffolk, Virginia, 2008), p. 27.
6   J. Handler, A. Wickenheiser and W.M. Arkin, 'Naval Safety 1989: The Year of the Accident', *Neptune Paper*, 4 (Apr. 1989); G. Allison and A. Kokoshin, 'The New Containment', *The National Interest*, 69 (2002), p. 39.
7   http://www.naval-technology.com/projects/akula/
8   K. Booth, *Navies and Foreign Policy* (London, 1977), p. 15; E. Grove, *The Future of Sea Power* (Annapolis, 1990).
9   *Indian Maritime Doctrine*, 2004.
10 *Future Navy Vision* (London, 2006), p. 3.
11 War Cabinet Minutes, 29 July 1942, Canberra, National Archives of Australia, p. 1404. See also, e.g., 30 June 1942, pp. 1378–9.
12 G. Till, *Seapower. A Guide for the Twenty-First Century* (London, 2004), p. 368.

Chapter 9

1   J. Glete, 'Bridge and Bulwark: The Swedish Navy and the Baltic, 1500–1809', in G. Rystad, K-R. Bohme and W.M. Carlgren (eds), *The Baltic and Power Politics, 1500–1890* (Lund, 1994), p. 56.
2   M.S. Navias and E.R. Hooton, *Tanker Wars: The Assault on Merchant Shipping During the Iran–Iraq Conflict, 1980–1988* (London, 1996).

Selected further reading

The following is a brief introduction to a highly talented field, albeit one that is disproportionately devoted to Western naval powers and to deep-sea fleets. Other works can be pursued through the notes of this book and the notes and bibliographies of those cited here. Anything written by Jan Glete, Colin Gray, Eric Grove, Richard Harding, John Hattendorf, Nicholas Lambert, Nicholas Rodger and Larry Sondhaus is well worth reading. Unless otherwise stated, all books are published in London.

Asada, S. *From Mahan to Pearl Harbor: The Imperial Japanese Navy and the United States* (Annapolis, 2006).
Baer, G.W., *One Hundred Years of Sea Power: The U.S. Navy, 1890–1990* (Stanford, California, 1993).
Boxer, C.R. *The Portuguese Seaborne Empire, 1415–1825* (1973).
Bracewell, W. *The Uskoks of Senj: Piracy, Banditry and Holy War in the Sixteenth Century Adriatic* (Ithaca, New York, 1992).
Bruijn, J.R. *The Dutch Navy of the Seventeenth and Eighteenth Centuries* (Columbia, South Carolina, 1993).
Chaudhury, S. and Morineau, M. (eds) *Merchants, Companies and Trade: Europe and Asia in the Early Modern Era* (Cambridge, 1999).
Cipolla, C. *Guns, Sails and Empires: Technological Innovating and the Early Phases of European Expansion, 1400–1700* (1965).
Dorman, A. et al. (eds), *The Changing Face of Maritime Power* (Basingstoke, 1999).
Dull, J.R. *The French Navy and the Seven Years' War* (Lincoln, Nebraska, 2005).
Earl, P. *Corsairs of Malta and Barbary* (1970).
Forbes, A. (ed.) *Sea Power: Challenge Old and New* (Sydney, 2007).
Fuller, H.J. *Clad in Iron: The American Civil War and the Challenge of British Naval Power* (Westport, Connecticut, 2008).
Gardiner, R. and Morrison, J. (eds.) *The Age of the Galley: Mediterranean Oared Vessels since Pre-classical Times* (1995).
Glete, J. *Navies and Nations: Warships, Navies and State Building in Europe and America, 1500–1860* (Stockholm, 1993).
Glete, J. *Warfare at Sea, 1500–1650: Maritime Conflicts and the Transformation of Europe* (2000).
Goldrick, J. and J.B. Hattendorf (eds), *Mahan's Not Enough: The Proceedings of a Conference on the Works of Sir Julian Corbett and Sir Herbert Richmond* (Newport, Connecticut, 1993).

Goodman, D. *Spanish Naval Power, 1589–1665: Reconstruction and Defeat* (Cambridge, 1996).

Gordon, A. *The Rules of the Game: Jutland and British Naval Command* (1996).

Gottschall, T.D. *By Order of the Kaiser: Otto von Diederichs and the Rise of the Imperial German Navy, 1865–1902* (Annapolis, 2003).

Gray, C. *The Leverage of Sea Power: The Strategic Advantage of Navies in War* (New York, 1992).

Grove, E. *The Royal Navy since 1815* (Basingstoke, 2005).

Guilmartin, J.F. *Gunpowder and Galleys: Changing Technology and Mediterranean Warfare at Sea in the Sixteenth Century* (Cambridge, 1974).

Halpern, P.G. *A Naval History of World War I* (1994).

Harding, R. *Seapower and Naval Warfare 1650–1830* (1999)

Hattendorf, J. and Jordan, R. (eds) *Maritime Strategy and the Balance of Power: Britain and America in the Twentieth Century* (Basingstoke, 1989).

Hattendorf, J.B. (ed.) *Ubi Sumus? The State of Naval and Maritime History* (Newport, Connecticut, 1994).

Hattendorf, J.B. (ed.) *Doing Naval History: Essays Toward Improvement* (Newport, Connecticut, 1995).

Hattendorf, J.B. and Unger, R.W. (eds) *War at Sea in the Middle Ages and Renaissance* (Woodbridge, 2003).

James, A. *The Ship of State: Naval Affairs in Early Modern France, 1572–1661* (Woodbridge, 2002).

Jenks, T. *Naval Engagements: Patriotism, Cultural Politics, and the Royal Navy, 1793–1815* (Oxford, 2006).

Jones, J.R. *The Anglo-Dutch Wars of the Seventeenth Century* (1996).

Lambert, N. *Sir John Fisher's Naval Revolution* (Columbia, South Carolina, 1999).

Love, R.W. et al. (eds) *New Interpretations in Naval History* (Annapolis, 2001).

Neilson, K. and Errington, E.J., *Navies and Global Defense: Theories and Strategy* (Westport, Connecticut, 1995).

Parker, G. *The Grand Strategy of Philip II* (New Haven, Connecticut, 1998).

Parkinson, R. *The Late Victorian Navy: The Pre-Dreadnought Era and the Origins of the First World War* (Woodbridge, 2008).

Phillips, C.R. *Six Galleons for the King of Spain: Imperial Defence in the Early Seventeenth Century* (Baltimore, 1992).

Pritchard, J. *Louis XV's Navy, 1748–1762: A Study in Organisation and Administration* (Quebec, 1987).

Pryor, J.H. *Geography, Technology and War: Studies in the Maritime History of the Mediterranean, 649–1571* (Cambridge, 1988).

Reynolds, C. *Navies in History* (1998).

Rodger, N.A.M. *The Wooden World: An Anatomy of the Georgian Navy* (1986).

Rodger, N.A.M. *The Safeguard of the Sea: A Naval History of Britain. I: 660–1649* (1997).

Rodger, N.A.M. *The Command of the Ocean: A Naval History of Britain. II: 1649–1815* (2004).

Sandin, B. *The Sea Dayaks of Borneo: Before White Rajah Rule* (1967).

Scammell, G.V. *The World Encompassed: The First European Maritime Empires, c. 800–1650* (1981).

Schencking, J.C. *Making Waves: Politics, Propaganda, and the Emergence of the Imperial Japanese Navy, 1868–1922* (Palo Alto, California, 2005).

Sondhaus, L. *Naval Warfare 1815–1914* (2001).

Sondhaus, L. *Navies of Europe, 1815–2002* (2002).

Sondhaus, L. *Navies in Modern World History* (2004).

Spector, R. *At War at Sea: Sailors and Naval Conflict in the Twentieth Century* (New York, 2001).

Sumida, J.T. *In Defence of Naval Supremacy: Finance, Technology, and British Naval Policy, 1899–1914* (1989).

Symcox, G. *The Crisis of French Naval Power, 1688–1697* (The Hague, 1974).

Till, G. *Seapower: A Guide for the Twenty-first Century* (2004).

Till, G. (ed.) *The Development of British Naval Thinking* (Abingdon, 2006)

Tracy, J.D. (ed.) *The Rise of Merchant Empires: Long-Distance Trade in the Early Modern World, 1350–1750* (Cambridge, 1990).

Tracy, J.D. (ed.) *The Political Economy of Merchant Empires* (Cambridge, 1991).

Trim, D.J.B. and Fissel, M.C. (eds) *Amphibious Warfare 1000–1700: Commerce, State Formation and European Expansion* (Leiden, 2006).

Turnbull, S. *Samurai Invasion: Japan's Korean War 1592–1598* (2002).

Vohra, R. and Chakraborty, D. (eds) *Maritime Dimensions of a New World Order* (2007).

Willis, S., *Fighting at Sea in the Eighteenth Century: The Art of Sailing Warfare* (Woodbridge, 2008).

Index

9 780230 202801